MOUNTAIN RESCUE

a TRUE STORY *of*

UNEXPECTED MERCIES *and* DELIVERANCE

COMPILED AND WRITTEN *BY* SHELLI OWEN
COWRITTEN *WITH* MARY OWEN GRIMM *AND* BRUCE OWEN

Developmental Editor: Linda Ruggeri, *The Insightful Editor*

Copy Editor: Jen Anne Becker

Book design services through Melinda Martin, *Martin Publishing Services*

Cover design by Rachel

Library of Congress Control Number: 2021907994 (for regular non-expanded edition)

ISBN: 978-1-7370542-3-8 (paperback), 978-1-7370542-4-5 (hardback), 978-1-7370542-5-2 (epub)

Color photos and additional material, including copies of police reports, news articles, and other items of interest may be accessed through the *Mountain Rescue* website at: https://www.mountainrescue.online/

To the Messianic Jewish woman
Who prayed this book into existence

and

To God, who sent our Rescue

CONTENTS

MOUNT HOOD WINTER

Mt Hood in Blue, by Katie Reim / "FinalSwitchback"

PART OF AN ANCIENT SONG

I love the Lord, for he heard my voice;
He heard my cry for mercy.
Because he turned his ear to me,
I will call on him as long as I live.

The cords of death entangled me,
The anguish of the grave came over me;
I was overcome by distress and sorrow.
Then I called on the name of the Lord:
"Lord, save me!"

The Lord is gracious and righteous;
Our God is full of compassion.
The Lord protects the unwary;
When I was brought low, he saved me.

Return to your rest, my soul,
For the Lord has been good to you.

For you, Lord, have delivered me from death,
My eyes from tears,
My feet from stumbling,
That I may walk before the Lord
In the land of the living.

❧ Psalm 116:1-9 ❧

A TAPESTRY

"Tapestry ~ a heavy ornamental fabric, often in the form of a picture... made by weaving coloured threads into a fixed warp; a colourful and complicated situation"

ॐ COLLINS ENGLISH DICTIONARY ॐ

This is the true story of the misadventure and rescue of our daughter, Mary Owen, a college student, who in the spring of 2013 became stranded alone on Sandy Glacier on Oregon's Mount Hood for six days and nights. It is also the story of her diverse community who united with us in prayer and support for her to be found, and then to be healed. Finally, it is the story of how God showed the reality of His Presence with us through His mercies and deliverance.

This story is a tapestry—a retelling that intertwines various sources.

I'm Shelli, Mary's "momma," the main narrator and weaver of the threads of this tapestry. Mary's dad, my husband Bruce, is another key voice, as is Mary because this story is based on events surrounding her choices.

Since much of this narrative is about how her actions affected other people, we have given many of those who were directly involved a voice in the telling.

I know many people prefer that God not be spoken of or believed in; however, from our perspective this account wouldn't be honest or complete without our recognition of God. Our purpose isn't to "convert" anyone, but to share our story and what we believe the Lord did for us. If you aren't a believer in God or His ability to work in unseen ways, I hope you will bear with us, and maybe even allow yourself to temporarily suspend an absolute conviction that the material world is all there is, that there *can't* be unseen, supernatural forces, and that only what the five senses convey to our minds is "real." Whatever your attitude is toward God, I invite you to consider all you can in a different light as you travel with us through this story, to figuratively wear our shoes—or our glasses, if you'd rather go barefoot like Mary.

After Mary's incident, many people told us that she owes us all a book! They wanted to know the entire story, and they wanted to hear it from her. However, she has been reluctant to share her story.

What she went through on the mountain is extremely difficult for her to retell. Whenever she does, in large measure, she relives what happened. It was both spiritually and literally an intensely cold, desolate, painful, and at times confusing experience for her.

Ever since Mary's incident on Mount Hood and the Lord's merciful intervention on her (and our) behalf, I've felt His nudge to compile and publish this story.

No story is ever truly complete or accurate. People see and remember things from different perspectives. We also acknowledge that there are always things we could have, and maybe even should have, added. For the sake of space, we had to compromise. If there are things you really think we should have included, or errors, please let us know. We will welcome any missing or corrected material as we may print a revised edition in the future.

If you're willing, we'd love to hear this story's significance for you. And we do hope it will be significant in some way. For anyone who reads this story, who recognizes their own natural propensity to err—sometimes majorly—we pray this story gives you real hope for your own deliverance from the immovable mountains in your life.

Author's Note: There were often Facebook posts and comments, also some emails I had to omit from those series which are included in this book. I had to leave some things out for the sake of readability and space. For the same reason, some of the posts, comments, and emails included are not in the exact order in which they were shared with us.

MY LIFE IS BUT A WEAVING

An Old Poem, first attributed to Florence M. Alt

My life is but a weaving
Between my God and me.
I cannot choose the colors
He weaveth steadily.

Oft' times He weaveth sorrow;
And I in foolish pride
Forget He sees the upper
And I the underside.

Not 'til the loom is silent
And the shuttles cease to fly
Will God unroll the canvas
And reveal the reason why.

The dark threads are as needful
In the weaver's skillful hand
As the threads of gold and silver
In the pattern He has planned

He knows, He loves, He cares;
Nothing this truth can dim.
He gives the very best to those
Who leave the choice to Him.

1

WHERE ON EARTH?

(THURSDAY, MARCH 28, 2013)

"Life is what happens to us while we are making other plans."

❧ ALLEN SAUNDERS, *PUBLISHERS SYNDICATE* ❧

O ur family was living in a tranquil, airy, cabin-like home that was situated in rural McMinnville, Oregon, amid the ferns, on a wooded hillside, and near a gurgling creek that ran year-round. The weather had been unseasonably warm and sunny all week, not like the usual mostly rainy, often stormy weather of springtime in the Pacific Northwest. While I was thoroughly enjoying the sunny days and a very peaceful spring break—having had the house to myself since the previous Saturday—a proverbial storm was beginning to brew only seventeen miles away in Newberg.

Tuesday (March 26th), Beth, a good friend and fellow student of Mary's at George Fox University (GFU) in Newberg, Oregon, sent this message to Mary via *Facebook*:

Hey friend, what's up!?! Haven't heard from you... still wanting to adventure this week?

Wednesday (March 27th), Izzy, also a friend of Beth's and a close friend of Mary's, as well as one of Mary's two college roommates, messaged her:

Alright. That's it. I am officially worried about you. Had dreams you had your foot cut off and that's why you're not home yet, because you're in some hospital. Where the heck are you?! Why haven't you emailed Beth or me? She relayed your last email to her about coming back Sunday or Monday and here we are at WEDNESDAY, MARY! Bah. ...I am really worried about you; it doesn't seem like you to just ditch us and not keep in contact. Please let me know you're okay. If I don't hear back from you by tomorrow, I'll try calling your padres. Sorry in advance for potentially worrying them, but if you're stranded or stuck somewhere you just might thank me later.

Love you always,

Izzy

Thursday morning, March 28, 2013, I got a phone call from Izzy, asking if I knew where Mary was. I didn't. I hadn't heard from her all week.

Izzy told me Mary was supposed to meet up with her and other friends on Monday and she never showed. She was also supposed to meet Izzy for coffee on Wednesday, though Mary had also said she might hike Mount Hood on that day, early in the morning. Either way, she hadn't been in contact with Izzy at all regarding any of these plans. She had also talked about revisiting a section of the Pacific Crest Trail (PCT) for an extended hike somewhere, and she hadn't indicated exactly where on the trail or how long a stretch she might do. Izzy was starting to get worried.

Izzy confessed Mary had asked her not to tell anyone about any of these plans, because she didn't want people (mainly Bruce and me) to worry. She also related that up 'till now, she and a few of her other friends had all been a little miffed at her, imagining she had gone off on some adventure without them. Although they were all still somewhat mad at her, they were also collectively beginning to worry. None of them had seen or heard from her since Saturday. In the last correspondence any of them had from her, she said she would meet up with them Sunday or Monday. No one else they had asked during the week had heard from her or knew her whereabouts either.

Izzy acknowledged it was still highly possible that at any moment Mary might reappear from an extended hike in the woods, or from some other roaming, and be perfectly fine; she knew that Mary'd be upset with all of them for contacting and worrying us.

That Mary was perfectly fine, and just on an extended hike somewhere, is what I thought was likely.

Mary, our then twenty-three-year-old daughter, could be best described as an outdoor adventurer, and she pursued her ventures without reserve. Being a middle child of five, she had certainly overcome being "lost" in the middle by then. She was her own person, loving and caring, but not a crowd follower, including at GFU where she was studying.

She occasionally and intentionally took time out of her busy life to spend part of a weekend or other time with us (her family). We were still very close, even though we didn't get to see much of each other.

I explained to Izzy that Bruce had been the last one of us to talk with Mary. On Friday before she took off for spring break, she had stopped by his office in the finance department at GFU. Friday evening, Bruce shared her plans with me, and I told Izzy what I could remember of them. Besides those things Izzy had mentioned, I thought Mary had communicated to Bruce that she wanted to climb Mount Adams (WA), possibly revisit the area around Snoqualmie (WA) where we had stayed at a ski lodge once, and something about some hot springs, and going out to the coast. Bruce might remember or think of something I was overlooking.

Bruce and my son Elijah (Mary's only brother and youngest sibling) had gone down to southern Oregon for a four-day speech tournament in Medford, which was five hours away. Neither Bruce nor I had cell phones, and I was not expecting them to be home for several hours. After telling Izzy all this, I promised her I would have Bruce call her as soon as he and Elijah got home.

When Bruce called to let me know they were just leaving Medford I told him about Izzy's call. Neither of us were overly concerned because Mary disappeared all the time. Even though my first inclination was to think Mary's friends were probably overreacting, they were the same friends she had said she was going to spend most of her spring break with. For this reason, I called our daughters, Jessika, Rachel, and Ruth, to see if any of them were with Mary or knew where she was. She wasn't with any of them, and none of them knew anything concerning her whereabouts. However, since she was attending GFU at the time and was super involved with the community there, this was not unusual. Rachel thought I should call the police and report her missing—*it would serve her right for not telling anyone where she was going.* I didn't think this was a good idea at the time.

Both Bruce and Elijah arrived home dead-tired after the extreme expenditure of energy that a four-day, early-morning-to-late-evening speech tournament required. The long drive had only added to their exhaustion. After Bruce was done unpacking the car and had gotten situated a bit, he still hadn't called Izzy. I suggested maybe he should—just in case her concerns were valid. I knew he was really tired, and I still wasn't thinking we should be concerned, but I had promised Izzy I would have him call her once he was home.

Bruce ——

I called Izzy, and she told me something similar to what she had told Shelli. The last time she had seen Mary was early Saturday morning when Mary was on her way out the door while Izzy was still half asleep. She said somebody else had gotten an email from her on Saturday or Sunday about getting together Sunday or Monday. It was a little confusing. I wanted to know when the last time was that anyone had heard from her. Izzy and I agreed that we needed to talk with more of Mary's friends to see if anyone else had heard from her. Izzy said she would gather everybody she could and call me back.

Shelli

In the meantime, I sent the following email to Mary:

> Hey Mary, if and when you get this message, please call or email or FB us to let us know you're OK and where you are and what your plans are, especially for Sunday.
>
> No communication with those who love you about your whereabouts = we get worried.
>
> Love you,
>
> Your Mom-e

Bruce

Mary and I had many "friends" in common on *Facebook*, from homeschooling, church, family, and from George Fox University where I worked. I thought one of these friends might have some information on where she might be. I thought perhaps she might even be with one of them. So, while I was waiting for Izzy's call back, I decided to post something on *Facebook*.

> I would appreciate it if anyone out there who may know where my daughter Mary is would contact me. She may be hiking with friends near Stehekin, WA. We do not know which friends she went with or when she was planning to be back. Roomy called us today wondering if we knew where she is. Now we are officially concerned. Any info would be helpful.

Izzy called a short time later. She had gathered everybody she could. Beth and some of Mary's other friends were there. They put me on speaker phone so everyone could hear me. I asked them questions, trying to pin down exactly when the last time was anybody had heard from Mary. They began talking back and forth between each other and it was difficult to organize what they were saying to me, so I asked them to answer my questions one at a time. As we talked, the mood of the conversation remained calm but became more serious. It quickly became clear that the email Beth received on Saturday March 23rd was the last communication anyone had had from Mary. Beth read the email to me:

> "Hey Beth,
>
> It looks like the forest roads in the Hood wilderness are closed during the winter—they don't plow them. What are your thoughts on a trip to the coast instead? I was looking into other hot spring options but haven't found anything much. I'm going to try and be back in Newberg, either Sunday night or Monday morning. We could maybe rent a yurt on the coast and do some hiking in the area?
>
> Love,
>
> MaryO"

The email was sent on Saturday. When I realized nobody had heard from her for almost a week, I told them I had to file a missing person's report.

What also came up during our conversation with Mary's friends was that she had borrowed a truck from a friend named Beau. Beau was with a group of other (GFU) students who were on a serve trip in Washington for spring break. (Serve trips were a Christian volunteer, interactive-work opportunity offered to GFU students during school breaks.) I was able to get Beau's phone number from them and wanted to call him first to see if Mary had been in contact with him before I filed a missing person's report.

I tried contacting Beau but kept getting his voice mail. While I was waiting to hear back from him, I posted again on *Facebook*:

> More accurate information about Mary. She has not been heard from since Sunday. She emailed a friend and said she would [be] back in Newberg no later than Monday (morning) but she never showed up or contacted any [one] since. It turns out her roomy and other friends were the ones she was planning on maybe going to Stehekin with. They are worried as well.

After not being able to get in touch with Beau, I called the university and was able to get contact information for his serve-trip leaders. This was how I finally got in touch with Beau. He didn't know what her plans were. She just asked him if she could borrow his truck while he was gone, and he agreed. Since clearly Beau didn't know anything about her plans, I went ahead and decided to file the missing person's report.

I didn't really know where to begin, so I called the state police, who said I had to call the local police. So, I called McMinnville police, but since Mary didn't live in McMinnville, they said I had to call the Newberg police where she actually lived. I called the Newberg police and made the report with them. I was afraid they were not going to take my report seriously, and that they were going to tell me that because Mary was an adult there wasn't really anything they could do, but they were extremely helpful and thorough.

They asked me when the last time was that we'd heard from her, if I knew who she might be with, and the name of the person was who was supposed to lead the hike on Mount Hood. I anxiously went through the papers on my desk over and over again, now feeling like I had missed something that was very important. I couldn't remember the guy's name, and I couldn't find the paper I wrote it down on.

They asked for her banking information including her bank account number so they could analyze where she had been spending money over the last week. From this they thought they might be able to obtain video footage and see where she had been and if she was alone. Fortunately, since she had given me that information in the past, and I immediately knew where to find it, I was able to give it to them. Being able to quickly lay my hands on those papers made me feel at least a little useful.

They asked me to send pictures of her; they wanted all the information I had about Beau and his truck; they asked me for the contact information of her friends who had contacted us. Because they questioned me in such detail, I felt like they were taking me very seriously and that was really encouraging to me.

Shelli ───────────────────────────────────────

Bruce gave the police all the information we had on Mary's possible whereabouts. He also shared what Izzy and her friends had told him. It was when Bruce was relaying this information to the police that we both realized, Mary could be anywhere!

Bruce commented on his own *Facebook* post, and others commented after that.

Bruce: (5:36 pm) I just placed a missing person's report.

Sarah H. (Rogue Valley, NCFCA,* family friend, GFU student): The whole H—— family has you in our prayers.

Bronwyn D. (Portland area friend): We are praying!!

Robin F. (Rogue Valley, family friend): Praying.

Isaac A. (Rogue Valley, NCFCA friend): The A——s will be praying as well.

Theresa S. (Bruce's friend from high school): Praying too.

Bruce: (7:18 pm) Thank you all!

Esther P. (NCFCA regional director): We will be praying ...

Neil M. (Rogue Valley, family friend): Knees bent. Prayers sent!!!

Scott W. (Portland area, family friend): Bruce, I will be praying for your daughter. God will protect her. Let me know if I can help in any way!

From this time forward, these and other friends and family began responding to Bruce's posts, asking questions, wanting updates, and offering prayers and support. What Bruce and I both really wanted was information that might help us locate Mary. But while that wasn't forthcoming, it was very reassuring to know so many people cared about her.

We didn't even think about dinner that night. Both Bruce and I continued trying to contact people who might know where Mary was. Bruce tried getting in touch with her acquaintances and advisors at George Fox who were involved in Christian Services, her previous winter serve team, or Urban Services. Each contact led to a dead end. A lot of students and faculty were out of the area on spring break serve trips.

Bruce and I continued brainstorming for names of people she had recently gone "adventuring" with. Bruce looked at her past *Facebook* posts to see if we could find clues there.

The last four friends who had commented on a relevant post were some of her former PCT hiking companions. Bruce endeavored to reach them. He retried calling friends who had not answered their phones. We tried reaching friends from the Rogue Valley, where we used to live. We tried long-

---

* National Christian Forensics and Communications Association (Forensic: "belonging to, used in, or suitable...to public discussion and debate" [*Merriam-Webster online dictionary*]).

time friends, ultimate frisbee friends, and former homeschool speech club (NCFCA) friends. Using *Facebook*, Bruce tried finding names and contact information for anyone Mary had been in regular correspondence with. Each person Bruce was able to reach (only a few) did not know where she was or her plans for spring break. With each dead end our concern steadily grew.

Bruce then put forth considerable effort to contact some of her close friends who were out of town on serve trips in Washington, Oregon, and California. He tried her GFU pastors (mentors) and some of her homeless friends from the outreach in Portland. He tried Wycliffe staff who had recently been working with her, and he tried her previous employer at Visiting Angels. There were no leads.

Throwing the net wider, Bruce attempted to contact someone who had gone snow shoeing with her in January 2011. He tried friends who had hiked the Cascade Range with her in the Sisters area. He tried members of the student team who had done the Wycliff "Race 2012" with her in Montana. He tried friends who responded to her *Facebook* post in February when she said she was "jonesing for some mountain time." At each turn he was either unable to connect, or just like us, those he could reach had no idea of Mary's possible whereabouts.

When Bruce wasn't making phone calls, I was. I was also sending emails and *Facebook* messages. After all these efforts it was disconcerting not to have come across even a tiny hint of where she might be. We were thoroughly perplexed and becoming increasingly uneasy. We completely abandoned our normal schedule and activities, and all other concerns. Finding Mary became our sole focus.

At some point Bruce and I began asking friends and family not only for information they might have on her whereabouts, but also if they would pray with us.

We had been through some really difficult situations before this. Approaching God through prayer had gradually become a "go to" for us. Not only through personal prayer, but also through group prayer and through the intercessory prayers[*] of others in the family of God. We understood we weren't meant to go through our trials alone, but just the opposite. Imperfect as we all are, God still works through the prayers of His people. Prayer and prayer support had become our lifeline.

Because of our past experiences, we trusted God could and would somehow help us, even if it might not be in exactly the way we might expect. We knew He could work in ways and through means outside our own abilities or control. This situation was beyond our abilities or control! We knew we needed to ask in faith—or for faith—and God would help us, so we began asking and inviting others to call on the Lord with us for His help.

---

[*] In one definition, "intercessory" according to the *Merriam-Webster online dictionary* means: "prayer, petition, or entreaty in favor of another" (https://www.merriam-webster.com/dictionary/intercessory).

Facebook at that time, was still a venue where people who really were friends could post and share. I posted the following on *Facebook*, hoping Mary or one of her friends might see and respond:

Shelli (5:50pm)

Please pray with us that we will be able to find where Mary is soon, or that she would contact us or her roommates. regarding her whereabouts. soon. We have officially filed a missing person report with the police, because all the people who should know where she is, don't know where she is, and haven't heard from her...We are not sure that she didn't try to hike Mt. Hood.

Many friends and family members responding to our requests for information and for prayer were Christian believers, but not all were. We were asking people to petition God in Mary's behalf, but we valued the expressions of concern and empathy from each individual.

We can only include a few of the responses here (and in sidebars later) to give an idea of the tremendous support, which meant so much to us.

Karen E. (Shelli's friend from high school): Oh no! I will put this in a prayer right now. Please keep us posted.

Larry C. (GFU student, family friend): Praying! This post just tugs at my heart. Shelli, is there anything that I could do to help?

Wendy A. (Rogue Valley, NCFCA friend): We will pray Shelli.

Christine C. (Rogue Valley, family friend): Oh, my goodness! PRAYING!!!

Roy Z. (long-time family friend): There for you guys...

Yadira I. (GFU student, family friend): I'll be praying! God is watching after her.

Bronwyn D.: We are praying for her safe return.

Shelli: (6:18pm) If any of you heard any other plans she was making and might be able to give us a lead on where she might have gone (other than Mt. Hood or the places Bruce mentioned in his post), please contact us.

Heath L. (Rogue Valley, family friend): Lord, be with Mary; bring her home safe. Lord, comfort the Owen family.

David "Davy" P. (Rogue Valley friend, featured in a later chapter): I am praying.

J.S. (Rogue Valley friend): Would it be alright if we ask our church to pray...?

> Shelli: Please, yes, do, J—— ...! Thank you! ♥

Darrell P. (long-time family friend): Awaiting positive word from you that all is well. Certainly scary and you have our most positive thoughts there for you.

> Shelli: (7:39pm) The police here are in contact with the personnel at Mt. Hood's Timberline Lodge, etc. to see if she might have checked in at one of the points where climbers/hikers are supposed to check in, and they're putting the word out in that area concerning the vehicle she might have been driving.

Kevn L. (Mary's uncle): Thanks for the updates, Shelli. The anxiety at this end is difficult to bear; here's hoping for the best...

McKaylee A. (Shelli's sister): My prayers are with you! Love you!

Wendy T. (Utah, long-time family friend): Fervent prayer and faith in your and her behalf. The Lord knows all. Hugs.

K.T. (Rogue Valley, NCFCA friend): Praying, praying, praying for all of you.

Elisabeth P. (Rogue Valley, family friend): So sorry to hear about Mary. She and the rest of your family are in my thoughts and prayers, and I hope that she will be able to be found soon.

Julie J. (Rogue Valley, family friend): Oh, my goodness.... I'm so, so sorry to hear this. I really hope and pray that she comes home safely and for the Lord to comfort you. Jesus be with Mary please!

Kelly P. (Rogue Valley, family friend): Shelli, I just read this. Bob, Robert, and I all prayed and will continue to pray for her safety and return. Praying that she is safe maybe just off doing her own thing and forgot to check in. Does not sound like her though. So very sorry this is happening to you. Know how very worried you must be. Please keep us posted.

Becki D. (Rogue Valley friend): Praying for her safety Shelli.

Amy S. (Portland area, family friend): Shelli, we are praying! ♥

Victoria D. (Rogue Valley, NCFCA, family friend): I've been praying and praying...

Peggy S. (Rogue Valley friend): We're praying. The Lord is near!

After all our other efforts, Bruce and I both began to try for possible leads through people who, to our knowledge, Mary had *not* had interactions with recently. These included PCT "trail angels" (people who graciously provide food, drinks, or board for PCT through-hikers); extended family and relatives in and outside of Oregon; any one we could think of who she had *ever* gone hiking or climbing or "adventuring" with, and *anyone* we could think of who had any substantial connection with her.

Bruce --

I talked with the police again later Thursday night. They said that they had put out a B.O.L.O. (be on the lookout) in Oregon and in Washington state for the truck. They asked for pictures of Mary with identifying details, so I emailed them the following two pictures. I chose these because of the clothing she is wearing in them, which was typical of what she would wear when hiking. Also, she often wore glasses.

(left) Mary hiking one of "The Sisters," Oregon, carrying a friend's backpack
(right) Mary (Dad in the background) wearing her favorite beanie and a smile

Shelli _____

It was getting too late to be calling people anymore without being rude. And both of us had run out of steam and ideas. We were worn out from efforts that had all been fruitless. Bruce was beyond exhausted. He had been running on adrenaline for six days straight.

We went to bed, but I wasn't able to sleep. Laying there in the dark, at first my mind ran repeatedly through all the people we had been able to contact, had tried to contact, and who we might try the next day; the frustration of not knowing where Mary was or how to find her kept returning. I realized I was trying to figure things out all on my own; I began to talk to God with my mind and heart variations of a prayer that He would somehow lead us or others to find out where she was.

Somewhere in the midst of my ponderings and pleadings the phone rang—a potentially promising yet fearful interruption to the quiet of the night.

2

ON THE ROAD TO DISASTER

(FRIDAY TO SUNDAY, MARCH 22–24, 2013)

"The mountains are calling, and I must go."

✤ JOHN MUIR ✤

Mary

I had told a couple of my friends I was going to be climbing Mount Hood that weekend before spring break. I had an experienced guide who was going with a crew of people. Two of them had already been up the mountain. One of them had summitted Mount Hood over one hundred times! I'd also told Beth and Izzy, two of my dear friends, that I was going to be back on Monday to hang out and do something fun for spring break, maybe go on a beach adventure or go camping.

Friday night I read an email from my climbing friend. He was canceling on me. He said the weather didn't look good, and he didn't feel good about the conditions the snow would be in. That should have been my first heads up to not go.

I didn't tell my roommates about the email, so they didn't know I didn't have a crew. I'd been wanting to climb "the Hood" for about three years. I had it in my head that I was going to summit. I would have to summit by myself, since nobody would go with me. I was feeling very isolated and antagonistic towards humanity in general. I felt like I would never be able to go if I waited on other people to do it.

That night, I went ahead and got all my gear together, crowing all the while about the upcoming adventure. I avoided praying about the trip. I had a feeling God would tell me not to go.

I got up early Saturday morning around 4:00 AM and drove two-and-a-half hours from Newberg (OR) to the base of Mount Saint Helens (WA) with all my snow and climbing gear. I knew I was technically under-equipped and was trying to figure out if I really needed to get other gear. I didn't have a whole lot of money in the bank. I was testing out, *What I can make do with?* And, *What do I absolutely need to get?* I went and monkeyed around in the snow for a few hours on Mount Saint Helens. I wandered around and climbed up and down a few boulder outcroppings. It was foggy, almost a whiteout that morning, and the snow was deep and powdery. I had to follow my own footprints back down to the car. They meandered all over the place. I led this poor snowshoe-er, who was following my tracks, on a horrible climb for him. That was all Saturday morning.

I stopped at a gas station on the way back through Washington and paid with cash. That was good, because if I'd paid with a card, it would later have thrown off the whole search trying to track down where I went. I drove back down into Oregon, stopped that afternoon at the Tualatin REI, and picked up some microspikes, an ice ax, wool tights, Solomon Trail Runners, and gaiters (pieces of fabric that wrap around the top of your boots, so they don't get snow in them). I was just pulling together the absolute necessities of what I needed. I would have liked to have gotten better gloves and extra batteries and a better map, or rather, *a* map; I didn't have a map. But I was short on money and had to forego purchasing those.

I got a giant Chipotle burrito with what I had left so I would have lots of fuel inside of me. I used my debit card to pay for gas and then drove out to Mount Hood. It was a beautiful evening. On the drive, I could see the mountain all lit up by the sunset. I told myself I was going to be on that summit the next day. It was dark by the time I got to the Timberline Lodge parking area. I parked my friend Beau's truck that he had lent me in the lower lot, rolled my sleeping bag out in the back, and prayed God would wake me when it was time to climb.

Something woke me that morning. I rolled over and looked at the time. It was 2:00 AM. The perfect time to climb. I was cold and really tired, so I went right back to sleep and didn't wake up again until around 10:30 AM. Looking back, I think that two o'clock wake up was the last time I heard from God for several days.

It had been light for a while when I got up, and there were tons of people at the ski resort. I gathered my gear and stalked over to the lodge. I felt defiant towards everybody around me. I knew I appeared under-equipped. I was under-equipped. Judging myself from the perspective of another climber, I would think, *That person is doing a really stupid thing.*

In the ski lodge there is a place that posts notices about snow levels, avalanche danger, and cautions about different aspects of climbing the mountain. One of those was a caution about the fumaroles, "Do not linger by the fumaroles. The sulfurous gasses can cause asphyxiation and death." For some reason that stuck in my mind.

I went inside and filled out the self-registration. I didn't answer truthfully about whether I had a beacon. You're supposed to have some kind of signal device in case you go under in an avalanche or fall into a crevasse. I filled out the form and wrote on it that I had enough on me to make it through to the next day, until 5:00 AM on Monday. I figured that would give me enough time, even if something went wrong, to get back down again.

I was under the assumption they actually check those forms daily. Apparently, they don't check them unless they receive a call from somebody asking about a person, and then they'll go through and look. In my case, there was no one to make that call. I had trained all my friends and family not to worry about me when I was gone. I wanted the freedom to be able to disappear for a couple of days and go adventuring. The void I created around myself was all my own doing.

Looking up Mount Hood (Mary's photo)

I headed up the mountain from the lodge. It was a gorgeous day, sunny and—in my memory— clear (though looking back at the picture I took, I'm surprised at my own assessment). There were lots of people on the lower ski lift. I was hiking up, to the right side of the lift line. I didn't want to be in the main climbing track because I did not want to undergo the scrutiny of other climbers. There was a group I could see all roped together, proceeding up the main climbing track.

I was out of shape. I hadn't worked out or climbed or hiked or done anything most of that semester or the semester before because it was wintertime. So, I was going slow, heaving and panting. I also hadn't eaten anything for breakfast that morning because I didn't have very much food. All I had were some Keebler crackers, Nutri-Grain bars, and some chia seed. I had intended to get more food, but I ran out of money. I needed to have enough to put gas in the truck so I could get it back to Beau.

I probably started out from the lodge around 10:40 AM. It took me almost two hours to get to the top of the upper ski lifts. It was late March, and these were closed for the season. There was a building at about 8,500 feet where the snowcats* are kept. I stopped under the eaves of the building and pulled out some crackers for lunch. By that time, the temperature had begun to drop. The clouds I had not really registered as being there, had now settled in on the top of the mountain. Little flakes of snow were falling, and there was a thick mass of clouds rolling up from below.

There was a man who'd been climbing below me, he'd started later than I had. He had these seal-skin slip-on skis that could snap together to make a snowboard. He was slowly gaining ground on me and finally caught up to me when I stopped at the hut. We started chatting.

I asked him if he'd ever climbed Mount Hood, and he said he had summited. He asked if I was going to, and I told him I was just going to see how high I could get. I knew I didn't look well equipped, and I knew he would probably think it was a bad idea and tell me not to go. He told me it looked like a whiteout was coming in, and I said, "Well, it might blow over. Maybe the sun will come back out." I kind of blew him off. I wasn't being disrespectful or rude to him, but I was pretending not to catch his drift. He was trying to caution me without overtly doing so. I was so dead set on going to the top. Even as we were talking, I was thinking through what I had on me. I knew I could survive for a day or two if I needed to. I wasn't going to turn around.

As we were talking, another climber came into view making his way down the mountain. The snowboarder called out to him, asked him what the conditions were like up there. The guy didn't even stop moving. He shouted out as he passed, "It's not good, really windy. I'm heading down." The snowboarder had already begun preparing for his decent. He shot me a look. I shrugged and didn't respond. I don't remember what he said in parting as he clicked his board together and glided off into the thickening mist. The climber was already gone.

I had gotten chilled just sitting there. I wrapped my poncho around me, put my head down, and started climbing again. I was frustrated by how little progress I had made up to that point. *I have to do this.* I wouldn't admit to myself I was socked in. I was willing the clouds to thin out and roll away. It wasn't a full-on whiteout at that point. Visibility was probably about fifteen to twenty feet or so. I felt like I was in some bizarre dream, climbing up this ice field where the wind whipped across the ice and

---

* A snowcat is a vehicle with multiple tracks used in severe winter conditions and snow grooming at ski resorts (See http:// sno-cat.com/).

made patterns like flames along the ground. As I walked, the fog around me grew thicker. Strange rock formations coated in jagged ice would appear out of the mist and fade back again. They looked like something from an alien planet. It was very surreal.

I was at the limit of what I should have been doing with microspikes. The ice was rigid, and there wasn't much to grip. I had one hand holding my ice ax the whole time, and the other hand I was keeping inside of my poncho for warmth. My gloves were horrible. They weren't actually snow gloves; they were dirt-bike gloves, useless for keeping out the cold.

I kept going up, and it kept getting colder, and the fog kept getting closer. There came a point where I could smell sulfur. I knew I'd gotten up towards the "Hell's Kitchen" area. Sure enough, as I kept going, these big patches of bare steaming rock would emerge out of the mist and then fade back out. I thought it would be so nice to go over and put my hands on those rocks and warm them up. Then I had that little phrase from the poster in the lodge float through my mind like an advertising jingle, "Do not linger by the fumaroles." So, I kept on going.

The wind was whipping around me in strong gusts, and I didn't realize it, but there were snow drifts that were sifting in and out of my path. Occasionally I'd be walking, and it would be a couple inches deep, and then it would be ankle deep, and then it would be up to my knees, and then maybe back to a couple inches. As I trudged through one of those drifts I came up on a berm of snow. The mist revealed a cave with a brilliant blue pool of sulfur water beneath it. It was beautiful. I skirted around that and headed straight up the glacier to the right side of the "Hog's Back." But I didn't know where I was at that point, so I was heading up the center of the glacier instead of cutting over to the ridge with the most common summit approach.

I kept slogging on. I lost track of time and direction. I wouldn't be surprised if I zig-zagged up that glacier, but I was trying to go straight up. It seemed like it was getting dark really fast. My gloves had been soaked through for quite some time. I was cold and wet but still in this bull-headed frame of mind. *Turning back is not an option.* I knew I was going to have to change my mind at some point, but I was putting it off. I was watching as the snow drifted over my footprints. It didn't register at the moment; I would not be able to follow them back down again. I wasn't thinking about going back at all.

I kept on going, going, going, and I got really, really tired. I knew I must be near the summit. Eventually I dragged to a stop and just stood there panting. At that moment, the mist thinned a little and I found myself standing in front of a dark wall of sheer rock and ice.

3

HOW IT BEGAN

"How Do You Solve a Problem Like Maria?"

❧ Rogers and Hammerstein, *The Sound of Music* ☙

Mary posted on *Facebook* right before spring break:

Mary · Friday, March 22, 2013 · Newberg, OR

In need of a crazy and well-equipped adventure buddy. Where are all my PCT* people?

She was attending George Fox University (GFU) in Newberg, Oregon, and had been making plans for spring break, but no plans that were solid; she always resisted being tied down to a definite schedule. And this is how it all began—no one ever knew for sure what she would end up doing or when—not even herself. Bruce and I, as well as friends who were supposed to join her for some of her adventuring, understood her plans were usually tentative. This had become a pattern of hers over the last few years.

To her, adventuring usually meant doing something outdoors—usually something like hiking, climbing, rafting, camping, and so on. Because of an obsession with spontaneity, she would get an itch for adventure and just take off without telling anybody where she was going. Later, she would show up, refreshed, lively and happy. But Bruce and I couldn't simultaneously share her joy because we had spent that same time wondering where she was, and whether or not we should be worried about her.

She didn't want us to worry—in her mind she would be perfectly safe and was fully capable (which in truth, she mainly was). But she would sometimes take off for the wilds when we thought she was doing something else with friends. She wouldn't straight-out lie to us; she would just add her adventuring to the something else she had told us she was doing. Then, only afterward, she would narrate her adventures to us.

---

* Pacific Crest Trail

We genuinely appreciated when she would take a spontaneous, courageous, or similarly adventurous friend with her, but too often she couldn't find anyone to accompany her. When she had really tried and still couldn't find someone to join her on an adventure, she felt like her only choice was to go alone and just not tell us—so we wouldn't worry. So, a pattern began developing.

For a significant portion of Mary's childhood and youth, we had a home in the beautiful, forested hills of the Rogue Valley between Grants Pass and Rogue River, Oregon. One day when I was out on my daily walk, I heard her exuberant voice exclaiming, "Hello Momma!" It was coming from at least a hundred feet up in a sugar-pine tree! She was around eleven or twelve years old then. Of course, I ruined her "fun" and told her to carefully climb back down to at least a height that wouldn't kill her if a branch broke and she fell.

Our children did a lot of adventuring in the area surrounding our home. Climbing trees, rocks, and all kinds of terrain was a common and loved part of their childhood. And when it came to climbing anything (trees, rock faces, ladders), Mary was especially fearless. Sometimes it worried us that she didn't seem to have the usual fears other children did.

Bruce and I (mostly I), homeschooled all our children, including Mary, and I elected to spend as much time as possible out-of-doors for science and other activities with the children. As part of the science curriculum, the children and I would observe, draw, and journal what we saw in nature. We investigated the woods around us and explored other places as well, including city, county, state, and national parks.

Among some of the more well-known parks we explored were Great Basin, Zion, Bryce Canyon, Grand Teton, Yellowstone, Arches, Mesa Verde, Crater Lake, and the Redwoods. Wherever we lived or traveled, hiking was one of our favorite pastimes. Some of the trails we most liked revisiting were those to Big John Flat in the mountains near Beaver, Utah; also in the Telluride, Colorado area; trails near the Mount Ashland ski resort in Oregon and in Ashland Oregon's Lithia Park; the Table Rocks near Medford, Oregon; and various trails along the Rogue River and the Oregon coast in southern Oregon.

Of course, homeschooling was not only an outdoor activity. We studied mostly indoors. While I was schooling the children at home, Bruce worked full-time in Medford, a forty-five-minute drive away. We still managed to discuss and plan this important element of our children's lives together and implemented a solid core curriculum. At the junior and senior-high levels, we also facilitated our children's enrollment and involvement in various community classes.

In middle school, Mary completed a series of science classes (chemistry and biology) at the Rogue Valley Community College. She was also active in, and did a lot of traveling with, a nationally affiliated speech and debate club (NCFCA) during her high school years. And she completed a high school astronomy class, taught by an eminent astronomer and geologist, Barry Setterfield, at a local private Christian school, which had a large telescope housed in a professional observatory. She excelled in all areas, and during high school she was hired to help tutor other students.

Mary was hard working and resourceful, as I think all our children were. This was necessary for them growing up in our home. Bruce and I had made the decision early on in our marriage that one parent would be at home with our children as long as they were dependent on us. So, by choice we were a one-income family, which meant we needed to stretch and supplement the (lower to middle-class) income we had. The children, including Mary, took part in this and helped with what they could.

Depending on age and ability, indoor and outdoor chores were everybody's responsibility. We clothing shopped at Goodwill and Walmart (our children didn't have to worry about ruining their clothes being children); exchanged babysitting when the kids were little and when the children got older, they babysat for us; bought dry goods in bulk (the children helped us make mixes); made food from scratch, so the children learned how to cook and bake; usually had a garden the children helped with; sometimes dried clothes on a clothesline (with the children's help); drove older cars (we didn't have to worry about the minor dings that came with young people learning to drive); built and repaired things ourselves when we could (including our home and car); lived in small towns and in the "country" away from city centers where our rent or mortgage was less expensive (the children played outside instead of playing video games); prepared and brought our own food when traveling and tent camping (staying at a motel or hotel was a rarity); generally did without extras such as cable TV, video games, packaged snacks, dessert every night, eating out, cell phones, recreational vehicles, and so on. Mary, with our other children, learned many skills, from how to build their own forts, to how to (at least in part) build a house (we did most of the building of our own home in Grants Pass).

Our children also learned a sense of community and responsibility through the lifestyle we had chosen. We never received any local, state, or federal money for homeschooling books, supplies, or classes. We worked instead to fund supplies and extra-curricular activities in other ways. We sold and exchanged books and supplies with other homeschoolers. For a while we ran a bookstore and bought many of our own schoolbooks at the retailer's forty to fifty percent discount. We participated in volunteer homeschool co-ops and did activities together with other families for group discounts. Skiing and snowboarding lessons, for example, were free or deeply discounted for our children because of parent coordinators and volunteers. For speech tournaments we brought our own food, stayed with kind host families, and hosted other families ourselves in turn. We also did a lot of free outdoor activities.

Besides outdoor science studies and hiking, our children liked to participate in almost any other kind of physical activity outdoors—except maybe some chores. We often joined other families and friends to do things together. We facilitated group sledding, ice-skating, and skiing/snowboarding in the winter. In other seasons, on weekends, breaks, and vacations, we would go swimming, river-rafting, beach combing, camping, stargazing, and picnicking. The Rogue River and the Oregon coast were favorite spots. Our children always enjoyed playing at any park, and they liked trying out various sports with other young people. Ultimate Frisbee became immensely popular with them.

Mary always loved being outside and active. She still enjoys the rejuvenation of being in the "out-of-doors"—in God's creation. During her teens, her friends and siblings gave her the nickname "Maria"—as in the song "How do you solve a problem like Maria," from the musical, *The Sound of Music*. This was because of her free, exuberant spirit, and need to always be participating in some kind of outdoor activity.

"Maria" wasn't the only nickname she was given. Every person has their strengths and weaknesses, including her. During her childhood, despite her many good qualities, the nursery rhyme "Mary, Mary, quite contrary…" also sometimes characterized her outlook. She tended to be over-sensitive, a tattletale, and obsessed with "fairness." But during her early teens she came to a place of spiritual decision. She made a personal commitment to follow Christ, which to her meant dedicating the rest of her life to being His disciple, putting aside her own will in order to seek and do His will (usually a life-time process).*

After she had given her life to Christ, we began to see a marked change in her. As she grew in her understanding of and relationship with Jesus, she began to develop a new outlook on people and on life. She began to be more compassionate and self-controlled, less rigid or ready to judge others, more empathetic and thoughtful of other people, and much more cheerful and positive in her overall outlook.

This transformation didn't take place overnight, but it was a definite, real phenomenon. As parents, intimately involved in her life since childhood, we could see by her attitude, speech, and actions that she was developing a humble responsiveness to God's Spirit, and that He was helping her character and mind to deepen and broaden beautifully. He began to give her an ever-expanding heart for others and for their cares and concerns. She was becoming a true example to others of what it looks like to love and obey God and grow in love to Him and to others.

When she was fourteen years old, she looked into, and then went with Calvary Crossroads Church's youth group on their annual short-term mission trip to Mexico. She came back home with a strong sense that God's purpose for her life involved long-term Christian missions. Later, when she

---

* "Then he [Jesus] called the crowd to him along with his disciples and said: "Whoever wants to be my disciple must deny themselves and take up their cross and follow me. For whoever wants to save their life will lose it, but whoever loses their life for me and for the gospel will save it. What good is it for someone to gain the whole world, yet forfeit their soul?" (Mark 8:34-36).

was fifteen or sixteen years old, an opportunity came for her to go to Papua New Guinea (PNG) with a group from our congregation at Jerome Prairie Bible Church. She took it.

The purpose of the trip was to rejuvenate the missionaries who were serving there (in PNG) by providing a weeklong, spiritually refueling retreat for them. This required people on the church team who would babysit children; prepare, serve, and clean-up meals; and do general set-up and clean-up for the event. Mary helped with all these things, and by all accounts, she was a huge help. This extended trip helped her to get a feel for what mission life was like and to determine whether the compelling desire to go into missions was just a passing phase or a true calling on her life. And it was her first introduction to PNG.

Through these kinds of experiences and her growing love for and skill in learning foreign languages (Spanish, Latin, German, Greek, and some Japanese and Pidgin), which had been part of her homeschooling and exposure, she gradually grew confident she wanted to serve in this way. When we asked her what she wanted for a high school graduation present, without hesitation, she said she would like funds for a summer-long trip to serve in PNG. She had been researching a group set to go there, which she wanted to join for the summer. Their express purpose was to support prospective missionaries at a training camp in PNG. Through the generous help and support of friends and family, she raised enough money to go. That summer of serving in PNG confirmed her calling to long-term missions and, specifically, for Bible translation (translation into which language remained yet to be determined).

After returning home from that summer in PNG, and while waiting for tuition remission to kick in so she could start college, she decided she wanted to travel—to do something epic. She began working to save up the money for that "something." Eventually, she settled on hiking the continuous 2650-mile-long Pacific Crest Trail.

Once she had settled on that, she began doing research and acquiring her gear. She wanted to have her dad's full approval and support for this venture. His stipulations were that she:

1) wear shoes—she had begun to go barefoot after her time in PNG

2) carry a SPOT Finder—a GPS tracking and emergency signaling device

3) find and hike with a partner—not alone

She mainly agreed to abide by these.

So, twenty-year-old Mary and Dani, a young woman she met through the PCT website, began the trek early the following spring at the U.S.-Mexico Border. They both finished the trail about five and a half months later at a park just north of the U.S.-Canada border.

Mary's time on the trail had been ultra-challenging at times. For most people, it would have been the adventure of a lifetime. We should have known she was not going to be like "most people." For a start, as part of the trail ritual, hikers give each other a trail name. The trail name that the *PCT hiking community* gave Mary was "Dare Devil" (DD). This was a bit alarming. Instead of helping to satisfy her thirst for adventure as Bruce and I had anticipated, the PCT trek only seemed to have heightened it.

By the time she had finished the PCT, it was beginning to occur to Bruce and me that we might have an adrenaline junkie on our hands. This was borne out when shortly after she was home from the PCT trek, she was already looking for more adventure. Soon she had talked some of her friends into going skydiving with her. Then it was bungee jumping, mountain climbing, spelunking, and so on. She supported this obsession with various part-time jobs, though she was also saving money for college.

It wasn't so much the activities themselves that concerned us. In fact, Bruce had given her the information on the skydiving and bungie jumping venues (making sure they were reputable first). It was her overall approach and response. She seemed to have no sense of safe limits, nothing like a healthy fear for herself, and she could never get enough. She always wanted more. Mary expressed to Bruce and me, more than once, that since God had a calling for her life, He also had her back. She seemed to think this meant she could do anything and everything without fear.

This began to cause occasional tension between us. There was a stretch of time when Bruce or I had to "warmly persuade" her to wear a seatbelt when we were going anywhere in the car. It was also around this time that she began hiking and climbing alone and stopped telling us where she was going. These behaviors did not go over well with Bruce or me; she would get upset with us if we asked about her plans because she didn't want us to worry—though she would usually be glad to tell us after the fact about her latest adventure.

To be fair, Mary saw herself as a responsible person, and this was true in many regards. She never had a car accident in all her years of driving, including her teen years, which is remarkable by itself. She didn't abuse substances or, by her assessment, take willfully ignorant or stupid chances. When asked, she told the truth, and she generally kept her promises. She was confident and capable, mindful of other people's safety, and Bruce and I—and others—could justifiably trust her abilities. She mindfully assessed her own skills and those of others before undertaking any adventure where others were involved—even if she didn't always communicate this to us or to others. To our knowledge she had never caused injury to others or seriously hurt herself.

Because Mary perceived herself as being a responsible person, it is understandable that she disliked and couldn't comprehend it when either Bruce or I would express what we saw as a reasonable concern. We believed our concerns could be greatly alleviated by her communicating better. At other times, our parental judgment of "reasonable care" was just not the same as hers. She also equated our input with worrying, being overly concerned, and fearful—which are all things, she would remind us, that *Christians shouldn't do if they really trust God*. But as her parents, her arguments didn't always convince us that we were wrong or unduly concerned.

We felt that our few real concerns—her hiking alone and not telling people where she was going— were not nearly as extreme as she seemed to think they were. We wanted her to display a reasonable amount of care about her life and safety in *all* events—not only in those *she* considered care-worthy. We were concerned her lack of precaution in just these regards could possibly lead to serious or permanent injury to herself, or premature death, or it could lead to the same for others who might become involved with her. I specifically worried about potential mission field scenarios.

Another element that came into this mix was that she was almost impossible to get in touch with. She rarely had her phone turned on or charged. She checked her emails and *Facebook* sporadically. There was no reliable way to reach her. This medley drove many of us who loved her crazy—her friends, siblings, employers, and later her school associates, but especially, Bruce and me. Maybe this element helped make things seem worse to us than they really were. It certainly magnified the concerns we had. We saw this combination as a recipe for disaster.

One of my continual prayers came to be that God would give Mary a *healthy* fear, both for her own benefit and for any people she knew or who she might eventually be working or living with during her lifetime. I saw God honor my prayers. Several times He gave her opportunity to learn this lesson through significant scares (without serious harm coming to her). However, she seemed to recover from these experiences rather quickly. And with time, they no longer fazed her at all—but just provided "proof" God would keep her safe.

I concluded then, that on this matter, she wasn't willing to listen. But in looking back, I think Bruce and I were at fault too. We would undo the impact of a scare God had allowed by also chastising her. So, rather than her fully considering and realizing the dangerous situation(s) she had put herself into, she would dig in and defend herself and what she had done to get us off her back. With perspective, I believe Bruce and I, even in our rightful concern, were getting in the way of what God was trying to do in answer to our prayers.

Despite Mary's apparent lack of reasonable concern for herself and her continual drive for more adventure, she was never a heartless or uncaring person. She cared deeply about other people and was fully invested in helping and serving others, especially those she considered to be down and out, or those who were having great difficulties in their lives.

In 2011, a few months after hiking the PCT, Mary began attending GFU where Bruce was working. Her aim was to prepare herself to be a linguist and Bible translator* in Christian missions. During college she was also a regular volunteer with Habitat for Humanity, Wycliffe Bible Translators, and Urban Services—an outreach at GFU for giving ongoing support to homeless individuals and communities in Portland and Salem. She had also grown close to her college roommates, some of her classmates and co-volunteers, and others at the university. Her heart for others was a part of who she was and this was apparent in her daily life.

Intermittently, while she was attending GFU, on top of her very full schedule, she had sometimes worked part-time too. She had worked in the GFU cafeteria helping with food preparation and for an in-home care organization staying with people who needed someone close-by at night and sometimes during the day, for health-care reasons.

Her life was not only closely bound up with her family, college friends, recent coworkers, and clients, but she had developed close ties to quite a few other individuals. Besides her own blood relations, who are not few in number, she had made good friends through homeschooling, home fellowships,** church, and service communities—friends who were like family. She had worked at "Cary's of Oregon," a friend's candy factory; "Stu-de-bakers," a home-grown bakery; as a tutor for homeschool students, and she did yard and garden work for another good friend. She had also stayed connected with most of her former employers, coworkers, and clients from her high school days.

Bruce

The week before spring break, Mary stopped by my office at the university to see me. She told me about her plans for the break. Most of the plans were "ifs," "maybes," and "mights." She told me she *might* go hiking up near Stehekin, Washington. She *might* go try to find some hot springs, or she *might* head out to the coast. The only thing that was certain in her plans was that she was going to climb Mount Hood.

---

* Bible translation is the work of transmitting the original languages that the Bible was written in; Hebrew, Aramaic, and Greek; into a target language (for example: English, Spanish, French, Yamano). Translations can be literal (for example: keeping all the translated words as close to the original words as possible), or interpretive (for example: translating words, phrases, and figures of speech to have equivalent meanings in the target language). Usually, translations use some mix of these two methods. Most Bible versions describe the method used (and why) in the front of each edition.

** Fellow believers in Christ who meet in each other's homes, usually on a weekly basis.

She saw a shadow of worry on my face and quickly tried to reassure me by telling me that she was going with a group, and that they would have a guide—someone who had summited Mount Hood more than a hundred times. She even told me the name of the guide and somewhere, on a piece of paper, I wrote it down.

Mary and I had often disagreed on what reasonable safety precautions were. What I called reasonable, she called living in fear, and she was not about to live in fear. She had committed herself to a life of service to God as a missionary and she often told me, "God has me here for a purpose, and He isn't going to take me until I fulfil that purpose." Some of the activities she called living without fear, and in faith, I called tempting God. That's just where we stood.

Despite our disagreements on reasonable safety precautions, I felt very close to her and truly respected her outdoor skills. Nevertheless, I made her promise me, out loud, that she would not climb Mount Hood alone. No matter what we may have disagreed on, I had always known her to be truthful and to act with integrity. When she gave me her word that she would not climb alone, I had no doubt she would keep her word.

Shelli ————————————————————————————————————

Later, Bruce shared with me the gist of his conversation with Mary that Friday afternoon. Like many moms and dads all over the world, I pray for all my children every day—sometimes many times during the day (while walking or driving or doing other habitual things). At the beginning of each day, I would spend at least an hour reading the Bible and in prayer for the purpose of seeking to learn more of God's heart and will. Along with trying to listen, I would talk with God aloud or in my mind about what was in my own heart—good or bad—towards others or towards Him.

At the beginning of spring break that Monday, in the quiet and solitude of my bedroom with my prayer journal open, I didn't know where to begin concerning Mary. How should I pray her? My emotions all weekend had been a mix of frustration and anxiety because of her growing history of uncommunicated, spontaneous, and fearless adventuring.

Like God so often does, He brought me back to reality. He reminded me (by bringing past incidents to mind) that no one else's life has ever been in my control—including Mary's. After giving me the strong but gentle prompting (thought or impression) that I should put her activities for the rest of the week in His hands and leave them there, He gave me the affirmation of His peace. This answer from God was not unusual; it was just like Him—except the impression to leave off praying for Mary for the week. That was unusual.

Though the impression to leave off praying for Mary every day, for the time being, seemed strange, I knew (by experience) God understands my humanness even better than I do. I figured it might be His foreknowing that if I picked this up again—at all—my frustrations and anxieties would just escalate all over again.

It seemed like God wanted this to be an exercise for me in waiting on Him. So, that Monday morning I put and meant to leave my daughter, Mary, in God's hands for what I thought would be the rest of spring break.

However, before letting go, I sent her an email that morning so she would know I had been praying and thinking of her (this version is slightly altered to help add clarity):

> Hi Mary,
>
> I hope your day and week will be blessed. And I want you to know, because I know it is your heart's desire to glorify the Lord (show the truth about God by seeking, hearing, and doing His will) in and through all things that you do; that I am praying for you that this week you will remember while you're adventuring and enjoying God's creations, to hold up (elevate)—even above your joy in adventuring—the contentment, the sufficiency (total fulfillment), which you have in Christ (through following and being led by Christ) as surpassing all things—even surpassing the adrenaline rush of novelty, adventure, and danger...
>
> BTW, I don't know whether Friday will work for going to the coast, but if it looks like it really might work for you, then give me a call and we will see what things are looking like when it's closer to the day.
>
> I love you dearly and miss giving you hugs!
>
> Your Mom-e

I didn't get a response. I mostly expected I wouldn't, for a time anyway. I imagined she was out and about without her phone or computer, she just wasn't checking her email, or she was intending to talk with me later in the week. I didn't worry about it. With God's help, I pretty much just left it (and her) in His hands. Until Thursday.

INTRODUCING MOUNT HOOD

"What are men to rocks and mountains?"

❧ JANE AUSTEN, *PRIDE AND PREJUDICE* ☙

Mount Hood, a Portland landmark; photo by Sean Pavone

Bruce

Mount Hood is a deceptively dangerous mountain to climb. Its proximity to the Portland area and several popular ski resorts lulls many into a false sense of security. It is easy to not take seriously the challenges and potential dangers of climbing this mountain that is just right over there, in our own backyard. All too frequently, people lose their lives because they fail to give the mountain the respect that it demands.

Shelli ──

Mount Hood is the highest point in Oregon. There are no other mountains of comparable height within miles of it. Hood's outstanding grandness can be seen from 100 miles away on a clear day. Beautiful in all seasons, it's a prized landmark of the Willamette Valley. The summit lies 11,249 feet (3,428.8 meters) above sea level. It is not that high compared to other mountains in the world, or even compared to other mountains in the United States, or in the Cascade Range where it is situated.[1] However, it is a more difficult climb than many mountains that are much higher. There are no clear paths or trails to the top at any time of the year. Even with the right equipment, an ascent or descent attempted without enough training, preparation, knowledge of the mountain, attention to conditions on the mountain, and so on, can end up being deadly. Between the account of Palombo with *The Oregonian/OregonLive.com* and that of *KATU* staff, records indicate that since 1883 up until February 2018, it has been a fatal climb for over 146 mountaineers.[2]

In May of 1986, as reported by Toutonghi with *Outside Magazine* "the second-deadliest alpine accident in North American history," occurred on Mount Hood.[3] A group of fifteen well-prepared teenagers, a mother, an administrator, and a priest gathered in Portland at their Episcopal high school. They were all set to summit Mount Hood as part of an adventure program required for sophomores.

On Mount Hood, with the addition of two guides, this group had begun their ascent when a sudden, unanticipated, and very violent Pacific storm swept in. Most in this group wanted to turn back immediately; only seven gradually did.

Twelve, keeping with a beloved but overly zealous leader, continued their course. When they could no longer proceed in the extremely hazardous conditions, or endure the freezing, hurricane winds, they decided to turn back, but it was too late. Members of the group were already succumbing to the cold. They built a snow cave, but it was too small, and they had to take turns being outside.

Meanwhile, a valiant rescue effort was made by trained personnel, despite winds that even over-turned a snowcat and blew out one of its windows. Of those recovered during the next three days of this tragic event, four barely survived after hospitalization, one of them with his legs amputated, while seven students and two adults had frozen to death.

Another notable disaster on Mount Hood occurred in December 2006. Various persons have pieced together separate accounts of this incident, including Karen James, the wife of one of the deceased climbers (in her book, *Holding Fast: The Untold Story of the Mount Hood Tragedy*).[4] Kelly James, who had climbed many of the tallest mountains in the world, and two other experienced climb-ers, Brian Hall and Jerry "Nikko" Cooke wanted to summit Mount Hood by its north face gully. They planned two days for this more technical climb and brought only the equipment needed to do it safely and in good time.

They made it to the summit but did not make it back down. Two unplanned things happened. James sustained an injury on the way up, and a widespread winter storm settled in ahead of time on the mountain. They were supposed to meet up with a friend at Timberline Lodge on Saturday, December 9, for a ride back to their vehicle on the other side of the mountain, but they never showed. James called his wife and two older sons on his cell phone on Sunday, December 10, to tell them he was waiting in a snow cave while Brian and Nikko went for help.

Due to heavy snowfall, winds up to 140 mph (230 km/h), poor visibility, and freezing rain at lower elevations, no immediate attempt at rescue could go forward. Finally, on Saturday, December 16, the weather cleared, and nearly one-hundred Search and Rescue personnel began efforts to find the climbers. On Sunday, December 17, about 300 feet (90 m) from the summit, rescuers found an insu-lating sleeping pad, a rope, and two ice axes in what appeared to have been a snow cave. Not far from there, at around 3:30 PM, they found the body of Kelly James in another snow cave. Bad weather set in again on Wednesday, December 20. The Hood River County sheriff transitioned the mission from rescue to recovery. Brian Hall and Jerry Cooke were declared dead. Their bodies remained missing, though later efforts were made to find and recover them.

These are two incidents in a long list of climbing mishaps and fatalities that have happened on this deceptively benign-looking mountain. To the loved ones of those taken by the mountain, these were not just "incidents." Their lives were changed forever.

Of course, many people have safely ascended and descended this mountain. But it is a feat which requires specific instructions and training or a guide, as well as appropriate climbing preparations. A climb to the summit can be initiated from high up on the mountain's side because ski resorts there have roads that are passable most of the year. Though it might appear to be a relatively short climb, it is a technical climb that, as Mesh and Palombo have reported, can be risky for many different reasons.[5]

High avalanche activity, falling rock and ice incidents are the most common threats happening on Mount Hood during a large portion of the year.

Besides winter snow, sleet, and ice storms on the mountain, the micro-climate of the mountain itself, with its own weather system, is unpredictable and can change suddenly. Gusts or sustained winds up to 60 mph, drastic temperature changes in a short period of time, and sudden low to no visibility are some possible hazards any day—and are prime conditions for a person to unwittingly walk or slide off a cliff or into a crevasse, which too many have done.

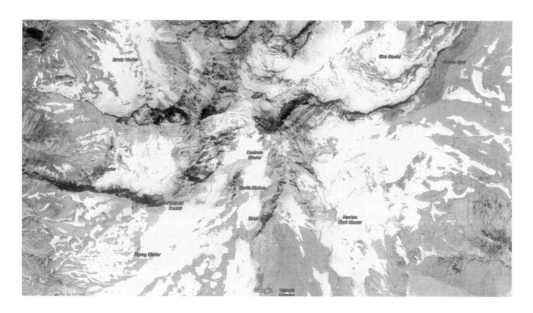

Google Maps, satellite view of Mount Hood glaciers

There are at least eleven glaciers on Mount Hood (see above map). Some have very deep crevasses and large internal caverns. Highlighting Mount Hood's Sandy Glacier (on which Mary became stranded), Tom Kloster details in his *WyEast Blog* that "Cavers have surveyed (to date) well over a mile of caves in the network, with parts of the cave system nearly 1,000 feet deep." In 2013, when Kloster wrote this article, Explorers were saying that this ice cave complex, consisting of at least three intersecting caves "is the largest…in the lower forty-eight states, and one of the largest in the world." Within Sandy Glacier they found "icy passages ranging from huge, ballroom-size open spaces with 40-foot ceilings to narrow, flooded crawl spaces only a few feet high, and passable only with diving gear." They described these caves as dangerous but also a "fantastic landscape of streams and waterfalls flowing under a massive, sculpted ceiling of ice."[6]

Other beautiful but hazardous aspects of the mountains are the large unstable cornices of overhanging snow created by the near-constant winds. These can protrude sometimes up to 40 feet out from ridges or other breaks in terrain. To the inexperienced hiker they might seem stable and strong, but as observed by *Avalanche.org*, because they are "cantilevered out over nothing but air" if you walk out too far on one, "zoom, down you go."[7] Walking out on a cornice or being below one that suddenly releases and comes crashing down, are both potentially and highly dangerous situations.

Like many high mountains, Mount Hood has its share of exceedingly steep terrain, perilous cliffs, and unexpected drop-offs that regularly claim human life (see examples in the endnotes).[8] Even during the short window of time considered to be optimal for climbing Mount Hood, when most people make the attempt, there have been a significant number of associated deaths.

The worst known accident to occur in prime climbing conditions happened in 2002. According to various reports from those involved or eyewitnesses, the following is roughly what happened.[9] In what must have been one terrifying moment, the *misstep* of one mountain climber, who was connected by rope to three other climbers, caused him to slip into an uncontrollable descent. His extreme momentum propelled his three partners, as well as five other climbers tethered together below them, into one entwined mass of unstoppable downward motion. They all slid about two hundred and fifty feet directly into a crevasse called the Bergschrund. This sometimes twenty- to thirty-foot-wide crevasse, which opens in the spring snow melt, lies approximately eight hundred feet below the summit of Mount Hood. It can get up to fifty feet deep. Five of the men hit bottom, three of them did not survive the fall. The other four that landed higher up in the crevasse on ledges all survived.

This already horrific situation was compounded when during the rescue attempt the helicopter, preparing to collect and carry the third and last critically injured person out of the crevasse, lost air lift. With its five-member crew, it crashed into the snow and began rolling down the mountain, throwing out parts and crew members as it went.

Miraculously, because of the soft snow, all five members of the helicopter crew survived, though one was critically injured. Because the astute pilot cut loose the tether as the helicopter was going down, the already severely injured individual they were about to lift out of the crevasse was not dragged down the mountain with the helicopter. As the helicopter was going down, the pilot also managed to avoid hitting any of the emergency crew on the mountainside who were assisting with the rescue.

Those who saw one or the other of these accidents that day, and those who were involved and survived, later expressed complete amazement that of the fourteen total people enmeshed in these two connected accidents, only three of them perished. All who were involved unanimously acknowledged that as awful as these combined incidents were, it could have easily been much worse.

Fumaroles on Mt Hood, photo by Mary (2015)

Besides normal mountain hazards, Mount Hood is also a volcanic mountain with active fumaroles. Magma relatively near the surface causes the water in these openings in the earth's crust to boil. Steam and sulfurous gases rise out of them and can cause vomiting, asphyxiation, or death to climbers who venture too near or slip into one of them. Two of the most well-known, "Hot Rocks" and "Devils Kitchen," lie on the most frequently used southern approach to the summit. Tomlinson, a reporter with *The Oregonian/OregonLive.com*, wrote a timely article in 2015 describing "new protocols" SAR was developing "to save fallen climbers from toxic volcanic vents" on this mountain.[10]

Earthquake swarms, though generally small quakes, are frequent in the Mount Hood area according to Hartog with the *Pacific Northwest Seismic Network*,[11] and may also occasionally trigger snow or debris avalanches.

There are debris avalanches of various sizes in connection with the volcanic formation and structure of this mountain, especially in the spring when terrain has been loosened by repeated winter freezing, thawing, and moisture. Once lahars—large debris flows made up of volcanic rock, ice, water, and mud—begin their rapid flow, they can be devastating. *United States Geological Survey* reports indicate that lahars are generally released by heavy rains.[12]

In recent recorded history there have been no climbing fatalities in connection with lahars, but there has been one recorded death and a great deal of damage, when lahars have broken loose from the sides of Mount Hood.

One of the larger Mount Hood lahar flows recorded by *United States Geological Survey: Volcano Hazards Program,* happened during a rainstorm on Christmas day in 1980. According to this summary, the heavy rains…

> …triggered a landslide at the steep head of Polallie Creek on the east flank. The landslide transformed into a debris flow [or lahar] that scoured sediment from the creek's channel banks and entered the East Fork Hood River, carrying a volume 20 times greater than the initial landslide. The debris flow temporarily dammed the East Fork. About 12 minutes later, the dam was breached, and a flood surged down the East Fork, destroying about 10 km (6 mi) of Oregon Highway 35—a total of $13 million in damage (in 1980 dollars). One person was killed. Similar events have swept down most of the valleys on Mount Hood during the past century, but flows on White River, Newton Creek, Eliot Branch, and Ladd Creek have done the most damage to roads and bridges.[13]

In Kloster's above mentioned article on the Sandy Glacier caves, he says:

> The downstream effects in recent years from Mount Hood's melting glaciers have been startling, and the Sandy Glacier is no exception. Sometime during the winter of 2002-03, a massive debris flow was unleashed from just below the terminus of the Sandy Glacier, and roared down the Muddy Fork canyon. The wall of mud and rock swept away whole forests in its wake, burying a quarter mile-wide swath in as much as fifty feet of debris.[14]

With all of its beauties and all of its dangers, Mount Hood is a mountain to be respected, and the goal of summiting this mountain is not appropriate for *spontaneous* hiking or climbing. It should only be climbed at the right time of day (or night), when the conditions are right, never alone, and by someone or with someone who not only knows the ins and outs of mountain climbing in general, but also those of Mount Hood in particular.

In 2009, not long after our family had moved to northern Oregon, I was clued-in to how dangerous Mount Hood could be. It happened on of one of the first homeschool skiing/snowboarding days that I took with my daughter Ruth and my son Elijah at Timberline ski park. In front of Timberline Ski Lodge, as we were entering the lodge at the start of our ski-day, we encountered Search and Rescue personnel with trained dogs. They were preparing to search the mountain for three missing climbers, Luke Gullberg, Anthony Vietti, and Katie Nolan. There was still some hope of finding them alive then. All three were experienced mountaineers.

Later we learned that during this search, Luke's frozen body was found, and that the search had to be called off because of severe weather conditions. The other two, Anthony and Katie, remained missing for many more months.

That following summer, on August 26, 2010, Elijah and I were back on Mount Hood again. This time, we were there with some family friends, the Swarts. At the time, Mary was in the midst of hiking the PCT, the trek she had begun in April at the Mexican border. Our plans were to intercept and then share lunch with Mary and her hiking buddy "Shades" (nicknamed for his sunglasses) at Timberline Lodge.

The PCT traverses the west side of Mount Hood. Mary and Shades were slated to arrive in the Mount Hood Timberline ski park sometime towards late morning. We had planned to meet them on the trail below the lodge, so we could hike with them, eat lunch at the lodge together, give them some "joyful" food supplies, and then possibly hike a little farther with them before all going our separate ways.

Elijah and I met members of the Swart family in the Timberline ski area parking lot as planned. Then together we hiked down the trail into the forest until we encountered Mary and Shades. On spotting each other we all erupted into expressions of gladness at seeing each other again. Smiling and laughing, we began waving and calling out our lightheartedly silly greetings. Even as dirty and odorous as they were, from hiking and camping for days without showers, there were uncontainable hugs and squeezes all around.

During our return hike up that beautiful mountain in the sunshine, and while we were eating lunch together at the lodge, we continued to notice a helicopter and rescue workers occupied with something higher up on the mountain. From inquiring, we learned that the bodies of Anthony and Katie, the remaining two missing climbers from the previous winter's incident (2009), had been found on the mountain the day before, and a recovery team was in the process of transporting them down off the mountain. (See endnotes for reference to *The Oregonian/OregonLive.com* report.[15])

Our inadvertent presence on Mount Hood, at the beginning and then again at the end of the search for these three young mountaineers, was sobering for me. Our being on Mount Hood on these two significant days embedded this heart-breaking event in my memory. It was my first personal exposure to the potential perils of Mount Hood. It did not escape my notice that the young people who were lost were experienced climbers. It gave me some serious respect for the hazards this mountain could hold. Because I was aware of Mary's growing predilection for climbing mountains, I shared what I knew of the beginning of this incident with her while we were all witnesses to the end.

Earlier in the year, while hiking the PCT through the Sierra Nevada mountain range in California, Mary, with her hiking companions Dani and Louis, had climbed Mount Whitney—which at 14,505 ft (4421.0 m) is the highest peak in the continental United States. The PCT through that range already traverses the terrain at some very high elevations. It was a relatively small jaunt up to the summit of Mount Whitney from the PCT for Mary and her companions. She had climbed a few other mountains along the way as well and seemed to be forming an obsession with summiting mountains.

When Mary and Shades passed through the Mount Hood area, they were on a time crunch, nursing slight injuries, and low on motivation for extra physical exertion. Their eyes were on reaching their destination in Canada before the early snows began to prevail in Washington's mountains where they were headed. Bruce and I knew then that even though Mary didn't stop to climb to the top of Mount Hood during her trek of the PCT, she would want to climb it sometime—probably in the not-too-distant-future.

While the Swarts and Elijah and I were eating lunch with Mary and Shades that day on Mount Hood, a bank of low-rolling fog began to move in. After lunch at the lodge, we headed north on the trail with them. We hiked the trail together for a mile or so before we, the non-through-hikers, needed to return to our vehicles and homes. Mary and Shades continued towards Washington in the by-then soupy fog and drizzle. Before the rest of us got back to the lodge parking lot, we could hardly see our way on the trail, and we were completely soaked by the dense, wet fog.

We wondered if Mary and Shades were still hiking in heavy fog. They still had a fair distance to go for the day. Just imagining what they must be going through in their current condition, with their injuries and weariness, on top of the cold, wet weather, caused me concern the rest of that day, and really until we heard from them again. Until they got safely to the next rendezvous point a day or so later (in Oregon still), where we were able to see them again and could know they were okay, I found myself, many times, asking God to heal, strengthen, and help them.

Mary

The first time I thought about climbing Mount Hood was when I was on the PCT. I had hiked around the base of Hood with my friend, and the experience had been awful. This thick cloud came down and sat on top of us. We were already hurting from overuse injuries,* and the bad weather just added to our misery. It wasn't until the next day that we got out from under the cloud cover and, looking back, could see the mountain. It stood, clear and gleaming in the sunshine, as if taunting us. At that moment, I determined at some point I would go back and redeem my experience by climbing it.

During the next couple years, I tried multiple times to pull a few friends together to climb Mount Hood. Occasionally there were climbing crews who invited me along. Inevitably, the timing wouldn't work out, and they'd end up going without me. I began to grow frustrated and even a little obsessed with that beautiful, snow covered face that constantly beckoned to me from the horizon.

In 2013, it looked like my chance had finally come. I had made a friend while climbing North Sisters. He was an experienced mountaineer who had guided crews up Mount Hood over one-hundred times and had offered to take me on the next trip that they did. I asked him if he'd be willing to lead one up on spring break, and he said that he would. I was going to climb with him and a couple of other friends of his.

Then, at the last minute, a day and a night before we were going to leave, he cancelled the climb. He said he didn't like the conditions. I'd already told everyone that I was going to climb it. I had bragged that I would climb it by myself if people didn't come with me. I was so excited about doing it and so determined to succeed, I wasn't going to let this be yet another failed attempt. I decided that I'd just go by myself.

---

* Overuse injuries are caused by repetitive trauma to muscles and joints, such as the impact on feet, ankles, knees, and even hips from hiking too far beyond one's conditioning in a day. Initially they cause pain and tenderness but can eventually cause stress fractures or small cracks in the bone, so they're not taken lightly.

5

"THIS IS WHERE PEOPLE DIE"

(SUNDAY TO EARLY MONDAY MORNING, MARCH 24–25, 2013)

"I suppose I'll have to add the force of gravity to my list of enemies."

୬ LEMONY SNICKET, *THE PENULTIMATE PERIL* ୭

Mary

When I found myself stopped, cold and wet, standing there panting in front of that dark wall of sheer rock and ice more than a thousand feet from the summit, I thought, *You know I'm not going to climb that in this condition.* I finally let it sink in, *I can't do this.* It was relieving. I didn't have an option other than to turn around. I felt like a spell had been broken. Whatever desperate determination had been driving me suddenly fled, and I was left feeling the stupidity of my situation.

I turned around and headed back down. I tried following my own footprints, but they were already effaced by the snow. I was relying solely on my sense of direction, which didn't count for anything in a whiteout. I was purposely edging to my right as I went down, because I had been cautioned by several people about the tendency people had to drift into White River Canyon on the south-east side of the mountain. A lot of people in low visibility have died down there on the glacier or in the canyon. There are a lot of crevasses, and the canyon is sheer, prone to rockslides and avalanche. I was worried about not being able to see my way and accidentally ending up down there, so I kept going right. I was over-correcting.

I knew that when I started down, I was on the south side of the mountain. I didn't know I was as near the summit as I was. I ended up drifting all the way around to the northwest side of the mountain, going up and over the Hog's back, traversing the little glacier on the other side and scooting down a narrow chute of ice and rock that lets out under a series of rocky cliffs above the Sandy Glacier. I've looked at that chute in the daylight on a subsequent climb. I never would have dared to go down it if I could have seen what I was doing! At the time, I had no idea where I was. With the snow drifts, the whiteout, and the growing darkness, I was completely disoriented. At one point I made a little snowball and started rolling it in front of me just to get a read on what direction was downhill.

I started to worry about getting down off the mountain. I was so cold and poorly equipped. Once I went down that ice and rock chute, I started doing controlled slides with my ice ax. I would slide for a little bit and then stop, edge further to my right, then slide for a bit, and then stop again. I was repeating in my head, *You've got to get down as fast as possible. You can hike out of anywhere, just get down.*

I sincerely believe God was protecting me the entire time. There was one point where I was sliding, and I stopped. I realized it was dark around me. I pulled my headlamp out and turned it on. I was only a few feet away from the edge of a crevasse. That was sobering. I already knew the situation wasn't good, but at that moment it finally hit me, *I could die out here*. If I had not stopped my slide, I would have gone right into the crevasse with no warning. Who knows how far down I would have fallen? I said a short prayer of thanks and began to edge around the crevasse. I kept going down, but slower and more carefully. No more slides.

I was still drifting to the right. I don't know how it got so late so fast. I lost track of time and direction. I was just wandering in this fog. And then, abruptly, I was out on a glacier in the moonlight. There was a cap of thick cloud sitting down on the top of the mountain, and I had just walked out from under it. I could see the lights of Portland in front of me, so I knew I was on the west face of the mountain, the wrong face.

I had a number of different things running through my head. In my registration, I had put down 5:00 AM as the time people should start looking for me. I knew it was late, so stopping wasn't an option. I needed to get back before I put other lives in danger looking for me. I was working through what my options were. *I could try to get over to the ridgeline and follow that down until I find the PCT wrapping around the mountain. I could try to go up and over the ridgeline and onto the next glacier and find my way back towards the Timberline ski park. I could head down the canyon until I hit a trail.* The terrain situation made my decision as to whether to try to go over the ridgeline. The snow was so deep that going any direction but down was like swimming through mud. It was up to my hips at most times.

I found a snowboard track that went across the glacier, and I figured rather than keep slogging through the snow that was so deep, I'd use the snowboarder track to make my way easier. I was beginning to feel my exhaustion, though I truly had no idea how bad it was at that point.

Even though the snowboard track was going across the glacier in the wrong direction, I started following it. The track was skirting down to the right again, heading North. I followed it down to the ridge on the other side of the glacier. That snowboarder was doing some crazy zig-zagging stuff all over the top of that ridgeline. Finally, I decided, *This person's crazy. I can't follow this.* So, I decided to jump down off the ridgeline, back onto the glacier, and try to make my way, either down the canyon, or up the other side. I jumped. I don't actually know how far the drop was. I think the helicopter crew saw it when they were looking for me, because they said they saw where I fell. It looked like there was a snow drift at the bottom. I couldn't see the tops of pine trees or anything poking out. I said a little prayer then jumped out. I was really relieved it was just snow I landed in.

I started wading across the glacier again, and again found that any direction except for straight down was almost impossible for me. I kept going down, and pretty soon I could hear water underneath the snow. I was getting down to where the glacier was starting to break up. I was scrambling down snow covered boulders now. I stopped to get water where the glacier started to fall down into the canyon. There was a spot where I could reach with my water bottle through the bigger boulders to where the water was running below.

As I kept on heading down, I started thinking about the Jack London story, "To Build a Fire," where a man punches through the snow into water. He gets hypothermia, he can't build a fire, and he dies. I could hear the water running beneath me as I worked my way down the canyon. The further down I went, the louder it got. I knew the stream was getting bigger. The canyon was getting narrower and narrower, forcing me to walk on the layer of snow over the water. I started to worry that if I went further down, I wouldn't be able to navigate around the stream. It would be too big. So I started to look around at other options.

There was a spur, or ridge, coming up from the river to about halfway up the canyon wall on my left side (the side nearer to Timberline Lodge), and up on the canyon wall there was what looked like a clean snow chute leading to the top. *Maybe if I could get up to that chute, I could use my ice ax to climb out onto the canyon ridge, then walk down the ridgeline to trail.* All this time, I was feeling the urgency to get back to the lodge before they sent searchers out for me. I didn't think stopping to wait for daylight was an option.

I started climbing up that spur. Slogging up through snow covered brush. There were trees along the spine of it. And once I reached them, the snow was only a few feet deep. I stopped then, under the trees, too exhausted to go on. I would have to rest just for a little while.

I tried to make a fire, searching for anything in my pack that I could burn for a fire starter. I tried my climbing permit, but it was soggy and wouldn't light. Then I found a Nutri-Grain wrapper, and that was good tinder for getting my little fire going. I pulled out my tarp, curled up in my poncho, and slept for a while. I lost my glasses there. They tossed out of my pack when I pulled my tarp out. I was so tired I just thought I would get them later, and then I didn't.

I probably didn't sleep longer than forty minutes. It occurred to me to check the time, so I powered up my phone (the battery was dying). I checked if there was a signal. There wasn't. It was 2:00 AM on Monday morning. I had been on the move for fifteen hours before stopping to rest there. But the thing going through my mind was, *I have three hours to get down this mountain and back to the lodge.*

So, I packed up and kept going up the ridgeline to where it met the canyon wall. There was a good size snow field between me and the snow chute I had seen earlier. I started traversing this, working my way over to the right and up. The slope was on a forty-five- or fifty-degree angle. The snow was so deep, it was up to my chest. I would climb up, and then slide back, then climb up and slide back. I didn't have any kind of flat surface to pound the snow down and give me some purchase. I battled and battled and battled, trying to make my way up. By the time I had made about forty feet I had spent any energy regained by my short rest. It was pretty ridiculous. I realized the snow chute was only going to be more of the same on a steeper angle.

I started thinking, *Okay, if the snow chute is like this, I'm not going to make it up the snow chute, at least not in the time that I needed to make it.* So, I changed tactics. There was an area of rock and trees above me and to my left. I figured the snow would be thinner underneath the trees, and I could use the terrain to get some traction going up. I fought my way over there, then began to climb the canyon wall. I was scrambling up, climbing from tree root to tree root, to branch to rock. It kept getting steeper until I was climbing vertical. I started using my ice ax in places where there wasn't a tree to hold onto. I jammed it into the ice and rock and used it like a hold. That was working pretty well.

Then I got to a place where there was a significant gap between tree roots. I slammed my ice ax in and put all my weight on it to lever myself up to the next hold. It slipped out, and I started to fall.

Everything went into slow motion. I had all these decisions going through my head. *Lose the ice ax; it's going to hurt you at this point.* I didn't trust myself to do a self-arrest without skewering myself. *Turn around so you can see where you're going. Tuck your arms in so you don't break them. Don't scream.* Then I was pin balling between the trees and rock I'd just climbed up. I was bouncing from one trunk to the next, mostly hitting what I thought was my torso. I hit one trunk extra hard and made a weird grunt. It sounded strange to my ears, like the sound a gorilla might make. Then I was sliding out onto the field of snow. There was a place where the snow ended abruptly at a steep drop carved out by water or rockslides. I splayed out my arms and legs and dug them in so I could stop my fall before I went over the edge.

I skidded to a halt and just lay there breathing hard for a minute. Then I got up and tried to walk. Right away, I could tell there was something wrong with my left leg. It didn't hurt, but there was this weird tugging sensation when I tried to move it. *Okay, I need to stop and wait until daylight and figure out what's going on—if I make it to daylight.* So, I used my right foot to pound out a flat area with a concave back in the snow. I was using my foot like a hammer, just slamming it into the wall of snow. I just needed a platform so I wasn't sinking four feet down every time I moved, and a bit of an overhang so stuff trickling down off the canyon wall wouldn't be hitting me directly.

I pulled myself together and assessed the situation there. I pulled out my climbing harness and put that down, and then put my tarp on top of that to create some space between me and the snow. Then I pulled out my camera and made a video for my parents. I realized after I stopped moving, *This is where people die. This is where people get hypothermia and they die, and they end up being found weeks later with no explanation.*

I've never been afraid of death, but I didn't understand until right then that death isn't just between you and God. That when you take your life, like I kind of had, in a way, by going up that mountain alone and being so careless. It impacts a whole world of people. I wasn't sure what was going to happen. I knew I was hurt and cold and I was really poorly equipped for snow. So, I made this recording for my parents. I wanted them to know how I got where I was, and what my mental state was. You hear stories of recovered climbers' bodies, and people wonder: "What were they thinking?" "How did they end up over there?" It was also important to me to know that I could say *God is good*, that I could say I trusted Him when I was actually looking death in the face. I made my parents a video telling them, "I'm sorry for being so careless," and letting them know, "I'm not, I'm not afraid, but I am sorry."

Then once I started talking, all the loose ends of my life came rushing in on me: the job I had arranged to work that summer, the ministry I was in in Portland, the last conversations I'd had with my siblings and friends, people I wished I'd treated differently, things I wished I would have said. It was hard to process what I needed to say. I was crying, but I was trying not to make it come out in the recording, so the recording sounds really weird. I recorded all this as video, but you cannot see anything but the darkness. When I was finished, I had to wrap my head around the idea that I probably wasn't going to make it through the night. I wasn't really certain how that works. When would death come to me? Would I know its approach?

The thought occurred to me to put my camera batteries into my GPS to figure out my location. I hadn't had enough money to purchase batteries for it. I don't know how accurate that GPS was, but it told me there was a town three miles away from me, somewhere down below. *I could crawl three miles.* I got situated to make the most of my body heat. I had my poncho over the top of my North Face jacket. I was wearing tights and running shorts and three layers on my torso: a tank top, under armor, and a T-shirt. I had my buff covering my neck and face and my hat on. I stripped my gloves off because they were just making things worse. They were soaked through and freezing cold. My tarp was underneath me and folded up behind me as well. I had my poncho over the top of everything.

I tucked myself into the jacket so only my feet were sticking out, and just kind of breathed into that space trying to keep my warmth inside.

I dozed in and out, sometimes leaning against the wall behind me, sometimes hunched forward balanced on my feet. I dreamt about finding a pathway off the mountain.

I dreamt somebody came along and said, "Hey, there's a path right there."

Man, I totally didn't see that. I actually woke up and packed my bag. Then I realized it had been a dream and there wasn't any path there. I felt really dumb for having wasted my energy and heat doing that. It was dark and there was a wet snowfall pattering down on my poncho. I was shivering so hard that my whole body was spasming. I was glad I was shaking like that because it meant my body was fighting the cold.

6

"SHE'S MISSING!"

(THURSDAY EVENING, MARCH 28, 2013)

How little we know the ones we love.
How little we know of anyone, in the end.

✎ ARIA BETH SLOSS, *AUTOBIOGRAPHY OF US* ✎

Case Report

Case Number : _____   Run Date : _____

Description :   MISSING PERSON

Report Date / Time :   3/28/2013 5:24:00PM   Related Cases :

Occurred Date / Time :   Beg DT :   3/28/2013 5:24:00PM

Location :   MERIDIAN ST, Apt , NEWBERG, OR 97132   Grid :   8

Case Status :   Case Disposition :   Located (Missing Persons and Runaways)

Offenses :

OTHER ACTIVITY-MISSING PERSON

OTHERS INVOLVED

Involvement Type: REPORTEE

Name :   OWEN, BRUCE THOMAS

DOB :   _____   Age : 50   Race : W   Sex : M   Height : 603   Weight : 275

Address :

Work Phone :   Cell Phone :

Beginning of Newberg Police, Missing Person Report

(For the full report, see *Mountain Rescue* website:
https://www.mountainrescue.online/official-reports

After Bruce filed the missing person report with Newberg Police late Thursday afternoon, other people besides Bruce and me, and her roommates and friends who we had talked to earlier in the day, began texting, calling, and asking around about Mary. The Associate Dean of Students at the university sent Mary an email:

Date: Thu, Mar 28, 2013, 7:46 PM

Mary:

We are trying to find you; please give your father a call.

Our friends who had learned Mary was missing began texting, calling, emailing, and posting messages on *Facebook* too. It was so encouraging to know we were not alone, and that other people were hoping and praying with us that someone, somewhere might know where she was. Following were some of our communications with friends through *Facebook*:

Roy N Hollie S. (Portland area, close family friends): Praying. Can you call and have them check the sign in log? ...Roy says there is a sign in log at Mt Hood. He is calling a friend to see if he knows where it is.

Shelli: Hollie, we will try contacting the lodge at Timberline [ski park], I know I've seen a sign in book there.

After this conversation Bruce asked the police about the log in book. They were already looking into it.

Guino G: (8:51pm) The Timberline Lodge has the Mt Hood rescue center in its basement. Did you guys get in touch with them?

Shelli: we have been in touch with Mt. Hood, or rather the police have. They don't think she tried to do the climb... because if she was with someone who was a professional climber (she said their prospective guide was), he would have signed their group in... and they're not signed in.

Jaime P. (Rogue Valley friend): We are praying for her safe return! Is there anyway her phone can be tracked? We have that feature on our phones. I would bet her cell carrier could do something! Lord, please bring Mary home safe and sound. Lord, please keep her in your care and bring her help if she's in need. Comfort and give wisdom to her family and friends and all who are searching!...

> Shelli: Unfortunately, she doesn't have a working cell phone. Thank you for any ideas though!

Scott W.: Bruce if you can post a picture of Mary, all of your friends can share the picture and get the word out. A lot of people on Facebook are great about helping find missing people. A lot of time people are found quickly after a picture has been posted. Praying for all of you.

Mary Beth J. (Bruce's sister): Bruce, what is going on??? Please let me know....

Bruce called his sister, Mary Beth in Arizona, who relayed the news Mary was missing to their sister, Vicki from Portland, who wasn't on *Facebook* then, but who was visiting family in Arizona at the time.

Then, he followed his friend's suggestion and posted on *Facebook* some of the same photos he had given the police. People continued to indicate through *Facebook* and email that they were joining with us in prayer and that they were concerned.

> Jodi K. (Rogue Valley, NCFCA friend): Praying for Mary's safe and speedy return home.
>
> Deana S. (Bruce's friend from high school): Sending SAFE vibes up your way, Bruce. ♥
>
> Janet M. (Bruce's friend from high school): Praying for her!
>
> Vance D. (Bruce's friend from high school): Dear Bruce, she is in our prayers.
>
> Amy S. (Portland area, family friend): Bruce, we are praying!
>
> Brad O. (Mary's cousin): My thoughts and prayers are with you.
>
> Cynthia K. (Bruce's friend from childhood): Keeping you and your family in close prayer.
>
> > Bruce: Thank you all for your prayers... we appreciate them all.

Emails:

Praying right now and will get this on a prayer chain.*

Kody & Amy F. (Rogue Valley friends)

———————————————

Just got your email and I will keep praying she is safe and sound. I am so sorry for this challenge for you...I love you all,

Janet S. (long-time family friend)

———————————————

Cole and I prayed for you and yours as soon as I opened this a few minutes ago...My heart goes out to you, and I pray the Lord give you strength and peace through this ordeal. Let us know if there is anything we can do

...In Christ, Neil and Cole

———————————————

Oh, Bruce and Shelli,

Praying hard right now and will continue to keep you in my prayers. Please keep us all posted as to how we can help.

Love, Kathleen E. (Rogue Valley, NCFCA, family friend)

———————————————

We are in prayer with you!

Monique (Portland area, family friend)

———————————————

I'll be praying for her safe return.

Love, Barb

Barbara R. (Rogue Valley, like-family friend)

———————————————

* A church texting, phone calling, or emailing network for passing on prayer requests.

Just saw this on Facebook. I am in my bakery, praying. Nonstop.

Sue M. (Rogue Valley friend, former employer)

———————————————

We will be praying for you for sure! We hope that you find her soon or that she contacts you soon! May God give you all peace.... Thinking and praying for you!

Alan W. (Portland area, NCFCA, family friend)

———————————————

Oh Shelli! I will be praying by faith! Please keep us posted. The Lord is greater and a very present help in times of trouble.

Cathy C. (California, NCFCA friend)

———————————————

Praying hard. We remember Bruce's kindness when Davy was missing. It's a horrible feeling... We love Mary and all of you so much. May the peace of Jesus Christ our Lord be with you.

Love, The P——s

Ann P. (Rogue Valley, family friend)

———————————————

Our prayers are with Mary and your family. We love you. Keep us posted please, and if there is anything we can do, just ask.

Jeannette C. (Shelli's sister)

———————————————

Our prayers are with you and Mary. We love you guys! Let us know if and when you find her please.

Love Candi (Mary's cousin)

———————————————

Gosh, I'm really sorry to hear that. J—— and I will be praying for you and her tonight. Maybe finding her car would help you know her approximate location. I will pray you find her in God Speed. God bless,

R—— (Rogue Valley, family friend)

———————————————

We're about to have family prayer time and we'll pray for her safe return! And we'll pray for you as well.

Jerrie L. (Portland area, family friends)

Wow...so sorry to hear this. I hope you hear from her very soon. You'll be in my prayers.

Love, Cheri (Mary's aunt)

Dear Shelli and Bruce,

I am so sorry. I will pray for God's direction!

Love, Cindy (Rogue Valley friend)

Shelli and Bruce—I saw your message on Facebook...I was totally shocked to read about this and am soooo very sorry to hear this news. Brad told me he'd read it first. I have relayed the info to Mike just recently at work and I know he's planning to call Bruce. I will be praying for Mary's safe and fast return. Please keep us informed on the progress of locating her. Was she going on a hike by herself? I hope they can send a search team out for her tomorrow if that was the case. If there is anything that we can do for you, please let us know. You will be in our thoughts.

Love, Nancy XOXO (Mary's aunt)

Bruce and Shelli,

I will and am praying even now!!!!

Carla D. (Rogue Valley, NCFCA friend)

Shelli, I'll be home all day Friday if you want to call.

Laurie C. (Rogue Valley, close family friend)

Bruce and Shelli, I will be praying for your family as you go through this time of uncertainty and concern for Mary. God's peace and grace be poured out on you all.

Love, Geri Ann (Portland area, homeschool friend)

We are praying!

Shelley M. (NCFCA Oregon Director)

[Holly A. (A close Rogue Valley family friend who was battling cancer)]

Dear Bruce & Shelli,

We are praying! Please let us know if you hear anything from Mary or her whereabouts. We know God is with her wherever she is. We have no choice but to trust Him and ask for His grace and mercy to cover her. Your whole family is in our prayers and close in our thoughts.

Our love to you all,

Holly, Doug, & Joy

Hi Bruce and Shelli,

We are praying! She did tell Sarah she was going to try to climb Mt. Hood with a fellow she met in the Sisters and a few other people. This was probably Friday.

Steve H. (Rogue Valley, NCFCA, family friend)

Praying for Mary and the whole family. We will put it on our corporate prayer at church.

Have a blessed day,

Dottie A. (Rogue Valley, NCFCA friend)

[David A. (Mary's grandpa)]

We just got home. Who saw her last, and what info do you have about her climbing Mt. Hood? She wouldn't do that alone. Our prayers are totally focused. Would you like us to come up [from Utah]? Please give us a call.

Love, Dad

P.S. When I heard Mary is missing, I had the strong impression: she is hurt and is alive.

A few of our friends were also asking others to pray that Mary would be found:

Stephanie M.

My friend Mary is missing, please pray for her safe return and for her family!

Christine C.: PRAYING!

Kelly P. (Rogue Valley, family friend): Yes, I...have been praying. Hope she is safe and found soon!

M.Z.: prayers for her and family.

J.R.: where was she last seen?

———————————

Julie J.

Some good friends of mine have filed a missing [person] report for their daughter Mary. She was supposed to return home no later than Monday morning & "no one" has seen or heard from her... PLEASE pray for Mary and her family. Thank you!

[Shared my earlier post: "Please pray with us that we will be able to find where Mary is soon..."]

———————————

Sue M. (Rogue Valley friend, Mary's former employer)

Praying for Mary.

[Shared Bruce's post: "We are still asking for prayer for the safe return of our daughter Mary..."]

We weren't thinking about it then, but thankfully our internet was working well at the time! So often we had trouble with bandwidth or connectivity. It was essential to us to have the means for disseminating and receiving information via the internet. We and the police were mainly communicating by telephone.

Bruce

Our house sits on the side of a hill, and we did not get good, or really any, cell phone reception. We used a landline to make and receive calls. As news of our missing daughter spread, we began getting calls. I thanked folks for their prayers and asked them to ask others they knew to pray. I also asked that unless they had some information about Mary's whereabouts to please help us keep our landline open for possible communications from the police.

Shelli

Elijah, who had just turned seventeen, was a junior in high school at the time and the only one of our children still living at home. He and Bruce had just returned from a four-day speech and debate tournament. Even though Elijah thrived on the social interaction and was becoming an excellent and confident communicator, tournaments were always super intense in every way. Each day began early and ended late. The adrenaline was pumping for all four or five days of it. Elijah had competed in several rounds for each of the three or four speech events (persuasive, humorous, interpretive, impromptu, historic, and so on) he had entered. As part of the huge volunteer force of homeschool families and friends who had been conscripted for everything from set-up to judging nonfamily or friend competitors, Bruce had worked nonstop each day in the ballot tabulation room (though he was never the one tabulating the judges' ballots for Elijah's events).

Since returning home, Elijah had been lying low in recovery mode, mostly sleeping, all afternoon and evening while we had been calling around and contacting people. When he finally rallied, and became aware of what was going on, he also posted on *Facebook* and many friends responded (only a few responses can be included in the side bar).

Elijah

My sister Mary has been missing since Monday. Please pray that she is ok and that nothing has happened to her. God is in control.

T.P. (Rogue Valley, NCFCA friend): We are all praying Elijah, and you are so right. God is in control.

N.H. (long-time family friend): We're hoping and praying she is safe.

Mercy K. (Rogue Valley, NCFCA friend): So sorry to hear that. Praying!

T.G. (Portland area, family friend): I just came from men's group where we prayed for her, will continue to pray!

Elijah _____

Right off everything was overwhelming, because I was still tired from the speech tournament and was still coming to terms with everything that was going on.

Everyone seemed to be franticly busy and no one knew anything. There was a lot of stuff going on with my parents calling and contacting people. I was aware that everyone was worried and it didn't feel like it was helping.

It was debilitating to find out Mary was missing, but I thought we just needed to let the situation play out. Of course I cared what happened and I was concerned, but I understood that it was kind of out of our hands, and that it didn't do any good to worry about it and to get all fussed up about it.

Shelli _____

Mary's younger sister, Ruth, who was twenty-one at the time, was living in Portland. She was renting a room from her older sister, our second oldest daughter, Rachel, and Rachel's husband, J——. Ruth and Mary had a lot of friends in common. After we told her that we had not been able to locate Mary, and that their dad had filed a missing person's report, she posted, then had the following conversation on *Facebook*:

> My sister Mary has been missing since Monday. My parents have filed a missing person report already. Please pray that we can get ahold of her soon!
>
> Guino G. (PCT hiking friend): WHAT!!!
>
> > Ruth: Yeah, Guino, have you talked to her lately?
>
> Guino G.: The last I heard from her was on March 16. On March 13 she said in regard to me being about to do a section hike:
>
> > **"Mary** • March 13
> >
> > 'Agh! So jealous. I've been thinking about the trail a lot. My Spring Break hasn't started yet, but I'm kicking it off by summiting Mt. Hood. Super stoked about that.'"

Ruth: You probably know a lot of her hiking buddies. If they don't have Facebook, could you spread the word and try to find out where she is?

Guino G.: I am, and I just texted your dad something interesting, that someone forwarded me.

Ruth: What's that? [gave her phone number]

Ruth

Seeing everyone else concerned made me concerned for them, but I wasn't really thinking much about how I felt at the time. I was upset that Mary was being careless, and I was concerned because no one knew where she was. Oddly, I felt like she was okay because I knew she could handle herself. I knew from growing up with her, and the way Mom raised us, that we were all kind of tough (we could take care of ourselves). I didn't ever have a feeling like she was dead, but something that did start to worry me around then was the thought someone else might have come into the mix. That she could have been kidnapped or harmed in some way by someone else.

Shelli

Eventually that day, we had learned that Mary was supposed to have climbed Mount Hood on a guided trip Saturday, but that it was canceled due to unsafe climbing conditions. Because she had promised Bruce she would not climb alone, we were trying to find out if anyone knew of anyone else who might have joined her in climbing Mount Hood or for any other adventuring she might be up to.

Other responses received around that time:

Tianna E. (Rogue Valley, NCFCA, family friend): Oh no! ☹️☹️☹️ Praying that God would let us find her soon!

K.B.: Dang baby. Praying hard!

Kelly P.: Ruth this is very concerning. Bob, Robert, and I are praying for her safety.

Elisabeth P. (Rogue Valley, family friend): Oh no. I'm so sorry. Will be praying. Your family is in my thoughts and prayers.

Marissa C. (Rogue Valley friend): Praying!

Julie J. (Rogue Valley, family friend): We prayed and will continue. Our hearts go out to you and your family.

Peggy S.: Praying here!

Stephanie M.: I'm praying so hard Ruth!!!! Where was she seen last?? Any idea where she was?

Mary's PCT hiking buddy, Guino, had suggested to Bruce to try contacting a PCT "trail angel"*
who he knew had been traveling through the Mount Hood area near Timberline ski park that week.
Guino thought this person could possibly have had some kind of contact with Mary, since Timberline
ski park was an area where Mary said she might be. We passed this information on to the police, who
were able to locate this particular trail angel in Bend, OR, but he hadn't had any contact with her for
a long time.

Several times the Mount Hood area had come up as a possibility for where Mary might be—more
than any other location, except for her maybe being somewhere else on the PCT on an extended hike.
Maybe this is one reason Mount Hood figured so strongly in Rachel's mixed memory of this time.

Rachel

As the sun set on the first day of the search, all I could think about was what Mary must be going
through. At the time I had a house in the west hills in Portland with a large picture window that
directly faced Mount Hood and I remember sitting there as the sun set, its final rays lighting up the
mountain.

...I felt so frustrated. I spent most of the evening feeling helpless, staring at the mountain, knowing
she was there, somewhere. That night I couldn't sleep. I couldn't imagine how she might be feeling.
I was worried she must feel utterly alone, worried she might give up. I felt like I would be leaving her
alone if I went to sleep so I stayed up, trying with all my energy to send her my thoughts, to let her
know that she wasn't alone and to give her a hug from far away, telling her over and over not to give up,
and to hang in there. I wished there was some way she could hear me, some way I could let her know
that people were looking for her.

Shelli

The Newberg police had assured us someone in their office would be working on Mary's case through
the night. All our own efforts that afternoon and evening had netted next to nothing, but we were
hopeful they would find *something* soon.

* Trail angels are hosts who live near the trail and supply water, food, and sometimes transportation, showers, and a place to
sleep to PCT hikers.

The long tournament days, the five-hour travel home, and the emotional rollercoaster finally caught up with Bruce, and despite everything he was able to fall fast asleep—at least for an hour or so. I remained in a state of wakefulness revisiting the day and conversing in my mind with God. Around midnight, the phone rang.

Bruce

The phone jingle woke me. I wasn't afraid when the phone rang, based on my understanding that "a phone call is good, a knock at the door is bad." I was hopeful of news of Mary.

The police had found the truck she borrowed in the parking lot at Timberline Lodge on Mount Hood. They told us that the Clackamas County Sheriff's office would now join the task force. They would be overseeing the search for Mary in the Mount Hood area and might be calling on various Search and Rescue (SAR) teams to help them. An officer from the Newberg police would continue working on Mary's case through the rest of the night and Clackamas officers would be meeting with the Newberg police first thing in the morning. All this was very assuring along with seeing someone really was working on Mary's case all night long.

I was sure the truck parked at Timberline Lodge meant Mary had been hiking along the PCT somewhere. She had promised me she wouldn't climb Mount Hood alone, and, between us and the police and Timberline Lodge, we hadn't found any traces of anyone climbing Mount Hood with her.

Shelli

Their finding the truck was very positive news, very heartening for us, because it narrowed down the search significantly. Until then, for all we knew, Mary could have been anywhere from mid Washington to northern California, in the mountains or at the coast. We had a starting place, which was huge and wonderful; at the same time it brought with it a whole new set of concerns.

7

THE SEARCH BEGINS

(FRIDAY MORNING, MARCH 29, 2013)

"There are no atheists in the trenches."

❧ ANONYMOUS, *WWI* ❧

Bruce

I woke up early Friday morning. I was too distracted to shower or shave. My mind was completely consumed with Mary and where she might be. After I got dressed, one of the first things I did was post the following on *Facebook*:

> We are still asking for prayer for the safe return of our daughter Mary who has been missing since last [Sunday]. Police called last night to tell us that they had located the truck she was driving in the parking lot at Timberline Lodge on Mt. Hood. I have not yet talked with police this morning, but I expect some sort of search will begin as soon as it is light enough.
>
> We still need information on who she might have been with and ask anyone with ANY information to contact Newberg Police or message us through FB.
>
> Please continue in prayer that she might be found safe. She is an experienced hiker with excellent outdoor skills.
>
> K.D. (Rogue Valley, family friend): Praying!!!!
>
> Kevn L. (Mary's Uncle): I'm relieved they found the truck; means they're getting close, I'm sure.
>
> > Bruce: It at least gives us a solid starting place. 7:23am.

After that, I called the Newberg police to see if there had been any new developments overnight. There was no new information to pinpoint her location. They had checked to see if she filled out a registration card to climb Mount Hood, but they did not find anything for her. The police told me there would be a meeting with Search and Rescue that morning to decide whether or not they would mount a full-scale search for her on or around Mount Hood.

I was surprised, and it made me anxious that there was even a question whether to search for her or not, because, up to that point, the Newberg Police had had people working her case around the clock. Their diligence had been very encouraging to me. It had not dawned on me that, in their view, the odds of finding Mary alive on Mount Hood were pretty slim. The thought that she might not be alive had not occurred to me at all. Perhaps this was just a father's desperate hope, but more than that,

> Sarai B. (Portland area, family friend): I am still praying. I am so glad at least you have a place to start looking now.
>
> Sterling A. (Shelli's brother): Glad to know you have something definitive. Our thoughts and prayers are with you. Makes me think of my foolish young adult days when I set out hiking without anyone knowing where I was going. Invincible.
>
> E.G.: The [PCT] Hiking Community is praying for Mary.

I did know that she had tremendous outdoor savvy and was, like her mom, incredibly resilient. The thought that she had fallen off a cliff or down a crevasse had not entered my mind. I believe that God kept that thought from my mind to keep me from despair.

I informed the police that if they decided not to mount a search, we would. I did not say this as a threat, but just a simple matter of fact. Since the news of Mary's plight had gotten around, I had received a lot of offers to help search.

I then made the half hour drive to Newberg to talk in person to the Newberg police investigators who had been working so diligently on finding Mary. They were very kind and truly concerned. Before I left the police station, I was convinced that they were doing everything they could to find her, and that a search would be mounted.

I headed over to my office at GFU only a few blocks away. It was Good Friday, and the university was closed. I was alone there for a while. I made more phone calls and monitored *Facebook*. The muscles in my neck and shoulders were tensing up. I was holding all my emotions in. I could not be terribly optimistic, because the outcome was still very much in doubt. And yet, I could not give in to despair for the same reason. Imagine being at the top of a roller coaster when the car has stopped climbing, but it has not yet tipped over into the big fall, and suddenly everything stops, and you are stuck in that place. Afraid and yet anxious to have it over with—drawing in the deep breath before the plunge.

My boss came in after a while and I told her why I was there. She said she was so very sorry for what we were going through. I'm sure she was imagining how she would feel if this were happening to one of her kids. Of course, she told me she would be praying for us too, and I really did appreciate that.

I didn't carry a cell phone, and because I felt like I should expect some news any moment, I was hesitant to drive home for fear that while I was driving home, I might miss the call that Mary has been found. Finally, feeling like there was nothing more I could do there in my office, I headed home, praying.

Praying, praying, praying.

When I say I was praying, what I mean is begging and pleading with God, sometimes out loud, sometimes only in my mind that God would literally intervene in a miraculous way and lead us to Mary. Like the leprous man begging Jesus, recorded in the book of Matthew. "A man with leprosy came and knelt before him and said, 'Lord, if you are willing, you can make me clean.' Jesus reached out his hand and touched the man. 'I am willing,' he said. 'Be clean!' Immediately he was cured of his leprosy'" (Matt 8:2-3). I'm a guy who believes Jesus really did those things, and still does. Somehow, knowing that a lot of people were also praying for Mary to be found was encouraging, sustaining. It helped me hold it together.

Shelli

Elijah and I were at home, but neither of us were thinking about his homeschool work. And I was there in case the police or SAR called. Many unknowns were still staring us in the face. We didn't know if Mary meant to hike the PCT or to climb Mount Hood. We didn't think she tried to climb Mount Hood. They hadn't found any registration for her, and we hadn't been able to identify anyone who might have climbed with her. This, along with the fact that she had promised Bruce she wouldn't climb alone—and that she had always kept her word—led us to believe that her intent had been to hike the PCT from the Timberline Lodge. But which way had she gone? Had she stayed on the trail? She had talked about wanting to go to some hot springs in the area between Mount Hood and the Columbia River, but the hot springs were more approachable from the other direction (from the Columbia River side of the trail). It was all very puzzling.

When a nonbelieving person arrives at a place of desperation, when all the human help and resources available remain insufficient, they'll sometimes try God, even as a gamble—in hope of possible help. As the day progressed, a few friends who had never indicated belief in God before this, indicated to us that they were also praying with us, and some were asking everyone they knew to pray too. This represented a huge amount of concern to us, and we appreciated it beyond measure.

When a person is a Christian, especially if they have a regular practice of honest, heartfelt communication with Jesus—who is even closer and knows them better than a best friend or lover—they most certainly will default to prayer, as we did in this situation. Prayer, in whatever circumstance, is an act of hope or faith that there is a God who is listening and who cares in some way about what happens to us.

That Friday morning, we also called our teaching pastor at Calvary Chapel McMinnville, and the head of Spiritual Life at GFU and asked them to pray for Mary and to put her on their prayer chains; everyone who had signed up at church or at the university to pray for people who wanted prayer could be notified and would be praying with us.

A pastor who knew Mary well when we lived in Grants Pass called and told us that he and Jerome Prairie Bible Church in Grants Pass were praying with us; we found out later that on Friday night they held an all-night prayer vigil for her. All the people Bruce worked with were already praying. Later, Bruce's boss's boss also called to let us know that he and others with him were praying and asked if there was anything they could do.

Friends from the Rogue Valley in southern Oregon also called to find out if there was anything they could do. Some people Bruce knew had a friend who went snowshoeing on Mount Hood all the time. He had offered to help with the search. Bruce's brother called asking if there was anything we needed. My Dad, Mary's grandpa, called several times checking up on the latest information we had. We appreciated all this support immensely, though we didn't talk for long with anyone who called, since we were trying to keep the phone line clear for calls from the police or SAR.

Meanwhile, family and friends including Mary's GFU friends, homeless friends, and friends from other communities were expressing their concern and support through *Facebook* and emails. Always, each person's caring comments and/or offers to pray meant a great deal to us. Their mindfulness included offers to help with the search, some truly thoughtful notes, and even some prayers sent and sought from sources we didn't expect.

Scott W.

Bruce, let me know if more searchers are needed or if any other help is needed. My son Trevor is involved in urban serve through GFU with her. We could both help if you need it. Just let us know. Our family is praying for her as well as the rest of your family.

> Bruce: Thank you Scott. We will let you (and everyone) know as soon as we know what the search and rescue plan is. 10:13am.

Teresa H. (NCFCA President): We are praying for you all...

E.G.: The Hiking Community is praying for Mary.

Mary R. (Rogue Valley, family friend): Shelli, we have just got back in town and heard the news. Lifting up your whole family in prayer. Wish we were there to help.

Emails:

Bruce/Shelli,

Is a search party organizing as yet? Please give an update as soon as you hear something as I am ready to pack my gear and head-up.

Praying, Keith

> Bruce & Shelli to Keith:
>
> Thank you, Keith, for the offer. what is your phone number? We will call you if / when they're ready for help looking for her…?

. . . I take it that this means no good news for an update as yet. Yes, please give me a ring if we can be of some help at all. My heart is heavy,

Keith

———————————————

Shelli, are they going to start searching for Mary? Do they need people [to help search]?

Jeannette C. (Shelli's sister)

———————————————

Hi, Bruce and Shelli,

Our prayers are with you and Mary, and our hopes that all is well. Please let us know if there's anything that we might be able to do to help! Thanks for keeping us in the loop!

Andrew P. (Salem area, family friend)

———————————————

We are praying for and with you for Mary's safe return.

M.B. (Rogue Valley friend)

———————————————

Hi Dear Ones!

Penny and I have been praying ever since your e-mail came in. Please keep us informed; we care about Mary and you all.

Our love to you all at this difficult time,

Barry & Penny (Rogue Valley friends, our former astronomy instructor)

Owen clan,

We are praying and we will not stop! God bless all of you and protect you during this time. You will continually be on our hearts and minds.

Becky, Jerrie and the boys (Portland area, family friends)

Hey, I am in Arizona with Mary Beth. Both Mike and Mary Beth have told me about Mary being missing up at Mt Hood. I had planned to return on Sunday. Do you want me to come home now and help in search? Let me know if you need some help.

Vicki O. (Bruce's sister)

Hi, Dear Ones,

we just want you to know that Mary and all of you are constantly in our prayers and thoughts. Would love to call and pray with you on the phone, but I don't want to have the phone ring because of my call. I know that, were I in your place, any phone call would fill me with hope and/or dread. If you need to pray or talk, though, please know that we'd love to be there for you ANY TIME, day or night. We love each of you very much. May the God of all comfort be especially close to each of you, and may He bring Mary safely home soon.

Lorrie, on behalf of the W—— family (Rogue Valley, NCFCA, close family friends)

We are praying for all of you. Please know how much we love you and love Mary. "We have an Anchor that keeps the soul steadfast and firm while the billows roll, fastened to the Rock which cannot move, grounded firm and deep in the Savior's love."

Waiting and praying,

Holly (A close Rogue Valley family friend who was battling cancer)

Dear NCFCA Family,

Our dear friends, Bruce and Shelli Owen, are in need of prayer for the safe return of their daughter, Mary, who has been missing since Sunday. Authorities have located her truck, which was parked at a lodge near Mt. Hood, and a search is now underway. Mary is an experienced hiker with excellent outdoor skills. Please pray that she is found quickly and in good health, as well as for the Owen family, as they await news. The most updated information may be found on Bruce's Facebook. Feel free to share this request with your friends and family. The Owens are trying to raise an army of prayer warriors on Mary's behalf.

In His service,

Esther P. (NCFCA Regional Director) to me/NCFCA families

———————————

Dear Bruce and Shelli,

Even though I'm going about my day as usual, my thoughts are continually with you. You are dear, dear friends and my heart longs for the miraculous answers that you are hoping and praying for.

With love,

Shelley (NCFCA Oregon Director)

Rachel

After Dad had filed the missing person report, information about the search started to trickle in agonizingly slowly. Once the truck Mary had borrowed was located and we knew for certain she was in the Mt Hood area, I couldn't stop thinking about every possible scenario. Mary is a very experienced outdoorswoman with excellent survival skills and many advanced treks under her belt so I was concerned that so much time had passed. If she was mobile, she would have almost definitely have been able to locate a road or a home or way station by now, so the fact that she hadn't resurfaced pointed to the high probability that she was at the very least badly injured, the worst-case scenario wasn't one I was willing to think about.

Bruce

The police learned through Mary's bank transactions that she went to a gas station in Sherwood and to the R.E.I. in Tigard on Saturday. She bought microspikes, boots, and a climbing axe there. The closed-circuit videos in both of those locations showed she was alone. Neither Shelli nor I ever saw the videos. However, now knowing the things she had purchased, I was forced to reconsider my strongly held belief that she would not have climbed Mount Hood alone. It made me feel confused. I had not known her to ever break a promise to me before. I was still reluctant to believe she had climbed alone. I wanted to believe she had climbed with another person, but no one else had been reported missing and no one had come forward from the climbing group she was supposed to climb Mount Hood with. There wasn't time to think about it or to be angry or feel slighted if she had climbed the mountain alone. We were just focused on trying to find her.

On the encouraging side, this new information argued against the notion that foul-play might have been involved in her disappearance. This was something the police had hinted might be a possibility.

The police also learned that the truck she borrowed had been in the same spot in the parking lot since at least Sunday. This was judging from interviews with lodge employees and from the amount of ice still under the truck.

The police had placed calls to Beau to get permission to open his truck. He wasn't answering, so they had left messages on his phone. This was not surprising to us. Students on serve trips were encouraged to leave their phones off so they could be more present and focus fully on what they were doing on the trip. And at this point, neither Beau nor his serve-trip leaders really understood the gravity of the situation. Later when Beau was made aware of what was going on, all he could really do to help was provide what little information he had to the police.

What they could see in the truck was not promising. They could see that her sleeping bag, new boots, and a hiking backpack were in there along with her laptop computer. From these it appeared, wherever she had gone, she had only intended a day's hike.

I called Beau's serve-trip leaders again until I could get a hold of one. He promised to pass on the message to Beau to call the police. Beau did call the police back right away and gave them permission to open his truck.

I had asked the police to find out for sure whether her poncho was in the truck once they got it open. When they did, they confirmed for me that it was *NOT* there. Shelli and I were so relieved to learn this. When Mary was trekking the PCT through Oregon and Washington, she had used it instead of a tent. She had also used it for insulation around her sleeping bag. She had used it, too, for its main purpose when she was hiking—to protect her from rain or snow. She loved that poncho, because of its versatility but also because it was so light weight and compact. We were all but sure she had taken it with her, wherever she was. If she had, we knew it increased her chances of survival.

The police asked for my permission to hack Mary's laptop, and I gave it to them. They hoped to find information about her plans and who she has been in contact with. They told me it might take hours, maybe all day. Though the computer crime specialist or computer tech was very good, Mary's computer was an Apple, which would be nearly impossible to get into. The police told us that Apple computers, more than PCs, were just innately harder to hack.

Shelli

While this was going on, other friends and family continued to send heart-felt, generous, and supportive replies to our emails and *Facebook* posts.

[Jim M. (Rogue Valley, close family friend)]

Bruce, Shelli, and Family. We are thinking of and praying for you guys. My gosh what an almost overwhelming turn of circumstances; can only be faced by the grace and power of God. You know all the promises of the Word, how He will strengthen us, etc. I also like the verses before Romans 8:28, especially verse 26 where it says, "In the same way the Spirit also helps our weakness" and in verse 27 "...He intercedes for the saints according to the will of God." We stand not alone but in reality, the Trinity is with us, especially the Holy Spirit stands alongside us when we are weak. He is with you and so am I.

Brother Jim

Bruce & Shelli:

Thank you, Jim, for your prayers and encouragement!

Alan-Gini W. (Portland area, NCFCA, family friends)

Dearest Owen Family,

We love you and are praying earnestly for Mary and your whole family. "On Him we have set our hope..." (2 Cor 1:10b). Thanks for keeping us posted. "Our help is in the name of the Lord who made heaven and earth" (Ps 124:8). On Him, we trust.

Heidy B. (Rogue Valley friend): Praying for your family Shelli....

Andrea B. (Rogue Valley friend): We are praying too!!!

Linda M. (Washington, close family friend): Shelli ~ You have been in my thoughts and prayers almost every waking moment ~ and will continue to be.

Darrell P. (long-time family friend): We are checking Facebook every 30 minutes hoping for some good news. We are also thinking of you 24/7

Bruce: Thank you Darrell.

Not only did all this support mean the world to us, but each individual also had their *own* `story, adding a great deal more significance to their comments and support. The following response was especially felt by Bruce and me, because only a few months earlier (Dec. 2012) Anne T., a friend from the Rogue Valley, who posted it, had been in an awful car accident. In it, she had lost her dear, sweet mother and suffered severe injuries, which took many months to heal. But this was not all. Earlier that *same* year (May 2012), she had lost a close friend to drowning, when he had slipped and fallen into the Rogue River above Rainie Falls. *She* wrote these words to encourage *us*:

> Praying continually for you. I know our God is sovereign and Mary is never outside of His reach. May all find comfort in a God who has a plan. Hope she is returned safe and sound!

We were feeling exceedingly blessed and grateful for each precious, caring person who was keeping Mary, those searching, and us, in their thoughts and prayers.

Another long-time friend commented:

> Janet S.: I am sharing your request on my Facebook page and praying for all of you! The Lord give you comfort and peace as you wait and pray.

Yes, the hardest thing remained—the waiting.

8

WE SURRENDER

(FRIDAY MORNING, MARCH 29, 2013)

"When a train goes through a tunnel and it gets dark,
you don't throw away the ticket and jump off.
You sit still and trust the engineer."

᠙ CORRIE TEN BOOM, *DON'T WRESTLE, JUST NESTLE* ᠗

Thursday afternoon and evening, as Bruce and I were coming to the realization no one knew where Mary was, we were sharing and comparing notes from our correspondence, but we hadn't really started processing, or talking together about what might be going on yet. We simply didn't have enough real information. The possibility that she could be in grave danger, or even be dead, had begun to hover in the air. But it wasn't something either Bruce or I were vocalizing.

Moving into Friday, these possibilities began to surface intermittently—and they remained "there," at least in the background, the rest of the time that we didn't know anything for sure. Thursday, we had been so busy, and everything was newly unfolding. Friday morning, while Bruce was gone, began a round of greatly fluctuating thoughts and emotions for me.

I really began to struggle. I contended, *If God really loves us, why is He allowing something like this to happen to Mary now?* But then I thought, *We don't even know what "this" is, for sure*, and I was hopeful again—for a minute. But then the weight of the undeclared possibilities began to press on me, heavier and heavier because of the information we had—and didn't have.

Thoughts and questions began to arise that made me feel frustrated and angry. *This is far beyond my strength to endure on top of everything else.* We had been going through some tremendous challenges, including deeply hurtful relational quagmires with a family member struggling with severe mental illness. *Enough is enough! Mary's being missing on top of everything else, is beyond anything I can endure. God, how can you allow this? Don't you care? Will You let me be destroyed?*

There still seemed to be no permanent or good resolution to our already-present-before-Mary-went-missing dilemma, and there probably never would be in this life. I began asking myself *What have I done to drive God away? Why is He letting this happen? Why has He abandoned me?* My focus was causing me to feel very isolated and alone.

Gradually, I was overwhelmed by thoughts like these and began to feel betrayed. *Is this all life brings? Darkness? Emptiness? Loss? Pain? And more pain?*

This is too much—way too much! If this is all there is, why have I ever believed a good God exists? Can God exist and allow this great, crushing pain and desolation at the same time? Has "God" ever really been there? Has the idea of "God" just been a delusion? I could always think of reasons to doubt my own sanity and everything else about myself. I had had dark struggles with suicidal depression since my late teens.

Eventually, in this passion, I allowed my feelings to come to an intensity, dryness, and harshness I had never permitted before. I was deeply angry and bewildered.

With a continuation of these kinds of thoughts, I found my mind and heart in a vast, black, and empty place. A place void of God and God's light. However, once I was in that dark place, I knew that ***nothing*** was worth remaining there! I had been in this place before. *This isn't the only "reality."*

Resisting God, being stubborn, wallowing in self-pity, pridefully holding on to my anger or even discouragement, maintaining my supposed "rights" to a pain free life, to my own view, to my often-wrong judgements, or to my "independence"—none of these (or other things like them) had ever held rewards that justified hanging on to any of these thoughts or attitudes.

Repelled, like the flip side of a magnet repels another magnet, I turned these thoughts away. I knew deeper still within myself this darkness was an emptiness caused by allowing my thoughts to turn away from God—the author of hope, the Creator of the other and better half of the story and the whole of reality. Returning to this realization was like waking up even though I was already awake. *The state of my own sanity or perception does not change whether God exists or not!* I was so relieved and glad of this! Again!

The existence of Jesus' Presence, love, and light had been imprinted on the very core of my being, even while His Being was (is) *other* or independent of my being. Jesus had only ever been a source of absolute, wonderful, beautiful soundness and sanity in my life. His love and Presence had been the one sure, unchanging stabilizer throughout my life, even when I was a child—even before I began to really know Him or experience the vicissitudes of life.

In my young adulthood, after some of the worst months of my life spent trying to be "worthy" of God's Spirit and not only failing but finding the distance between God and me greater than ever, I came to the soul-wrenching realization I would never be worthy—ever. It was shortly after this realization that, unexpectedly and despite my unworthiness, His Spirit first washed over, in, and through me and Jesus revealed Himself to me in a vision of pure, all-encompassing love and light.

This life- and heart-changing vision or revelation of Jesus not only changed my life from that time forward, but His Spirit of love and light also illuminated and brought the Bible to life for me as well. Since then, Jesus and His word in the Bible testament—which I am now convinced was inspired by His Spirit in the first place—has been more real to me than any material or immaterial creation of His. The greatest sense of peace, love, and joy I've experienced in my life has been while resting in the assurance of my true identity in Him and His Presence with me.

As I began to recall what the Lord is really like—as I remembered, *He is the only good and perfect One, who had always loved and taken care of me and my family, in all the essentials, independent of my fluctuating feelings and interpretations of my experiences.* I began to "see" again, what (who) had been there all along in Spirit—He had!

Besides His spiritual (unseen) Presence, there was right outside my window tangible evidence of His practical love and provision. The sunshine was sifting through a variety of beautiful trees and intricate ferns, and a bird was flitting here and there—and I noticed a deer, a chipmunk, and another bird. Seeing these things refreshed my mind again with the infinitude of God's works, His creations, and all He maintains, which encompass and extend far beyond the intricate detail and interworking of the beautiful and "joyful" things I could see just outside my window.

Awe and gratitude came sweeping into my soul. Like physical exertion these only require the initial effort of remembering to overcome inertia. Once a person begins revisiting some of the good things God has given and done for us, more remembrances are triggered. In a moment I was remembering past financial, temporal, relational, physical, mental, emotional, and spiritual blessings (many, many good things) the Lord had poured out on me and on us (my family and loved ones). All which had demonstrated His living and active faithfulness, goodness, love, infinite wisdom, and power exercised on my and our behalf.

Many of these blessings had been a result of directing my thoughts, desires, and words towards God in prayer and were His answers. *Many people are praying with us for Mary right now. God hears sincere prayers. She is in His hands.*

By this time, Bruce had returned home, and not long after I had regained my senses, he sought me out. In the privacy of our bedroom, he finally brought "it" up. He shared with me that this situation—with its awful possibilities concerning Mary's welfare—had once more brought him to a place of decision—like the time before Elijah was born. I knew immediately what he meant. My heart sped up in both fear and anticipation.

Before Elijah was born, for reasons unknown to me, Bruce had a very strong impression that I was going to die in childbirth or from complications. It brought him to a place of decision.

As he described to me later, he somehow knew he could let his very real fear and anxiety develop into anger and bitterness against God, especially if anything "bad" really did happen to me. Or he could take a chance on God and trust in His character—that He is good and that His will and purposes are always what's best for us in the long run, eternally, no matter how things might appear or turn out presently—even if He should allow death to intervene.

Ultimately, he took the risk, he placed his bets on God being "there" and being good. He took the position of trust. And God was "there" and able, because of Bruce's responsiveness, to ease his fears and give him peace of mind and a sense of His immanent Presence.

There were complications after Elijah's birth—though (obviously) I didn't die—but because Bruce was trusting God, he was able to receive His comfort and strength through everything that transpired, and to continue in the assurance that all would be well in the end, whether in this life or the next.

I believe the slight, but real hesitancy Bruce had perceived in the police and SAR to search for Mary, and her being so utterly and unavoidably missing had brought him to that place. Again, he was choosing to trust, no matter what the outcome might be. He had completely submitted himself to accepting God's will, whatever it was, in her situation.

God's peace isn't something that comes through human reasoning. It cannot be humanly generated. The enemy of our souls cannot imitate it. God's peace somehow allows a person through spiritual (immaterial) means to be assured of His unseen, but very real Presence. Only His Presence can give one's soul the true and comforting reassurance that all that isn't *presently* well with us now *will* be well in the end.

When Bruce shared his decision to trust in God's will and goodness with me, it was a freeing, terrible, and wonderful thing all at once. It is hard to describe the simultaneous joy and terror I felt, and the encouragement in seeing the Spirit of peace and comfort God had already given him. I greatly appreciated and honored his courage; I knew in the core of my being that this was the only way we were going to get through this situation—and life—whole and intact.

Simultaneously, I couldn't believe how far my own mind and heart had been from thinking of God's will or purposes in all this. Where does a person's mind and heart go in such a crisis? God and I were seeing where mine went (reaffirming God still has a lot of work to do in me)! I believe true followers of Christ are meant to live in this place of surrender on a continual basis, but how easy it is to "forget" and to habitually substitute one's own "righteous" desires and agenda instead.

As soon as Bruce shared this, I knew I needed to do the same thing. I knew it was the only sound, sane way I was going to be able to deal with something so out of our control (which is the opposite of how "the world" teaches us to think).

In all our struggles God has been with us and helped us. Even though some of those challenges have been hard and painful, and it wouldn't have been my conscious choice to go through them, they have deepened and expanded my empathy, understanding, love, and relationships—especially my love for and appreciation of Jesus (God's revelation of Himself to us). They have created a foundation Bruce and I can rely on between us and God. Like nothing else could have, my worst trials have brought the most valuable, good, and lasting results into my life. They have refined relationships and my character in ways I desperately needed. No, I wouldn't trade any of these hard things for all the short-lived comfort and pleasure in the world.

I didn't know what this situation would bring with it for Mary or for us, but I knew every one of the painful and uncomfortable things I or we had gone through in the past were temporary. They eventually passed—and even those that hadn't yet, I knew would end when this mortal life is over, if not sooner. *This too shall pass.*

Knowing and remembering all these things, I also chose to surrender Mary's situation into the Lord's hands and to commit myself to His wise, all-seeing, perfect will. I had returned to a substantial hope that all wrong and evil things would be redeemed by God's grace through Jesus if we were willing to seek, wait for, and obey God to receive it. Through releasing control of the situation to God, I came to a place of understanding that we needed to wait on Him to direct things, and of believing He would.

From then on Bruce and I were on the same page. It brought us closer to God and to each other be able to verbalize to each other the assurances God was giving each of us separately. Assurances that wherever Mary was, she was in His hands—even if she was dead (even though neither of us believed she was); that He was bigger than any circumstance she might be in; that He had been faithful in the past, and He would continue to be; that the comfort, peace, and assurance God was giving us, He could give to her too; that she wasn't "lost" to God; and that through our communion with God we were connected to her, since God was with her too, wherever she might be (see Ps. 139).

Returning to rest in God's will and absolute goodness again, opened our eyes to what He might be doing and calmed our spirits. His gentle, quiet Spirit was able to speak to our souls just what we needed when we needed it, to guide us, to assure us, to hold us, to comfort us, to teach us how and what to pray, to help keep us sane. In truth, there is no earthly comparison to heavenly Presence and help!

9

GLACIAL SILENCE

(MONDAY TO THURSDAY, MARCH 25–28, 2013)

"But my words, like silent raindrops fell
And echoed in the wells, of silence…"

❧ PAUL SIMON, "THE SOUND OF SILENCE" ❧

Mary—Monday (on the northwest side of Mount Hood)

I must have slept at some point that night or Monday morning, because when I woke up it was starting to grow light. *Okay, well, I'm not dead. I guess I'm not gonna die. Now what?* First, I took a look at the gash on my leg. It was about 6 inches long, and I could see red, and then there was white underneath, which I assumed was fat. *Well, thank God for fat*, because it was all closed up, there wasn't any blood. I figured I'd leave it alone, because I didn't want to mess with it and open it up or get it bleeding or anything. I just covered it back over with my tights.

Next, I began experimenting to see if I could walk with my leg like that. I wasn't aware of the state of my legs and feet because they were numb. I got up and went to step forward but stumbled instead. I immediately punched through the surface crust of the snow and sank in up to my thigh. That's when I realized my right foot was sprained. It took me only a few minutes, but it felt like twenty to pull myself out and to get back up onto the snow platform I had made.

Because my left leg had this big old gash in it, I hadn't done a full evaluation of everything else. I just started moving, and then realized I couldn't get very far. *Okay, maybe it's better to stay put, since I don't know how mobile I can be in this situation.* I was already concerned about the canyon narrowing and dropping into the tree line. I figured that by now someone at the lodge must have read the climbing report I had filled out on Sunday morning. *I put down I would be back by 5 o'clock Monday morning, which was several hours ago.* I think it was 7 o'clock at this point. *They're going to be looking for me soon, if they're not already. If I go any lower than where I am right now, I'll be below the tree line and it will be harder to see me from above. I know it's pretty difficult to get up this canyon. There's not going to be anyone on foot looking for me here.* I figured the best thing was to stay where I was. So that day, I stayed put, hunkered down in my poncho on top of my tarp and climbing harness.

At some point that morning, I started praying, "God, please help them find me." That's when I realized God wasn't answering. It was quiet. I'm not sure how else to describe it. Every time I'd pray it was like the prayer would flutter upwards for a moment and then drop dead to the snow. The Presence I've sensed all my life was just gone.

Once I realized that, I started getting all panicky and frantic. It was like drumming on a ceiling or pounding on a wall. I was trying to find some trace of Him; looking back I realized He hadn't spoken with me in quite some time. I hadn't really spoken to Him either. I had been in this crazy blindered state, so focused on the summit, I hadn't realized He wasn't talking to me.

I started going through all the things I knew I needed to repent of, trying to get Him to talk again and to be present.

Silence. More than silence. Void.

I haven't questioned God exists. I've known that *He Is* since before He introduced Himself to me when I was a child. I've questioned a lot of things about Him, but not that *He Is*. This was the first time in my life I didn't have that knowledge inside of me. That was terrifying.

That whole day I wrestled with the blankness inside and out. Occasionally I would yell out, "HELLO!" "HELP!" just in case there was somebody looking for me. It was quiet. Then I'd yell again, and it was quiet. Then I'd try to pray, and it wouldn't work. Then I'd yell again, and it was quiet.

The only sounds were the white noise of the stream below me and the occasional rumble from the canyon walls. I strained my ears for any voice other than my own. Nothing. No bird song. No airplanes. No rescue team shouting out for me. No God to tell me it would be alright.

It was cold, and it was overcast. It was snowing/slushing on me most of the day, so a big portion of that time I was shivering. Occasionally snow would come trickling down off the canyon wall on my side. Every now and then it would come sliding down into my little concave slot there. I'd have to push it off and dig it out from around me, wasting energy and heat. Always, I was fighting to stay warm. I started to melt snow in my water bottles. I'd put a little bit of it in each of them, and then let it melt. I wasn't holding them against my body because I didn't want to use my body heat for that. I ate a Nutri-Grain bar and a pack of Keebler Crackers. I had three of each with me. I figured I'd ration them out; every day I'd get one of each. I didn't know how long I'd be there, and I didn't want to run out of food. I ate some chia seeds and that was that.

The day went by in this long, tedious sequence of shouting and listening and having the horrible sound of the stream just going and going below me. I didn't have anything I could use to divert my attention. I spent some time trying to search through all my memories of scripture verses I had memorized. I couldn't remember any of them. That was disturbing. For some reason I hadn't packed my Bible, my little pocket one, which I always pack. And I hadn't packed my notebook, which I always pack. It wasn't a very interesting day. I was just sitting and listening and hoping and being scared that God was not talking.

Then it started getting dark and colder, and I was shaking again. I was dozing in and out, too cold to sleep soundly. I had dreams about getting off the mountain. I dreamt my friend had a dragon, and I was telecommunicating with her. She agreed to have her dragon come and get me off the mountain. But then the dragon came, and he didn't want to pick me up because I stank. This was after I had been sitting there for a day. I had gotten up once to go pee, and it had taken so much effort, and I'd lost so much body heat that I decided it wasn't worth it. So I smelled like pee. I stank to myself, and I guess I was dreaming about that. I told my friend, "Hey, your dragon won't come and get me."

And she replied, "I don't know why. I told him to come."

That night was a lot of in and out, in and out, trying to come up with a way to get off that mountain. I kept thinking, *How long do I wait for them to find me? If I drop down into the tree line, if something happens to me, they won't be able to spot me.* Then I figured, it might take some time to get search crews together and they don't know which side of the mountain I'm on. *Should I go? Should I stay? Is there anything I can do right now?* Looking back, I wasn't thinking very clearly. There are things I probably would have done differently. I think I would have tried to crawl down the canyon if I was in that situation again. I would have just gone carefully and kept going. But that's part of the story. I didn't do anything heroic or smart. I just sat there and waited all day Monday, and tried to talk to God, and He didn't talk to me.

Tuesday

"My God, my God, why have you forsaken me?"

❧ Psalm 22:1 (ESV)

Tuesday morning was gray, but it felt a little bit warmer. There was a good rain, and I held my poncho out and caught as much of the water as I could. It was really great to drink, just to have full swallows of water.

It must have been getting warmer because there was more and more snow coming down off the canyon wall into my little concave. So much snow fell in that it went up to my knees, and I had to dig myself out again. *I need to move. This isn't safe anymore.* I packed everything up in my backpack. Then

I took that tarp and balled my fists up in it, and butt-scooted across the snow, using the surface area of the tarp to keep myself from sinking in too much. I was trying not to mess with my leg, because I didn't really know what state it was in—if it was going to open up, or if it was in danger of anything.

I was scooting back the way I'd come up, traversing along the snowfield under the canyon wall, trying to get back to the small, wooded spur I had climbed. There was a steep drop-off below me, so I couldn't just head straight down. I also thought if I could get to the spur, I could start a fire. If I could start a fire, there would be smoke, and people would see it and they could find me.

I started making my way across. It was slow going. My body had so little to give. Every yard took so much energy. I made it only about 20 yards before I was absolutely exhausted. It took me a good long chunk of the day to do that. I made myself another little ledge, another little concave area. I hunkered down in that and rested and ate my Keebler crackers, Nutri-Grain bar, and chia seeds for the day.

Looking back now, I don't remember the agony, but I know at the time I was thinking about tumbling all the way down, finishing the fall, because I just wanted to not be in pain, not be cold anymore. Then I thought, *if I did that, I'd probably fall to the bottom, and break a leg, and still be alive, and that would be even worse. I would just be in more pain with more problems. And if I did die, would there be anything on the other side?* All my life, I had counted on the reality of God—His Presence the safety net. "No fear in death." But where was He now? Did He even exist?

Sitting on my little shelf, I was saturated with cold, pain, and the terrible silence. I was thinking about breathing my CO_2 and suffocating myself. Then I thought, *what if they find me hours after I die, and they analyze how I died and realize I could have lived? What would it be like for my family to know I terminated my own life when I could have hung on a little bit longer and they'd have found me, and I would have been alive?*

I wanted—intensely at some points—to die. In the movies it's really simple. Somebody gets hurt or lost, and they fall asleep in the cold and just sort of drift off. But I would look inside and there was this horrible little ball of light that just kept going and going and going and going. It would never just go out. That was really frustrating at times because I was just… I mean hours and hours and hours of no comfort whatsoever, of just cold and pain and shaking.

The rest of Tuesday was the same as Monday. I was sitting on the snow shelf and little trickles of snow were falling into my snow concave. I was shouting out, listening, looking, hoping, and occasionally feeling out and seeing if I could hear God talking to me. I was trying to recall hymns and sing. I couldn't recall anything. I couldn't sense God, and all the things that were attached to Him were gone too. All my memorized verses, all the hymns, all the things I knew so well were gone.

I found myself crying out, "My God, my God, why have you forsaken me?"

He just wasn't there. That silence loomed over all my other thoughts. Hours and hours went by, my mind occupied with trying to make God talk to me, questioning whether or not He was really there, whether it was worth it to keep living, and whether I could even die if I wanted to. All the while I was listening and hoping to hear the sound of searchers, a plane, a helicopter, voices shouting. I thought somebody would be looking for me. It hadn't crossed my mind yet that they were not.

I spent Tuesday night on that second snow shelf I had made. I dreamt this cowboy-like, John Wayne person came along and told me that there was a Himalayan hot springs village up the hill from us, just a little way. "Well, I can't get up there," I told him.

He replied, "Well I guess I could have them bring a pony down."

"Yeah! That would be really great, please do that!" So he took off and never came back.

And then these Himalayan Sherpa guys came, and they brought this little pony, "Just get up on the pony."

And I was trying to. I would literally get up, only to realize there was no one there. I was losing body heat, and using energy, and getting really frustrated. I started coming up with little tests for if somebody came to me and told me something. I would ask them if they could say my name and ask them to give me a cup of water. If they couldn't do those things, then I would know it was just a dream and I wouldn't follow through in action and try to do the thing they said to do.

Wednesday

"To sleep, perchance to dream.
Ay, therein lies the rub."

✣ SHAKESPEARE, *"HAMLET"*

Wednesday morning, I got up, packed my things, and scooted across the snow some more. I kept butt-scooting along to try to get to that ridgeline, to get out from under the canyon wall. I was starting to worry there would be a bigger slide, something I wouldn't have the strength to dig myself out of. This time I made it to where the ridge met the canyon wall. I scooted down the spur as far as I could before I was exhausted. I wasn't directly under the cliffs anymore. I made my next little snow shelf. I was still up on the snow, but I was another increment closer to my goal: the little stand of trees down the spur and a bare patch of dirt beneath them. Now that I was no longer on the canyon wall, I could see out into the valley below and to Portland beyond that. I could see planes leaving from Portland International Airport and flying overhead. That was a really bizarre thing, to be on this little snow slope all alone and have hundreds of people with their toes up above my head. None of them were aware that I was there on that ledge. It was a weird feeling knowing about all those people and being very, very, very alone.

arial view of Mount Hood

I kept listening for the sound of a helicopter or the sound of a search plane. I kept shouting out. I kept going over in my mind, trying to figure out death and God and whether He really existed or whether I could get Him to talk to me.

That's pretty much all that happened on Wednesday. Not much. I ate my last Keebler Crackers and Nutri-Grain bar. I saved the rest of my Chia seed. I figured I could fast for the rest of the time until I really, really needed it. I had no idea how I would know when it was time to use it. I was starting to wonder if anybody was looking for me. I started thinking about going down into the canyon and what the best way to get down was. I figured I would try the fire thing before I went down into the canyon.

Wednesday night I tried curling on my side instead of sitting balled up in my jacket like I had been. It felt good to let my muscles loosen a little, but I paid for it in body heat. My whole body was spasming from the cold. My legs jerked uncontrollably. I balled myself up again and began to doze in and out.

I dreamt there was a secret celebrity hot springs resort up the mountain from me. They had known I was there the whole time, but they hadn't come out to help me because they couldn't risk leaking the location of this celebrity hot springs. Really famous people would go there, and the whole point of it was that it was away from the paparazzi. They finally had mercy on me, and some big bouncers came down and told me, "Hey, you can come up if you need to."

"I can't get up. I can't go."

"Well, you're just going to have to."

But every time I would try to get up, I would hear the sound of the stream below me, and I would come awake again and be on the mountainside. I got so angry at myself that I couldn't just make the sound of the stream go away long enough to be able to get up and go with them and get out of the reality of being on the mountainside. I was so convinced that if I could just make the sound of the stream go away, I could enter into the dream and not be on this ice shelf, alone and freezing to death.

Then, the woman who owned the resort came down and berated me for not having the mental oomph to muscle past my reality, and to get to the resort.

Finally, I told them all, "You know what? I'm happy where I am. I'm plenty warm here." And I did feel warm and pictured I was in my own little hot tub there on my snow shelf. I wasn't shaking anymore that night. Looking back, I wonder about that. Why I wasn't shaking. Anyway, I told myself, "I'm in my own little hot spring resort. I don't need to go to your hot spring resort."

Right before dawn, I dreamt the Jonas Brothers came (I don't actually know what the Jonas brothers look like). They said, "Okay, we're heading out, and you can come with us. We know a way down the mountain. We have this guide who's going to take us."

And I replied, "Oh man! That would be so great! Thank you so much! Let me get my stuff together."

But then U2 showed up and the Jonas Brothers told me, "We'd really like to help you, but we don't want to travel with them."

By the time I got my stuff together, they had left. It had taken me too long. Then it was dawn, and I really had gotten all my stuff together. So I figured I'd just get going on down to the trees below.

Thursday

"And your ears shall hear a word behind you, saying,
'This is the way, walk in it,'…"

❧ Isaiah 30:21 (ESV)

I started scooting along again and finally did get to the tree line and the patch of dirt. That dirt felt so good. The sun was out for the first time since Sunday and the dirt was dark and warm. I felt like I was in paradise. I had been curled up for so long inside of my poncho and my jacket. It felt amazing to just stretch my legs out. I filled my bottles with snow and set them in the sun to melt. I started building a little fire. I probably should have planned that better. I wanted warmth right away, so I built a fire with what was at hand. Once I had fed it with everything within reach of where I was sitting, I had to get up and go snag a couple of branches and feed it before it went out. I was stiff and sore, and my legs weren't working well. I would sit down exhausted from each little trip, then have to get up again and get more branches to keep it alive.

I moved my little fire to the base of this snag that was on the ridgeline there. It was maybe 15 feet tall. I figured if I could get that thing lit on fire, maybe just light the whole ridge on fire, that would get somebody's attention. I had given up on anyone looking for me. I got the base of the snag on fire, but it just burnt through the base and the snag fell down. That wasn't very useful. I tried lighting the branches of some of the other trees on fire, but they were too green, and they just crackled and went out. I did get my hands warmed up for the first time in days. I didn't take my shoes off though. I didn't want to see what state my feet were in at this point. I think I probably melted the side of my shoes a little bit, warming my feet near the fire. Between the sun and the fire, I was able to melt a fair bit of water and take big luxuriant gulps of it.

I was starting to feel hopeful, like I could maybe get out of there. I was gauging the slope off my ridgeline and figuring out if I could just slide down it on my tarp. There was a broad flat area scooped sharply out of the canyon. It was below me and parallel to the stream. I figured it was full of water and rocks under the snow. I could hear the water down there. I didn't know what it would be like trying to cross that. If I could get across that, I was eyeing the next hurdle. There were two bare rock outcroppings making a bottleneck where the stream shot through the base of them. I was trying to figure out if I would have to crawl up and over that, and if I would be able to do it in the state I was in.

I wanted so much to do the brave thing. Muscle my way out of there. I was teetering along this edge, part of me feeling reckless—what did I have to lose after all?—part of me paralyzed by all of the what-ifs: *What if no one is coming for me? What if I get injured again sliding down into the bowl below? What if I get stuck at the bottleneck and simply don't have the energy to navigate around that growing stream? What if there is a trail, just down there, and all I need to do is travel a few hundred yards to get to it? What if I get stuck somewhere under the tree line, invisible from above?*

That evening as it was growing dark, I thought with relish about stretching out flat to sleep for the first time in days, *I don't care if I'm cold. I'm so tired of being curled up in a ball.* There was a long thin strip of dirt I could stretch out on. I had my tarp underneath me and my poncho over the top, and I used string to tie down the sides of the poncho. But I was right on the crest of the ridgeline, and the wind was whipping up and over me, really chilling me, stealing all my body heat.

That was where the Trench Cat came along (I have no idea what a Trench Cat is; it just said it was "the Trench Cat").

"Silly human, you're going to freeze to death if you stay here."

There was a little bracket or cluster of pine trees a couple yards away and down off the edge of the ridge.

"You have to go over there."

"I don't want to, I'm tired. And I don't want to break the branches. I don't want to work anymore."

"You'll die if you stay up here," said the Trench Cat.

So I crawled down to the little thicket, and broke all the branches to make a space for myself.

"You need to put your tarp like this, so that it blocks the wind when it's coming down off the mountain."

So I did. I was in this little semi-circle of pine trees just big enough for me to curl up my whole body in there.

As I was trying to sleep, lying there on the ground, I had these different personalities inside of me that were disagreeing with each other on the best way to sleep. There was somebody named Alex, and she wanted to sleep on her side. And then there was a guy who wanted to stretch out; we were all arguing about how to position ourselves. One voice would get the upper-hand and I'd sleep like that, and then another voice would get the upper hand and I'd sleep like that for a while. All the while we were bickering, I knew it was just different parts of me wanting different things.

Then the Trench Cat told me to take my shoes off. So I took my shoes off. It really hurt, and again, I didn't dare look at my feet. I didn't try to figure out what was going on with them, because I was worried it would be horrible.

I kept dozing in and out through the night. There was the Mere Paper Cat that came along and thanked me for being so very polite.

And I said, "You're welcome." Because Mere Paper Cats are very polite.

That Thursday night was probably the oddest of the various dreams or hallucinations, or whatever it was, that I had while on the mountain. Because the Trench Cat (the Mere Paper Cat too) wasn't actually a dream, there wasn't any visual, it was just there. You know how when God talks to you, there's a voice that's not your voice that tells you something? It was kind of like that, but it definitely wasn't God's voice, and it wasn't my voice. So that was kind of weird. It was not dream and not reality. I didn't really know where to place it. I'm just glad it kept me from sleeping exposed out on the ridgeline.

That was one of the oddest nights.

I did have a real dream that night. I dreamt Megan Armentrout (a dear friend of mine) came up on the ridgeline and was talking to me. "Mary, what are you doing here?"

"What are you doing here? I thought you were on a serve trip?"

She said, "I was; but I came back early."

I asked, "Hey, can I use your phone?"

"Oh, yeah. Absolutely. Of course. Never have to ask." So she gave me her phone and I called 911,

"Hey, I've been out here for a long time, and nobody's looking for me."

There was a very apathetic woman on the other end of the line. She answered in this noncommittal monotone, "I'm sorry. We'll get on that right away."

"Good, because I've been out here a really long time, and it's not good."

And she continued in the same monotone, "Yeah, we'll get to you. Don't worry."

Then I asked Megan if I could use the phone to call my parents, and of course she said yes. I tried over and over again, but the call would never go through. I just wanted them to know I was okay, but it would cut off as soon as they picked up, or just ring and ring and ring. I was getting so upset. It dug up the memory of years ago when I was in Papua New Guinea. We were trying to Skype call. I could hear my parents, but they couldn't hear me. It was awful to be so close to reaching them. It filled me with this frantic, helpless feeling.

That night, Thursday night, was the first dream I had the entire time where I saw somebody that was close to me. Megan was the first person who said my name, who knew who I was, and I knew her. The other people in all my dreams, some of them were faces I knew but not good friends. So that was kind of an interesting thing.

That was Thursday night.

THE NEWS SPREADS

(FRIDAY AFTERNOON, MARCH 29, 2013)

"When I said, 'My foot is slipping,' your unfailing love, Lord, supported me.
When anxiety was great within me, your consolation brought me joy."

❧ PSALM 94:18-19 ❧

Earlier in the day, when Bruce still wasn't home, the police had called. Reporters from various news stations were seeking interviews with us through them. The police assured me we didn't have to allow reporters to have our contact information or interviews. After Bruce got home, we talked about this. I didn't want to give any live interviews, but Bruce didn't hesitate at all. He hoped that we might be able to reach *someone* through this means who may have seen Mary or who might have some information on her plans or whereabouts. So, Bruce called the police back and gave them permission to release our contact information to news reporters with the stipulation, per my request, that they only seek interviews with him, and not with me.

Sergeant Collinson, who was in charge of the search for Mary at Mount Hood, called to give us updates several times during the day. By early afternoon he informed us that SAR was fully organized and had begun their efforts. Bruce posted what information we had from him on *Facebook*. By this time many people had begun sharing our posts.

Bruce

I just got off the phone with Search and Rescue. Still no word on Mary. He did say that her pack was still in the truck, along with what looks like an empty boot box. They are opening the truck to see if she took her spikes and ice ax which would indicate she was planning to be climbing. They have clothing from her pack and are bringing in dogs.

Please keep praying.

Sue M. (Rogue Valley friend, Mary's former employer): Praying constantly for ALL of you!

Christine C.: Thank you for the update...praying, praying, praying!

Cynthia K.: Hugs to you and your family. I lit a candle for Mary.

Jilann C. (NCFCA Idaho Director): I am praying for you all, Bruce!

K.H. (Rogue Valley family friend): Thank you for the update ♥ Sending up prayers every minute!!!

K.P. (Bruce's friend from high school): Will be praying, Bruce. The Lord knows where she is. I pray He'll reveal it to you and the search party.

Cheri M. (Rogue Valley, NCFCA friend): We're all praying, Bruce.

Amy F. (Rogue Valley friend, Anne T.'s twin sister): Praying without ceasing. My heart aches for what you must be going through.

David A. (Mary's grandpa): Thanks for the update, Bruce. I went up in the mountains and prayed.

L.M. (Bruce's friend from high school): More prayers and intentions coming her way, Bruce.

M.L. (Bruce's friend from high school): Thoughts and prayers.

Barbara R. (Rogue Valley, like-family friend): Praying constantly.

J.C. (Bruce's friend from high school): Praying that Mary is safe!

Becki D.: Praying, praying, praying. Our family adores Mary!

J. A.: Praying for her safe return.

Tami G. (Rogue Valley, NCFCA friend): Praying!

Bronwyn D.: Not gonna stop praying 'til they find her!

J.M. (Bruce's friend from high school): Thinking of you & your family. Hope your daughter is found safe.

Mary Beth J. (Bruce's sister): Thank you Bruce for the update.

Marissa C.: Praying for Mary and the rest of you guys!

Bruce

Here is the latest update from SAR. They have the vehicle open. Her backpack was inside. Her sleeping bag was inside. They found out that she bought a pair of inexpensive hiking/running shoes and another (2nd) ice ax. They think they now know what she is wearing based on what they found in the pack, tights and running shorts. It appears by this information that she did not intend to be out overnight. That being said, she probably would still have taken her poncho as an emergency shelter and would know how to use that. Still trying to guesstimate what her intensions and possible route would have been. Please keep praying.

Yadira I. (GFU student, family friend): Me and friends are praying for you and your family. Thank you so much for keeping us updated. Mary and your family are greatly loved. God is watching after you all.

J.A.: I've asked friends all over the country to join us in praying for her safe return.

N.H.: Praying with urgency

Cynthia K.: Worried alongside you.

Heather F. (Portland area, family friend): Thank you for the update.

Jessica G. (Rogue Valley, NCFCA, family friend): We are praying that the Lord will be close to you and her, and that she will be found soon!

Anna G. (Rogue Valley, NCFCA friend): Praying!

Sergeant Collinson also called to notify us that along with the search teams that were out on the trails and up on the mountain, a search plane had gone up. He asked that we not encourage people to assist in the search for Mary unless they were trained SAR personnel. For our part, besides what they were sharing with us and a few pertinent questions we had, we didn't ask for more details about what SAR was doing at this time. We were trusting them and just trying to let them do their job.

Sometime that morning, we got a call from a person who offered the assistance of "intuitive" friends of his. Bruce and I believed that he and his friends meant well; however, just at that time, his offer of assistance was highly distressing rather than helpful, particularly to me. In the past, I'd had intensely negative experiences with spiritism.* I was wary of anything that appeared to be in that realm. Bruce saw this offer differently, mainly as a diversion, and in our situation, as a potential waste of valuable time, energy, and resources. Neither Bruce nor

---

* Spiritism is the practice of knowingly or unknowingly calling on spirits (unseen entities) other than God's Holy Spirit for help. Other spirits include those of demons, humans, or of the deceased. See Lev. 19:26, 31; 20:6-7, 27; **Deut. 18:9-19**; 1 Sam. 28:3, 7-17; 1 Chr. 10:13; 2 Kings 21:6; 23:24; 2 Chr. 33:6; **Isa. 8:19-20**; 19: 1-4; 44:24-26; 47:10-15; 65:1-5; Jer. 29:8; Acts 16:16-18; **1 John 4:1**.

I wanted to employ this approach to find Mary. However, because these services were offered with such good intentions, and we didn't know the source (as the "intuitives" wanted to remain anonymous), and because we were already under a lot of stress and highly preoccupied, we just let it be.

After a while, because we had not responded, this person called Search and Rescue. SAR called us and wanted to know if we wanted them to look for Mary in the area where this person's friends intuited that she was, using the coordinates they had given. We knew they all just wanted to help and figured it couldn't hurt, so we authorized this. The SAR plane didn't find her in the area of the coordinates they gave. (It was significant mountain miles from where she was.) That was in the early afternoon. We refused to receive any more guesses from them after that—though we appreciated the well-meant intent behind them.

Bruce

Later, in the afternoon, I gave interviews to several local television stations, who came out to the house. My thinking was that, if Mary was planning on climbing with a group, someone in that group would contact us and perhaps give us additional information that would help us find her. As far as I know, no one ever came forward, but the story started to take off in the news.

Shelli

In the afternoon while Bruce was giving interviews to news reporters at the house, I went for a walk. It was a clear, sunny day. I'd found that a walk is always good for the soul in every way—mentally, physically, and emotionally. I really needed one to help me get some exercise and perspective. I also wanted to be out of the house while news reporters were at the house.

Many thoughts poured through my head as I was walking. *Something must have happened to Mary, or she would have returned by now—unless she was just backpacking for the full week somewhere?* I couldn't get rid of the impression that she was in some kind of distress. *She often hikes alone, maybe something happened to her and she's stuck somewhere? Did she climb into a situation she couldn't climb back out of? Is she hurt? Badly? Has she broken a leg? Does she have food? Water? Is she in the snow? Is she cold? Is someone holding her against her will?*

Even with all the assurances we had been given, it was still very hard *not* to feel distress for what she *might* be going through. My mom-heart ached, and I wanted somehow to be able to reach out to my daughter, no matter what was going on with her, to hug her and hold her and let her know I loved her. I knew my speculations and wishes couldn't change her situation, whatever it was. But I also knew the cries of my heart would be heard by God and He could reach her.

As I was pleading with God that He might somehow let her know my heart and thoughts were with her, and that He would comfort her through whatever she might be experiencing, He once more reminded me that suffering isn't always bad or permanent. If it does last for this lifetime, it won't last after that. And He can use it to make lasting, positive changes in us through it.

It was about then He also gently reminded me about the impression He had given me when I was praying at the beginning of the week—to leave Mary in His hands. At the same time, He gave me the quieting impression that what was going on with her had to do with His meeting and teaching her in a way only He could.

It hadn't occurred to me until then that God might be in the process of answering our prayers to give her a healthy fear of danger, for her benefit and that of others. I knew prayers are often answered in ways we don't expect and sometimes in ways we can only understand in retrospect. *Is God doing something through Mary's situation? Is there a deeper, long-reaching purpose in whatever is going on with her?*

Though I couldn't be absolutely sure that these impressions were from God, or reflective of reality, I did recognize a familiarity with how God had worked before. It renewed my hope. *Perhaps God is using this crisis not only to meet and teach Mary, but also to teach me, and maybe others too.*

At that point, a past incident came clearly to mind, a time when some young friends of ours had been lost on another mountain and miraculously found. As I was thinking about what had happened back then, I realized God was assuring me He could do the same for Mary. He had also just given me a more specific way to pray.

I also pondered on something Bruce and I had discussed and would end up reiterating a few more times between us—the impression that Mary was still alive. We were both aware of the outdoor skills she had cultivated, and we had already gone through the agonies and ecstasies of her first backpacking trip—hiking the PCT. The thought of her being gone from this life did not ring true for either of us. Neither of us sensed in our innermost being she was dead. We still understood there was the chance she was gone from us, but neither of us believed we should allow the seed of this thought any ground while we had the sense of her being alive. The thought she could be dead continued to resurface, but each of us kept choosing with deliberation to reject it.

We didn't feel we were being unreasonable. We knew there was a very real *possibility* she was not alive on earth anymore. There was also the *possibility* she was in the hands of a person with evil intent. And there was the *possibility* she was critically, even permanently, injured. The *possibilities* were endless, including the possibility of her being alive and eventually restored to us!

This brought me to reflect on the extraordinary comfort, peace, and strength Bruce and I were experiencing during this time of uncertainty. I believed that in large measure this had to be due to God answering people's petitions and pleadings for us. "Even" His prompting us to surrender and to continue to submit Mary and this whole situation into His hands were likely part of His answer to people's prayers.

It seemed highly probable to me that if God hadn't been supporting us with a sense of His Presence, we would easily have become abject captives to the fears that had been trying to master us. This kind of thing had happened to each of us in the past. Left to our own imaginations and devices, we would probably have been going crazy with worry. I would have been inclined to give in to despair. I would indeed have been crushed by the weight of the unknown with its accompanying fears.

In realizing all this, I was even more grateful for the support and prayers of other individuals—for their hearts and willingness to call on the Lord with and for us—even some of them who didn't know us personally. There were times while Mary was missing that I could almost literally feel these prayers. If God was answering people's solicitations for us, Mary's parents, in this way, He would most assuredly be answering their importuning for her.

Returning home from my walk about an hour later, a news team was still at the house. Avoiding them, I went in a side door and upstairs for privacy. Checking the computer, I saw that our oldest daughter, Jessika, then twenty-seven years old, had posted on *Facebook* what she had learned from us. She had also requested prayer, and many kind friends had already responded.

She had then also posted:

Jessika

Thanks all of you!!! Right now, they are pretty sure that her truck has been there since Monday (at Timberline [ski park], Mt. Hood). They opened the truck and from the contents it looks like she was planning on just a day trip. REI (a hiking equipment store) said that she recently purchased an ice-axe. So not very good news, but on the bright side, Mary is a very experienced mountain climber, and hiked more than one mountain when she hiked the Pacific Crest Trail! Thanks so much all of you!

Please pray especially for my mom, she is really hurting—we all are, but being Mary's mom, she has that special bond. I will let you all know if I hear anything more substantial or hopeful at all.

May God bless you and please keep praying! Love you guys!

C.P.: Jessika, thanks for keeping us posted. Praying for Mary... and your family, praying for all involved searching.

Cheri A. (Mary's aunt): Praying for you all! We love you.

Meri N. (Portland area friend): Mary is on my heart and I am praying for her. She is a good friend and I care for her!

It wasn't long before the news Mary was missing began to surface in the media. Below is an example of a lead-in to a news bulletin for the Portland metro area that was posted on *Facebook*:

FOX 12 Oregon: BREAKING NEWS

29 March 2013

"If you have seen Mary Owen since last weekend, you are urged to call deputies at...

[Shared now-inactive link to *FOX12 / KPTV News* report:] **"Missing Mt. Hood Hiker has not been heard from since last Sunday**. Deputies found Mary Owen's SUV at Timberline Lodge, but the 23-year-old hiker is missing...." (*FOX12 Oregon / KPTV.com*).

Following is a link to the *KOIN News* TV segment, "Search continues for missing hiker at Mount Hood," that aired that evening: https://www.youtube.com/watch?v=Ab9YfD_dqsA. I posted a link to another news broadcast on my *Facebook* timeline following a brief update and prayer request, and friends responded:

Shelli

We are pretty sure now that Mary only intended a day hike (Sunday or Monday?) from what she left in the truck she borrowed, and that she's probably alone. She's probably injured or stuck somewhere. Please pray a search and rescue team will be guided directly to her, and that God will continue to hold her in his arms until they can get to her.

[Shared now-inactive link to *NWCN/KGW News* report:]

"Woman missing, possibly alone on Mt. Hood" A 23-year-old woman is missing and is believed to have gone hiking alone on Mt. Hood several days ago, officials said..." (www.nwcn.com / kgw.com).[16]

Wendy A.: We continue to pray. Lord, help them find her.

Mary Beth J. (Bruce's sister): Thank you Shelli. I am praying for her safe return.

Karen E. (Shelli's friend from high school): This is really affecting me, Shelli. As a mother this has to be such a heartache. I am sending your whole family big hugs and I am praying hard for Mary's rescuers to be led right to her. Hang in there and keep the faith. Love ya.

Anne T. (Rogue Valley friend): Still praying! I keep thinking about hiking out of Rainie Falls for help for Josh, not sure if he was safe or not; and just feel what you are going through as you wait on a loving God to see what He has in store. May you find comfort and peace tonight knowing God has you all where He wants you and will not let go. May you feel the God of all comfort more closely now than ever before.

Both Bruce and I were very grateful for the ongoing (what we have renamed) "mortal" support—support God was providing through other mortals. Our family, friends, and church, in fact our whole community, also many others, were being ultra-supportive, offering help, hoping, and praying with us for Mary's safe return and the best outcome possible. We also had full confidence in the professional work the Clackamas police department, SAR, and the Newberg police department all seemed to be doing. We felt there really was nothing more we or anyone could do for the time being. It was in God's hands.

At some point Bruce wanted me to come and read a comment on one of his *Facebook* posts. It was very short, but very significant to both of us because of who had written it.

Cheri A. (Mary's aunt): I sent a prayer request to *Guideposts* magazine. They sent me this:

"Use this prayer for safety and protection:

Those who go to God for safety will be protected by him. I will say to the Lord, 'You are my place of safety and protection. You are my God, and I trust you.'" Psalm 91: 1-4.

Janet S. (long-time family friend): My girls and grandchildren are praying as well as friends. I know your mother's heart is so hurt. Will continue to pray for her and all of you. Love and hugs, Janet S.

Lisa M. (Mary's cousin): I will keep her in my prayers for a safe return home, Aunt Shelli and Uncle Bruce.

Kelly P. (Rogue Valley, family friend): Have you heard anything yet? Do they have any idea where she may have hiked? Have been praying all day. The only real comfort I have in this whole thing is Mary's true love in Jesus. I know whatever she is going through she has been with Jesus the whole time. And he with her. Will keep checking until we hear from you.

> S. Eddy: Bruce, I am fervently praying for Mary's safe return. Our hearts are with your family. God is good—always.

Less than a year before, S—— Eddy had lost her 19-year-old son, Joshua, in the river accident that's been mentioned. We were with mutual friends when we learned he had fallen into the river at Rainie Falls. We all prayed fervently for this young man and for his family, with the hope he would be found alive. With others, we were deeply saddened when he was not found after several days. Then we were somewhat relieved with them when at least his body was recovered sometime later.

Since that time, Mrs. Eddy's and Josh's (pre-death) writings have been a great help and encouragement to many people walking through difficult times or trying to find meaning and significance for living.[17] Theirs is a unique and powerful message of trust in and surrender to God's will. The fact that Mrs. Eddy was reaching out to us resonated deeply with both Bruce and me. It must have brought back some very painful memories for her, and yet she was intentionally standing with us in prayer and encouraging us to remember God is good—always.

STILL MISSING

(FRIDAY EVENING, MARCH 29, 2013)

"Make friends with the angels, who though invisible are always with you.
Often invoke them, constantly praise them, and make good use
of their help and assistance in all your temporal and spiritual affairs.

❧ SAINT FRANCIS DE SALES, SWISS CLERGYMAN (1567-1622) ❧

B ruce and I half expected Mary would be found that Friday, especially with the plane up looking for her. But the sun had gone down, and Search and Rescue (SAR), for the safety of the crews, had stopped the day's search without a sight or sound of our daughter.

They'd had people searching along the PCT in the Mount Hood area and searching areas on the mountain where climbers usually ascend or descend. One crew had dogs. We never asked for, nor were we given details about the dogs. I assumed they were dogs who could follow a particular person's scent. I later learned they were probably the Mount Hood Meadows Avalanche (or cadaver) Dogs,[18] trained to find and dig for people, hopefully alive, but also dead, who are buried in the snow.

The police and SAR both had been out working to find Mary that whole day. Because they had simultaneously reiterated that they didn't want us or our friends who weren't trained in search and rescue out there "helping" them, the only thing we felt we could really do was to remain at home so we could be a contact point and a reference. Certainly, if the Police/SAR had any questions for us that we might be able to answer, that might be helpful in the search, we wanted to be there. We were also a go-between to receive and pass on information between the Police/SAR and some of Mary's/our friends and family.

Bruce had insured that the news Mary was missing became public, hoping it might trigger someone to come forward with possibly life-saving information; and now, the news was quickly spreading in the media. We had continued to do all day what we considered to be one of the most important things we could do—ask people to pray with us for her to be found.

Most of our friends and family had joined us in getting the news out that she was missing, and they were also asking others to pass on the word and ask God (pray) with us for her to be found. We never realized how many people were connected to her life until this happened. We felt a spiritual bond with all these people who also cared about our daughter's welfare.

> **Victoria D.** (Rogue Valley, NCFCA, family friend)
>
> An update on my friend, Mary Owen...
>
> [Shared Bruce's latest Facebook post:] "Here is the latest information I have from SAR. They have had two crews out since this afternoon and a plane. One crew checking the Pacific Crest Trail where it runs by Mt Hood. Another crew searching the areas where climbers usually come down the mountain, and a plane in the air. Newberg police has sent a computer crimes specialist out to hack Mary's laptop which they found in the truck. They are hoping it might have information on it to help narrow the search. They have traced her debit card activity to several places and reviewed video in each which showed her to be alone at the time she used her card. They have identified what she bought, (shoes and another ax) and are figuring that stuff in when they look at what was left in the truck. So far, we still do not have any info on the people she was planning on climbing the mountain with so we are still trying to find out who they are."

Later, we learned people from all over the world were praying. Friends in India, Kyrgyzstan, PNG, Africa, Mexico, South America, and others in churches everywhere had begun to ask God to keep Mary safe and for her to be found—and for us, her family to be sustained and upheld through it all. We'll never know the actual number of people who were concerned and calling on the Lord for and with us, but we were (and still are) grateful for the willingness of every single one who did.

> Melanie D. (wife of Bruce's high school friend, family friend): We are praying for her and your family. God Bless!
>
> Brenda K. (Bruce's sister): I'm thinking of all of you......I love you!!
>
> Nathan A. (Shelli's brother): We're praying too. What has the weather been like?
>
> Arden S. (Rogue Valley, NCFCA friend): Lord Jesus, have mercy on this family.
>
> Jackie E. (Portland area, close family friend): I have been praying for Mary and you all, all day.
>
> Cynthia K.: Bruce...any new developments?

That evening, all our children, but Mary, gathered with us at our home in McMinnville. All of us were needing the "mortal" support of being together in-person. Elijah, of course, was already with us when Rachel and Ruth arrived from Portland. They had picked Jessika up on their way over. Mary's not being there and being missing felt like a great hole in our family.

Rachel

It was sobering when we got to the house and the press was there. I was worried about how taxing it must be for my parents. While I was concerned about Mary, it was starting to sink in how brutal the toll would be on the whole family if something happened to any one of us.

I didn't "feel" as though Mary was gone though, and I wasn't going to grieve for her unless we actually learned otherwise. Everyone was calm, although the strain and concern were palpable.

Shelli

We were all subdued, talking between each other. At one point, Rachel started looking up past accounts on the internet of people who had been lost or stranded on Mount Hood and survived. It was a mercy to us that she didn't tell us most of the stories she ran across trying to find these.

One account she did share was of two people (in 1986) who survived three days after a major storm on Mount Hood by hunkering down in a snow cave. What she didn't tell us was that there were six others in that snow cave, and these two were the only ones out of the eight people in the snow cave, who did not perish (see chapter 4, "Mount Hood"). It was speculated, the reason these two survived was because they were higher in the cave than the others, and warm air rises, so they were able to stay warmer than the rest.[19]

Elijah

There were people who were out there working to find Mary, who were trained to look for people. I believed that if God wanted her alive or otherwise that was out of our control. I realized our power over our circumstances was limited. I felt like we should let go of control and leave things to God, since there wasn't anything we could do; unless we were going to go up and search—which would have worsened the situation and put us in danger.

It had crossed my mind that something like this was bound to happen to her sometime. She tended to go off without a second thought, and that was kind of frustrating, because she didn't seem to pay any attention to how much we cared.

I was resigned to the outcome being whatever it needed to be, because she made her choices and there was nothing I could do about it.

Shelli _____

After the SAR crew had a chance to regroup and report, they called us. Again, they weren't totally sure at first whether they should mount a search the next day, on Saturday. Mary had been up there at least five, maybe six, full days on the mountain. In their experience chances were slim to none of finding her alive at that point. They were concerned about risking lives of searchers for someone who, according to their experience, was likely dead. They were not saying this directly to us, but they didn't have to. A lot of people have fallen and died on Mount Hood, but this was not on our minds at all. The idea that she had possibly been injured was. Again, Bruce told them if they weren't going to search, we and friends would.

SAR called us back a little while later. They'd decided they'd go ahead with a full-scale search over the weekend. The weather was expected to be beautiful. The conditions would be as good as they get that time of year, even with the ever-present danger of avalanche. They'd have a lot more volunteers on the weekend. We were all very grateful they were going to continue the search.

We heard from SAR a couple more times that evening. Each time Bruce shared what we had learned from them on *Facebook,* and I also shared this information on email.

> . . . SAR says they will have upwards of 50 trained people out there [on Mount Hood] beginning at 4 a.m. tomorrow. They plan to have one crew brought to the summit to do a top down search of the mountain.
>
> SAR says more untrained searchers would not be helpful, but if you are trained in search and rescue, you might be of use up there. They said if folks wanted to go to Timberline [ski park] and just talk to people and show Mary's picture, that might be helpful in maybe coming upon someone who knows something. If people wanted to maybe bring food for the SAR folks that could be of help too.

Please keep praying and spreading the word. Please share this post to your *[Facebook]* wall so more people will see it. We are continuing in prayer and faith. We hope to find Mary soon.

Bruce also posted the two following photos of Mary on *Facebook*:

Mary on the PCT

PCT smile

Cynthia K.: I'm glad that the professionals are taking this seriously. Sounds like they are sending the very best up there to bring her back. 4 AM seems so far off for reinforcements. You must be wanting to drive up there tonight. Hugs to you and Shelli. Mary knows what to do in in the wild. Very nice photos of her that you have posted. Thinking of you all and praying for safe return home for Mary.

J.A.: The SAR people are near and dear to my family. Great people who will work hard to find her. Continuing in prayer.

T.A. (Rogue Valley, NCFCA friend): We are joining you in praying for the safe return of your daughter.

Bronwyn D.: Appreciate the updates. Praying!

J.F. (Bruce's friend from high school): Praying for a safe return Bruce.

Christine C.: Love to you ALL and MANY prayers!!! Thank you so much for the updates.

Scott W.: My family and I just had a great time praying for Mary and your family! God is so good, and I know He will protect her. Thank you for the updates, Bruce. My offer is still open if extra search team members are needed.

<u>Suzette J.</u> (Bruce's friend from high school): Praying for you and Mary.

<u>Sue M.</u> (Rogue Valley friend, Mary's former employer): Same here, Bruce. Praying and praying! Love you all!

<u>Christopher C.</u>:

[Shared the following post:]

<u>Jeremy Camp</u>

"I have told you these things, so you may find peace in Me. In this world you will have trials. But take heart! I have overcome the world" (John 16:33).

Friends offered what support they could:

Dear Bruce and Shelli,

Thank you so much for the updates on Mary. We are praying urgently day and night. May the Lord keep you tonight in his loving arms. Our God reigns.

With love,

The P——s (Ann P. [Rogue Valley, family friend])

> Bruce & Shelli to Ann:
>
> Thank you! 🖤

Andrew P. (Salem area, family friend):

Hi, Bruce and Shelli,

I have a day off tomorrow and would like to help however I can, with the understanding that I don't have any equipment or training for anything technical. I certainly wouldn't want to be in the way, but if you feel that I might be able to be of assistance, I'd be glad to help. Let me know the details by reply, if you're interested. If not, that's perfectly fine as well. Our prayers are with you and Mary.

> Bruce & Shelli to Andrew:
>
> Hi Andrew, if you can be at our house before 8:00 AM, you can ride up to the mountain with us. Or if you just show up there at Timberline Lodge, we are probably going to be handing out flyers and talking with people going up the mountain or hiking, or skiing, or snowshoeing, etc... You are welcome to come help us.

Andrew P.:

Hi, guys. I think it will work best if I meet you at Timberline tomorrow morning. I'll head on up there when I get up. Anything I can bring? I get email to this account on my cell, and

I can also be reached by phone/text at XXX-XXX-XXXX. See you tomorrow. Please let me know if there's anything I can buy or bring.

Thanks!

> Bruce & Shelli to Andrew:
>
> Maybe bottled water for the SAR people? God willing, we will see you up there then. Thank YOU!

Andrew P.:

I'll have water bottles. Let me know if you think of anything else. See you there!

Bruce and Shelli,

We are praying that she is found soon. Blessings to you all. Thank you for the updates.

Jerrie, Becky and the boys (Portland area, family friends)

> Bruce & Shelli to Jerrie L.:
>
> Thank you so much for your prayers and encouragement.

Darren & Brenda N. (Portland area, family friends):

Bruce, If extra bodies are needed to fan out in an area, let us know if that would be helpful. I am sure the officials will know what is best and if it would be fruitful to have extras up there. Call or e-mail us if we can help in any way. My cell is XXX-XXX-XXXX Brenda's is XXX-XXX-XXXX.

> Bruce & Shelli to Darren & Brenda N.:
>
> Thank you, Darren. Right now, they are asking that we NOT put a bunch of people in the field to look for her. They are concerned with other people getting lost and

there are avalanche conditions out there and they don't want anyone to get hurt. I will post on my FB account if we get to a point where they might need more folks.

Thanks,

Bruce

CHERISH (homeschool group) to CHERISH members:

Please keep holding this young woman and her family up in prayer. Thank you!

In Bruce's last phone conversation that day with the sergeant in charge of SAR, he had told Bruce that looking for Mary on that mountain was literally like looking for a needle in a haystack. They really didn't know where to start. There were just so many places she could be up there. Even though they had had several crews out, in the air and on the land that day (Friday), that hadn't even remotely begun to cover all the possibilities. As Bruce was sharing this with me afterward, I remembered the past experience that had come to mind earlier in the day while I was walking.

Some years back when we were camping with a large group of our friends at Lake of the Woods campground, a portion of our group did an all-day hike to the top of Mount McLoughlin and back.[20] Two of the young men, Davy and Brad, who went up the mountain with everyone else, never came back down that evening.

Brad's parents ended up calling 911. Search and Rescue (SAR) said they'd be at the base of Mount McLoughlin first thing in the morning and assured them that though night temperatures would be pretty cool on the mountain, the young men would be fine for one night.

The next morning SAR set up base in the parking lot where the trail to summit Mount McLoughlin begins. They asked hikers on the way up to keep their eyes open for the young men. They had some rescue volunteers hiking the trail and mountain too. They sent up an airplane in the afternoon when Davy and Brad still hadn't been found.

The plane eventually sighted Davy, alone, climbing up a scree field on the southwest side of the mountain. Volunteers immediately began working their way up and over to retrieve Davy from the side of the mountain.

It was bad news to learn that Davy and Brad had separated! One of best things hikers can do in such a situation is to stick together. Brad's parents were starting to feel desperate!

Shortly after Davy was spotted, a call was made to the SAR base camp from a hiker situated towards the top of McLoughlin. The caller said he could see someone with white clothing at the tree line down the mountain from him, and he gave coordinates.

Bruce and I were at the SAR base with Brad's parents when this call came in. SAR personnel showed us all where this hiker would most likely come down off the mountain, and where we could probably intercept him by driving up some jeep trails to reach him.

Bruce and I had been accompanying Brad's parents all day. We were with them when they drove down the mountain, then back up the indicated trails. We drove straight to where Brad, at the same time, was coming out of the woods onto the trail. Too little time had elapsed for him to be there already, and he was dressed ALL in black. His T-shirt and jeans were black. His hair is black. And even his skin, including his face, were close to black with dirt. There was no white anywhere on him!

We don't know who or what the caller to SAR saw wearing white, but it wasn't Brad. After that incident, we dubbed whoever or whatever had been at the tree line wearing white that day, an "angel." Providence had used this white-wearing entity to guide us directly to Brad. It was a small miracle and a big answer to our prayers.

Recalling this past experience, we decided to begin asking the Lord specifically that He would send an "angel" to guide SAR directly to Mary in their search on Saturday. For the rest of the evening when people contacted us, we also began asking them to join us in praying for this as well.

Afterward, we learned that even people who had not received this request from us were lifting this same prayer up to God. My sister Celeste was one of them. She later shared:

> On that Thursday late afternoon in March, Dad [Mary's grandfather] called me and told me that Mary was missing and had been since Sunday. He asked me and my family to please pray and fast for her. I had such a strong impression that I really needed to get on my knees and pray right away. I gathered all my family together and we prayed right then. Then I started my fasting and prayers. Thursday night ended and Friday, and still Mary wasn't found...
>
> On Friday night, after S&R had failed to find her, I felt impressed to be more specific in my prayers. I then pleaded with the Lord to send one of his specific messengers to lead searchers to Mary. I felt a conviction that it was now in God's hands, and He would show the rescuers the way...

I believe God's Spirit was inspiring us and others how to pray. In a sense, setting things up so we could see His hand in what happened later—so we would know it was Him answering our prayers and not just happenstance.

Bruce and I and our children also decided that we would all go up to Mount Hood in the morning. But because Search and Rescue has asked us not to try looking for Mary on the mountain ourselves, we settled on creating some flyers with her picture on it, along with police contact information to hand out to people. We thought we could pass them out in the towns and resorts up in that area in case someone might have seen her. We could also bring food and water to SAR workers. Rachel and Ruth volunteered to make the flyers first thing in the morning and bring them up to us on the mountain. We planned on meeting at the Timberline Lodge parking lot, SAR area.

At that point, we all agreed we needed to *try* to get some rest—if not sleep—so we would be ready for the next day. Before our girls headed home for the night, we gathered in a circle, joined hands, and prayed aloud together for Mary—expressly that God would send an "angel" to help SAR find her the next day. Rachel and Ruth took Jessika home to her place in McMinnville, then they headed back to Portland.

For reasons unknown to us, the news Mary was missing began to be picked up by the media nationwide. They were relying on our local news stations for their information. One of the final local online news reports for the day was this:

Search for missing Mount Hood hiker to resume Saturday

Updated Mar 29, 2013; Posted Mar 29, 2013

By Heather Steeves, *The Oregonian/OregonLive.com*

[with our photo of Mary wearing a beanie]

A search for a Newberg hiker who has likely been alone on Mount Hood for days will resume Saturday morning.

Search crews scoured the area Friday for Mary Owen, 23, who emailed a friend last Sunday to say she was going to hike on the mountain, said Adam Phillips, a Clackamas County Sheriff's Office spokesman, in a press release.

The friend called police Thursday when Owen did not return and an announcement for the suspension of Friday's search came around 9 p.m.

Owen's white 1998 Toyota 4-Runner was found in the parking lot of Timberline Lodge with her backpack inside. She is an experienced hiker, but is likely to be short on supplies, Phillips said.

A helicopter from the Oregon National Guard as well as search teams from Portland Mountain Rescue, Pacific Northwest Search and Rescue and others are planned to aid in Saturday's efforts.

Anyone who sees Owen is asked to contact the sheriff's office non-emergency line XXX-XXX-XXXX or Sergeant ███ Collinson at ██████@co.clackamas.or.us. She is described as blonde, wears glasses and likely a green beanie hat.[21]

– Heather Steeves,

12

HEADING UP TO MOUNT HOOD

(SATURDAY MORNING, MARCH 30, 2013)

"Hope is a passion for the possible."

ও Søren Kierkegaard, *Fear and Trembling* ৫

Bruce

I was up early, waiting for the time we agreed to drive to Mount Hood. I was holding it together so far, with the Lord's support and the prayers of what felt like thousands from around the world, but around the edges of my mind the thought was there. *What if God takes her?* As I wrote a *Facebook* post before we headed out to the mountain, I stopped pushing the thoughts away, and submitted to God's will, again.

> Nothing new overnight. We are heading up to the mountain this morning.
>
> Your prayers and support have been overwhelming, and we appreciate you all so much.
>
> I do ask that if you are experienced in SAR and can be of help with the team up there looking for Mary that you would come.
>
> I am conflicted on what to say to all of you who want so much to help, who want to search, but are not SAR trained. We desperately need to find Mary, but I would never want anyone else to be hurt or lost in the process. And so, I can only ask that you would prayerfully consider what God would have you do, how God would have you help, and to act accordingly. Please be led by God's Holy Spirit in you and not by your own emotions in making this decision. We love you all, and we believe your prayers are a help beyond all measure.

We beg of You Father [God], that You would hear our prayers, that You would hear the prayers of all those that are praying so faithfully. We pray that You would bring Mary back to us safely. We ask that You who know all things, would show us where she is. We ask that You would bless the hands and feet of all those who will search today. Keep them safe and point them in the right direction. We trust You, we praise You, and we submit ourselves to Your good and perfect will in this and in all things. We thank You God that you hear and answer the prayers of all those that love You and put their trust in You. Please hear us now.

Sarah B.: praying, Bruce (6:45 AM).

Sue M. (Rogue Valley friend, Mary's former employer): Beautifully said, Bruce—my prayers continue (6:49 AM).

D.G. (Bruce's friend from high school): Amen. Peace and His grace to you, friend (7:12 AM).

Becki D.: Amen (7:23 AM).

Shelli ———————————————————

Bruce is almost always up and going before me on any given morning. This morning was no exception. Knowing our own temperaments and predilections—so that there would not be undue misunderstanding between us or extra stress in the morning—we had talked over our plans and decided the night before what time we wanted to leave in the morning to go up to Mount Hood.

Unaccountably, Bruce and I had both gotten *some* sleep and had woken up with a sense of hope. We had no reason—yet every reason—to believe this day would be the day Mary would be found. Before going headlong into our preparations for the day, Bruce shared with me in a little more depth what he had already shared on *Facebook*. We reaffirmed that we both still felt like she was alive. Though we couldn't know anything for sure, there was a quiet glimmer of expectation in the air between us. It was a precious but tentative thing we couldn't quite put into words.

Soon after I was up, after dressing in layers of warm under and outerwear, I was gathering coats, hats, and gloves/mittens for being up on the mountain. If I remember right, Bruce had already filled our five-gallon container with the excellent, fresh well water from the tap at our large laundry-room sink and had grabbed a package of paper cups we had in our pantry. We wanted extra to share with others. I filled a plastic shopping bag with fruit to share for snacks later. I don't remember if we fixed or ate any breakfast that morning or not. We were all on autopilot as far as these kinds of preparations went that morning.

Elijah was also up and getting himself ready. I'm sure I probably reminded him to dress in layers for being on the mountain. He was probably helping Bruce load the car with the things we were gathering—anyway that's what he would have been doing on other occasions out of habit.

I called our daughter Jessika also, to confirm the time we had planned for picking her up. (She lived about twelve minutes away from us in McMinnville.) She had decided not to go with us. She didn't think she could emotionally handle going up to Mount Hood for however long we might be up there. She was really struggling. The rest of us had committed and were determined to go up. I told her we would double check with her right before leaving home in case she had changed her mind.

Izzy had indicated to us the night before that she wanted to go up to the mountain with us, so I also called her that morning to confirm the time we would be picking her up on the main street in front of their apartment in Newberg. Another friend of Mary's from Portland had asked Bruce if he and his dog could go up with us too. Bruce had prearranged with him a time and place where we could meet him on our route up to Mount Hood.

We decided I should be the driver since though we were all stressed, I had the most experience. Before leaving, we called Jessika. She still didn't feel up to going.

After a thirty-minute drive, we stopped in Newberg as planned to pick up Mary's roommate, Izzy. Bruce had to remind me to stop—I was so focused on getting to Mount Hood. One of the first things Izzy and Bruce did after she joined us was to ask God aloud, as voice for all of us, that Mary would be found—God willing—as soon as we arrived at Timberline Lodge, and that she would be alive and okay.

Driving through a suburb of Portland on our way up to Mount Hood, we picked up Mary's friend and his dog. Then we gassed up at what-turned-out-to-be the same gas station where Mary had last filled the white truck on her way up to Mount Hood! Bruce learned this from talking with the cashier there. This was one of the last places she had been seen before she disappeared. It seemed like predestination, or at least a hopeful sign, that we had inadvertently stopped at the same gas station she had.

When we were back on the road again, none of us talked much, but when we did, it was mainly about the weather. There was a light morning fog over us and hanging about the skirts of the mountain. We talked some about Mary, what we knew and what we didn't know.

Since Bruce and I didn't have a cell phone then, we didn't see these *Facebook* comments until later, but while we were on the road our family and friends continued to respond to Bruce's early-morning *Facebook* post and another he had posted right before we left home. Some people were also responding to the email we had sent the (Friday) night before, and to other of our family members' (Mary's siblings') *Facebook* posts.

Neil M. (Rogue Valley, family friend): Still praying with you... (7:35 AM).

Jeannette C. (Shelli's sister): Our prayers join in (7:40 AM).

M.L.: Continuously praying (7:48 AM).

Susie D.: Mary was on my mind—as were all of you as I went to sleep (7:57 AM).

Merino N.: Mary is a dear friend, and I am praying that she will be found safe. Praying for everyone who is heading in search of Mary (8:09 AM)!

Donna S. (Bruce's friend from high school): Bruce, I am going to put you on the prayer chain at church as well (8:12 AM).

Amy S. (Portland area, family friend)

I was awake many times during the night and used all those moments to pray for Mary and your whole family!

Roy N Hollie S. (Portland area, close family friends): Me too, Amy. Prayed most of the night (8:41 AM).

Bronwyn D.: Me too (10:29 AM)!

Barbara R. (Rogue Valley, like-family friend): My prayers are continual. I love you guys (8:37 AM).

Nancy O. (Mary's aunt): Very nice, Bruce. We are sending positive thoughts and hoping Mary is found today. Sending our love to the whole family (8:42 AM).

Therese S.: Amen. My prayers continue for Mary and for those who are searching for her (9:52 AM).

Karie C. (Shelli's sister): ...We are praying for her... (10:11 AM).

Monique G.: Amen (10:17 AM).

S.R.: Prayers for you and your family.

D.T.: Still praying. Peace. Be still and know that He is God! Praise Him in the midst of the storm. Oh Lord, You have Mary, for she trusts in You!

Sabrina D. (Rogue Valley friend)

Bruce & Shelli...our family is praying for you & for the team looking for Mary. We pray for her safe return. Thank you for your faith displayed even in this difficult time...what a blessing!

Emails:

Shelli,

Can I send $ or anything to help get food up there for the searchers? Would you like me to come up?

Jeannette C. (Shelli's sister)

Bruce, Shelli, and family,

We are praying for you all. Our men's group prayed this morning for Mary and for you. God Be with you all.

Ron S. (our pastor)

We will find her today, alive!

David A. (Mary's grandpa)

Thank you, Shelli, for the update. Continuing to pray for all of you and for my own daughter [one of Mary's best friends from childhood]. God will be glorified in this! Love,

Lori (Rogue Valley, close family friend)

PS: If there is anything we can do down here, please let us know.

Elizabeth W.

If you can use our house for anything, please know it is open for you or any need that you have. Our hearts and prayers are with you.

Alan-Gini W. (Portland area, NCFCA, family friends): Also, if our RV would be of any use to you, you are more than welcome to it (8:27 AM).

Also, while we were on our way up to Mount Hood Saturday morning, *The Oregonian* / *OregonLive.com* published the following update on the search for Mary:

Search teams fan out on Mount Hood, looking for missing woman, 23

March 30, 2013, at 9:08 a.m.; Updated Mar 30, 2013, at 10:08

By Lynne Terry, *The Oregonian/OregonLive.com*

[with our photo of Mary wearing a metal backpack]

Mary Owen, 23 of Newberg, was last heard from on Sunday. She's believed to be on Mount Hood.

Search and rescue teams fanned out on Mount Hood on Saturday morning in a massive effort to try to locate a missing 23-year-old woman from Newberg.

Crews set out on their search for Mary Owen just after 8 a.m. Dozens are taking part in the search, most of them volunteers. The groups include Portland Mountain Rescue, Pacific Northwest Search and Rescue, Hood River Crag Rats, American Medical Response Reach and Treat,

Mountain Wave Communications, Corvallis Mountain Rescue, Lane Mountain Rescue and the Clackamas County Sheriff's Office.

Steve Rollins, rescue leader for Portland Mountain Rescue, joined the air search in an Oregon National Guard Black Hawk helicopter.

"We're searching the entire mountain," Rollins said. "The theory is that she may have gone climbing on Mount Hood."

Owen, a senior at George Fox University, is an experienced hiker. She completed the Pacific Crest Trail from Mexico to Canada during a nine-month [sic]* adventure.

"That shows dedication," said Deputy Marcus Mendoza, a spokesman for the Clackamas County Sheriff's Office.

He said she was planning to hike and summit Mount Hood with friends but their plans didn't pan out. She was last heard from on Sunday when she emailed a friend saying she was going to climb Mount Hood [sic].**

Her friend [sic]*** called police on Thursday. That same day, they located her white 1998 Toyota 4-Runner in the parking lot at Timberline Lodge. They found various items inside, including her computer and a backpack.

Mendoza said Newberg police are checking the laptop for clues to her whereabouts. The backpack was empty. Mendoza said her friends and family believe she took another backpack with her.

She often set out alone, Mendoza said.

"It was reported to us that she's somewhat of a free spirit (who) often goes on hikes," Mendoza said. "So, this wouldn't be uncommon."

A search on Mount Hood on Friday found no sign of Owen. Saturday's effort on the ground will focus on the area from White River Glacier on the east side to Zig Zag Canyon and Paradise Park on the south. Conditions are sunny and clear but there is one potential problem.

---

* Six-month

** Mary did not say this. Part of the difficulty of the search was that Mary was not specific about what she was going to do.

*** Bruce, not Mary's friend, called the police.

"We expect high avalanche conditions later today," Rollins said.

The warmth of the sun melts the snow, which is transitioning from winter to summer snow packs, causing it to become heavy and unstable.

"Water can percolate to lower levels through the snow pack and can hit a weak layer and lubricate it," Rollins said. "That's what causes avalanches."

He said teams are armed with avalanche gear—beacons, shovels and probes. But searchers will need to avoid areas with slopes from 30 to 45 degrees during the day when the risk of avalanches is the greatest.

A four-person team from Portland Mountain Rescue set off at 4 a.m. to reach avalanche terrain before the sun beats down. Rollins said they probably had made it to the Hogsback area on the south side by about 8 a.m.

Rollins said the search could take time.

"I wouldn't be surprised if this goes past today," he said. "We have a large area to search and not much information to go on."

He said searchers believe Owen took basic climbing gear but they don't know exactly what she had and they've not been able to locate her through a beacon or cell phone. Mendoza said sheriff's deputies learned from her cell phone company that her phone has not been on since Saturday.

Mendoza said Owen did not usually carry a tent but would take other gear in case she had to camp out.

"We believe she has a sleeping bag with her," Mendoza said.

Police asked anyone with information about Owen to call 503-XXX-XXXX or email @ co.clackamas.or.us.

— Lynne Terry

We also didn't see this news article until later.

After about two hours of driving, the road began to climb Mount Hood. The fog started to clear, and the sun shone through. It would be a gorgeous spring day in the mountains of northern Oregon. Search and rescue teams would have a clear, sunny day for their search. This lifted our spirits. We knew the good weather would greatly increase visibility and the ability for sound to travel, even though it would also increase avalanche danger and the difficulty of traversing the snow as it softened. Even the well-trained searchers would have to be extra cautious.

At each turn in the road as we got closer and closer to the Timberline Lodge parking area where we were to meet the officer in charge of the SAR operation, we just wanted more and more to be there already. At one point I think I said something like, "I don't remember there being this many turns in the road." Our anticipation mixed with trepidation was mounting with each mile as our vehicle climbed the mountain.

Another half-hour later, when we were finally on the approach to the Timberline Lodge parking lot, we saw the cordoned off area first. We assumed this was for SAR and entered to park there. We weren't even all out of the van yet when an officer began walking towards us. He greeted us and introduced himself as Collinson, the sergeant in charge of the search; this was the same officer we had been talking with on the phone since Friday morning.

The first thing he told us, after brief introductions, was that a helicopter was at that very moment hovering over someone who fit Mary's description! They didn't say they were hovering over a "body"—which intimated to us that she was alive! It was like a beautiful, surreal dream. The world exploded with the light of possibility. They weren't sure yet if it was her, but he said they'd be able to tell us more in a few minutes. Our bodies immediately switched from neutral to high gear—our hearts and minds racing—hoping, hoping, hoping, almost certain but not yet…. Collinson needed to return to where the radio was, where they were receiving communications from the helicopter.

While we were waiting, all physically holding on to each other, we huddled together and out loud, prayed with all our hearts it might be so!

13

"YOU'RE ALIVE!"

(FRIDAY TO SATURDAY, MARCH 29–30, 2013)

You, Lord, brought me up from the realm of the dead;
you spared me from going down to the pit.
Sing the praises of the Lord, you his faithful people;
praise his holy name.
For his anger lasts only a moment,
but his favor lasts a lifetime;
weeping may stay for the night,
but rejoicing comes in the morning.

❧ DAVID (PSALM 30:3-5) ❧

Mary—Friday (Still on a narrow ridge of rock and dirt amid a Glacier on Mount Hood.)

Friday morning, I woke up, and the very first thing that happened was God spoke to me. He said, "Do not worry about what you're going to eat, or what you're going drink, or what you're going to wear tomorrow."* My entire being responded, *You're Alive!* And it was like the lights switched on. All of a sudden, the world came back into focus and vibrant color. All those days sitting in terrible silence, it was as if I had been underwater, partially deaf and blind. The world came back online, and I knew, *God is Alive, and I am going to live.* I knew. The next thing that came into my head was, "There are thousands of people praying for you right now." I knew with absolute assurance, *They're going to find me, and I'm going to be okay!*

I uncurled myself from where I had been hunkered down in the pine brake. I looked through what I had for anything with an ounce of color. I came up with my red microspikes and a mauve

* Paraphrase of Matt. 6:25-34

T-shirt that was in my bag for some reason. I stuck those on the end of the snag I had burnt down, and I propped it up so it was upright in the snow. It took me most of the morning, as I had very little energy and I was hobbling and crawling around, unable to feel either of my legs. I was hoping the snag would catch somebody's eye if there was a search plane flying over. At that point I had run out of Nutri-Grain bar wrappers to use as tinder and my lighter was out of fuel. I tried starting a fire a couple of times, but I wasn't able to get a flame going. So, I was waiting, and I was listening, and I was happy! I was actually able to talk to God and sing. I was certain they were going to find me.

Sure enough, that evening a search plan came over the rim of the canyon. *Yeah! They found me!* I waved my arms and shouted. I tried to stand up. It circled right over me, and then flew off towards Portland. After a while, another search plane came down the canyon, circled right over me, and then flew off towards Portland. It gave this little tilt to the wing as it flew away. *Okay, they've seen me. They're going to go get a search crew to come up. They obviously can't pick me up with a plane here, so they're going to go send a crew up the canyon to come and get me.* I packed everything up, and I sat up on top of that ridgeline as visible as I could be. I'd crawled up onto the snow again, so I was exposed and easily visible away from the tree line.

I was sitting out there waiting. Then it started getting dark. I was shouting out because I was hoping they were sending somebody, so they could hear me. It got darker and darker. *Well, is there any reason why they wouldn't send a crew tonight? I can't think of any reason why they'd have seen me and then left me here. But they must've seen me. They flew overhead and then circled.*

I stayed out there, hoping, worrying, wrestling with the cold and my own confusion. As the night grew darker the stars began to come out. It was the first time since I had gotten stranded out there that I saw the stars. I don't know if it was because the nights weren't clear before that, or I just wasn't seeing them, but seeing stars comforted me. Ever since I was a child, and especially during my time hiking the PCT, the stars have been like friends, companions, to me. So, seeing them that night was like seeing the face of an old friend when you're in an unfamiliar place. It was good not to be alone.

I stayed out on the exposed ridgeline and looked at the stars for a while, then finally let the realization sink in—they weren't coming for me that night. I went back into my little cove in the trees there and tried to sleep.

I dreamt of a helicopter landing on the ridgeline, one of those big Chinook military helicopters. The bay opened up in the back and a couple of people came out with a stretcher, with these really warm wooly blankets, and hauled me onto the helicopter. I remember saying something like, "Don't forget my shoes! I've got to have those!" I knew the guy who was the helicopter pilot. He was another student, an acquaintance from my work leading Urban Services at the University.

That was all I dreamt that night. I dreamt about being rescued.

Saturday

> *It is well (it is well)*
> *With my soul (with my soul)*
> *It is well, it is well with my soul.*
> ❧ HORATIO SPAFFORD ❧

Saturday morning, I woke up with a feeling like the moment when you reach the summit of a mountain and stand there just breathing it all in. Exultation. Peace. *Alright! This is it! They're going to come for me today.*

I rolled up and packed my tarp, poncho, and climbing harness, took the microspikes and t-shirt down off of the snag where I had hung them the day before, and squeezed my swollen feet back into my shoes with the laces as loose as they'd go. It was a cold, clear morning. I crawled out of the trees and sat out on that ridgeline strip of dirt where I had made my fire. I wanted to be as visible as I could get without going up onto the snow. The sun was starting to rise, but because I was on the west side of the mountain, I was still in shadow. I watched the sunlight stretch across the valley below me. I was singing, "It Is Well with My Soul."

Just as the sun hit my ridgeline, I heard the blades of the helicopter, *"tuka tuka tuka tuka tuka…"* The deep sound I had been listening for, for all that time! I had been waiting for it for so long. It fell on my ears like a cool drink of water on a parched throat.

They came down, straight down the canyon towards me. They flew through the same space where the search plane had flown right over my head, and they circled around to face me. I thought I could see the two people in the cockpit waving their arms. There was one terrible moment where I was afraid they'd fly away and leave me like the search planes had. It's strange that after being out there for so long, this was the first time I felt inundated by fear about the situation. I was almost panicky, imagining all the things that could go wrong. *What if they don't see me? What if they leave?*

I couldn't stand up, but I was up on my knees, yelling and crying and waving my arms, praying aloud, begging them to see me. When the helicopter turned around and faced me, I was sure they had seen me, but they began backing out of the canyon. Now the panic was up in my throat, "Noooooo! Please, please come back for me! Come for me! Come for me!"

Later, they explained that they had to back out of the canyon in order to get a signal out to SAR. They radioed out to get the go ahead for the maneuver to pick me up. It was only a few moments for them, but it felt so long to me. Then they moved back into the canyon, until they were hovering about forty feet above me and to the left. The side door opened and a man in military fatigues began

116

descending on a line. He landed on the ridgeline above me, so he was out of my sight for a moment. I was still panicky. *What if he falls in a tree well?* *What if he gets injured in the landing?* I had all these ridiculous fears crowding in during the last moments.

Then he came up over the ridgeline, and all my fearful thoughts just stopped. There was only joy and gratitude. He had a helmet and shades on so I couldn't see much of his face, but he smiled reassuringly. He had to shout over the noise and wind of the helicopter blades. He asked me if I was Mary Owen. The thought flashed through my mind, *What if I wasn't!*

He motioned for me to come up to where he was. I had my little tarp out and strapped my backpack on my back. I started crawling up the snow to him. My body had so little energy left, every move took a great effort, but at that moment I don't remember feeling any pain. I must have been pretty adrenalized. He crouched down with both arms reaching out to me, encouraging me.

When I got to him, he pointed to the place where the line from the helicopter rested on the snow. He shouted, "We need to get over to there." There was something like an anchor attached to the end of the line. "Can you make it? Do you need help?"

I told him, "No, I can do it." I was full of hope and focus, it felt like strength. I started crawling along, and he got down on his hands and knees and crawled along next to me. I thought that was so kind. I can't tell how far it was because for me in those moments every distance seemed ten times greater than it probably was. It could have been fifteen feet away, but it felt like fifty. We got over to the line, and he showed me how I needed to sit. He sat on one side with the arms of the anchor supporting his thighs, and I sat on the other side facing him, with my legs overlapping his. I was holding on to the center part of the anchor and he passed the harness under my arms and around me, "Alright, you ready?"

"Yeah!"

He made a motion with his hand, and we lifted up off the snow. We started to swing out over the canyon. I was totally absorbed in the experience, grinning like crazy and trying not to yell for joy or laugh out loud. It was crazy to be dangling hundreds of feet up off the canyon on this little, tiny line. I've always been a bit of an "adrenaline junky", and at that moment I was thoroughly enjoying myself, though it seemed like it would be disrespectful to the gravity of the occasion to show it. My relief had momentarily washed away the thought or memory of all that fear, cold, and pain.

---

* People of all skill levels get trapped and die in tree wells. A tree well is a pocket of air and snow that forms under the overhanging branches of evergreen trees that generally goes down to the base of the tree. The deeper the snow, the deeper the tree well (https://cwsaa.org/2019/01/16/tree-well-safety-education/). See this video by Goss on why not to ski alone: https://www.youtube.com/watch?v=NY6STzbolTU; and Davenport's video on how to get someone out of a tree well: https://www.youtube.com/watch?v=qnbju_AGwe4.

They started to reel us in. The man—he was a medic with a red-cross patch on his uniform—was swinging his legs a little bit to keep us from starting to spin. There was a metal brace extended out above the door of the helicopter holding our cable. As soon as we came up to the level of the door, the men inside reached out and hauled us in. The door slid to, and they started flying towards Portland right away.

Inside the helicopter all the men had these big grins on their faces. The roar of the helicopter blades seemed to echo the great swell of relief and triumph almost tangible in the air. The first thing I asked them, shouting over the noise and using my hands to motion, was if they'd call my parents. One of them nodded emphatically. "I think they already know."

14

A JOYFUL REUNION

(SATURDAY, MARCH 30, 2013)

"Every parting is a form of death,
as every reunion is a type of heaven."

❧ TRYON EDWARDS ☙

In the cordoned-off parking lot area on Mount Hood, while we were waiting those very few minutes which seemed an hour, Bruce, Elijah, Izzy, Mary's friend from Portland, and I barely had time to huddle in prayer before Sergeant Collinson returned with the news: "It *IS* Mary. She's alive!" He told us that according to the helicopter medic she had some injuries on both her legs and frostbite, but none of these appeared to be life threatening. She seemed to be in good spirits. The helicopter crew were taking her to Legacy Emanuel in Portland. They'd let us know more about her injuries once they got her situated and could better assess them.

Bruce and I both burst into tears of great relief and joy! I began shaking uncontrollably, Bruce fell to his knees sobbing.

Immediately, we verbalized what was in our hearts:

"THANK YOU, LORD!"

"PRAISE GOD!"

After recovering ourselves as much as we could, we immediately wanted to share the good news with family and friends. First, we called our daughter Rachel, and she and Ruth began to relay the good news by text, phone, email and on *Facebook*.

Mar 30, 2013, 10:39 AM

They just found her!!! Alive, she's got a leg injury and some frostbite - shes getting helicoptered off the mountain we are meeting her at legacy Emanuel hospital

Rachel's "They just found her alive!" text

We called Mary's grandparents, and they notified all my siblings and their families. Bruce contacted his sister Mary Beth, and she got the news to the rest of their siblings.

With great difficulty, because I was shaking almost uncontrollably and I was borrowing Izzy's puzzling-to-me cell phone, I posted for our communities using *Facebook*:

Mary is found alive on Mt. Hood! She is on the way to the hospital, should be ok.

Rachel

Ruth and I were on our way up to the mountain where the search was going on, and while we were still in the foothills below Mount Hood, I got the call from my parents that Mary had been found alive.

We took a moment to scream and cry in relief and text people to share the news. We were told she was being helicoptered to the hospital in Portland, so we turned around and headed there. We weren't sure what shape she was going to be in.

Elijah

When Mary was found, I felt very relieved. Before that, I had been thinking, *There is a 50/50 chance of things going really well or really poorly.* When she was found, besides feeling great relief, my main thought was, *She's a strong one.*

Shelli ———————————

After this, while still standing there shaking with relief, initially thinking I was speaking to SAR volunteers, I inadvertently gave an interview to a news team. They were in the cordoned-off SAR team base area; at that point I was glad to talk to anyone. I was somewhat alarmed when it dawned on me who they were. They were courteous and didn't push outside bounds, and apparently, they honored my initial request by not publishing this interview. In the end I had nothing to worry about.

Once the initial commotion was over, Bruce and I started greeting some of the people who were there in the parking area cordoned off for SAR. A few were people we had already met on the phone or by mention, but not in person. Some there were SAR qualified volunteers who had come later to help search. One was our friend, Andrew, who had brought water for the SAR volunteers.

While we were there talking with various people, we found out from one of the older searchers, who had been with SAR for over twenty years, that this was the biggest SAR group he had ever seen on the mountain.

Bruce and I also learned that the Oregon Army National Guard Blackhawk helicopter crew who had found Mary, had just been up on a preliminary flight-check

---

Ruth Owen (10:36 AM)

We found Mary, thank you, God!!!!!!!!!!!

I.D.: That's awesome!

Tianna E. (Rogue Valley, NCFCA, family friend): What?!?!?! Where?

> Ruth: On the mountain. She has a leg injury and possibly some frost bite. We are headed to the hospital now to see her!!!!!!!!!! I am so happy! Thank you, God!!!!

A.G.: Praise the Lord!

Tianna E. (Rogue Valley, NCFCA, family friend): Praise God!!!!

Mary Beth J. (Bruce's sister): Thank you! Thank you! Thank you! Yes, our prayers have been answered!!! Keep the faith.

Kody F.: Oh thank God! How is she doing? Is she injured?

Caitlin Q.: Omygosh!! Praise God!!!

> Ruth: Yes, she is injured I'm not sure how badly we are about to go see her I will update you all on how she's doing.

Kody F.: Strength in our Lord, to you and your family. Fast healing to Mary! Thank you for keeping us posted.

> Ruth: Thank you so much for all your prayers. Keep praying for Mary's quick healing!

Karie C. (Mary's aunt): I'm SO RELIEVED!!! God is GOOD!!!

T.M.: Praise God! I was praying.

T.A.: Praise the Lord!

Mary Beth J.: Tell her we all love her and are still praying for her. she is so loved…. I'm crying on my knees and in prayer for you all. Love you guys….

Elisabeth P.: What a huge answer to all our prayers. So glad that they were able to find her. God is good.

V.G.: PRAISE THE LORD!!!!!!!!

Ruth: God is so good! Thank you all so much for your prayers! Please be praying now for her healing! Such an amazing God we have! He is so good!

Molly S.: Thanks for the update, Ruth! I've been thinking about her a lot today. Tell her to get well!

Sarah W.: Praise God!

Stephanie M.: Where was she??

S.H.: That's awesome!!! God is great! ☺.

Janet S.: So very happy, and praise the Lord for this miracle on the mountain.

D.T.: Hallelujah!!!! Still praying and so thankful!

previous to taking a SAR team up to the top of the mountain. The SAR team they had expected to drop at the peak was going to search from the top of the mountain downward, on foot.

We also discovered that all the searchers who were on foot on the mountain had probes because of the high possibility Mary had been buried in an avalanche or in the snow. From past experiences, most of the rescue workers weren't expecting to find her alive.

Much later, Bruce and I heard from the helicopter crew they also "expected to find a popsicle," and when they came upon a person fitting Mary's description, alive, there was considerable celebration among them!

Before Bruce, Izzy, Elijah, Mary's friend and I headed down the mountain to drive to the hospital in Portland—at least an hour away for us—we were debriefed by the SAR sergeant and some of the volunteers. One of the SAR coordinators showed us the coordinates on a map—the exact location where the helicopter crew found Mary. It was inside the area covered by the Sandy Glacier.

The medics with the National Guard helicopter crew who were taking Mary to the hospital communicated through SAR personnel that she had sustained a large, apparently deep gash in the thigh of one leg, a serious injury to the ankle and foot of the other leg, and she had fairly severe frostbite on all her extremities. However, none of her injuries appeared to them to be life threatening.

Before we left the roped-off Timberline ski area parking lot, Bruce and I tried to thank all the rescue personnel who were there. We did not get to personally thank those who were still on the mountain. We felt a ton of gratitude to them all, gratitude we were never able to fully express, though later we tried to express some of what we felt through emails and letters.

Earlier that morning, Bruce and I and some of our friends had asked God to, please, keep safe all who would be involved that day. Bruce and I, and probably Izzy, Elijah, Mary's Portland friend with whoever was around us at the time, stopped and gathered to verbally thank the Lord, once more, and to ask Him again to watch over each one of the SAR personnel who had gone out or up on the mountain and to give them a safe, beautiful, refreshing snow day in the sunshine. Also, that He would bless them to be able to return without incident to base camp, then to their homes.

Mary

The sound of the blades filled the National Guard Blackhawk helicopter. I signed to the medic for some water. He shouted above the noise, telling me to drink it slow. Then he started cutting my mid-calf gaiter* from around my ankle. I started gesturing, "No! Argh!" They gave me headphones and I told him, "There's a Velcro strap on the back." So, he just took the other one off. Through the headphones, I could hear them radioing the hospital. They weren't getting anyone on the other side to give them the okay to land. The pilot said something like, "Well, we're going to land one way or another."

Meanwhile, the medic had cut the bottoms of my tights off. I could see my feet for the first time. They were all huge, and purple, and swollen, and gross looking. He also peeled back the tights around the gash on my thigh. I told him I thought my other foot was sprained. He didn't do anything to the sprain or the gash. Since it wasn't bleeding or anything, there probably wasn't much he could do.

We landed on the top of the hospital, and they brought a stretcher out. The medic walked along side as they wheeled me into a receiving room. I felt so deeply grateful to him. I didn't have any words. Seconds after we got to the room two of my sisters, Ruth and Rachel, came in along with the Clackamas County sheriff. He pulled out a recorder right away. My sisters and I were hugging and crying for a while. The medic with the National Guard must have left sometime during that reunion.

After we calmed down a little, the sheriff started asking me questions. I told him everything I could remember. I told him about how I turned around once I got to that wall, and he said, "You mean after you summited?"

And I said, "No. I didn't summit."

* According to Gritters: "Gaiters cover the tops of your boots [or shoes] to keep snow, water, dirt, sand and other debris away from your feet. If you're headed out for a hike or run on dusty trails with loose debris, a pair of low gaiters can make for a more comfortable experience."

He was confused, "Well, we found your sleeping bag print on the summit."

"I didn't summit, and I didn't have a sleeping bag, so it wasn't my print on the summit."

He said, "But those were the tracks the helicopter crew followed down to where they found you."

"I watched my tracks disappear in the snow, and I didn't summit. Sorry! I wish I would have summited."

The sheriff continued to question me, and I recounted the whole story. It took maybe an hour, but I was not thinking about the time.

My sisters told me that my parents were on their way from Mount Hood. The hospital staff put me on a saline drip and my sister Rachel asked me what I wanted to eat. I asked for French toast! I was craving something fatty and sugary. My sister's husband went and got me ice cream from Salt and Straw. That was pretty fantastic.

Shelli

While we were coming down off the mountain on our way to the hospital, I was almost hysterical with relief and exhilaration. If not all of us in the van, Bruce and I at least were intermittently laughing and crying tears of release and jubilation. We talked about the name of the hospital, Legacy Emanuel, which had stood out to us. Emanuel means "God with us." In my thoughts, and sometimes aloud, I was sending up expressions in prayer after prayer of gratitude to the Lord, from the depths of my heart. Bruce was too. I wanted to sing, but my mind was in a whirl, so I turned on a Christian radio station. The very first song that emanated from the speakers was "Gone," by the group "Switchfoot."* As the song came across the air waves, I laughed and cried all over again—the words were so descriptive of Mary—though with a unique significance in her context.

Bruce and I talked about what we should or should not say to Mary. We both felt she surely had been punished enough. What could we say beyond what she must have been through on that mountain?! We were just glad she was alive.

Rachel

As we arrived at the hospital, her helicopter was landing, and we were able to see her within minutes.

When we first saw Mary, she was surrounded by people. She was very shaky, and I imagined, overwhelmed, but we were also overjoyed to see each other. I can't put into words what it is like to lay

* For the lyrics to "Gone," see: https://www.azlyrics.com/lyrics/switchfoot/gone.html.

eyes on and hug someone you feared you may never see alive again. That feeling just filled the room and we were all in tears but couldn't stop smiling.

A sheriff came in and wanted to interview her while everything was fresh in her mind. Ruth and I stayed there listening. I recorded the whole interview on my phone and later shared it with my parents.

Shelli

When the hospital finally came into view, we also noticed news vans parked along the streets at a nearby park. They'd have to wait. We arrived at the hospital, found a place to park, then hurried into the Emergency Room. Only family was allowed to go in, so Izzy and Mary's other friends that arrived also had to wait to see her.

Mary

At some point, the nurses were taking my vitals. They helped me peel out of my filthy, smelly clothes, and get into a hospital gown. I was there with Ruth and Rachel. Then my parents came. My dad enveloped me in a huge hug, and the first thing I told him was that I was sorry. It was forefront in my mind because I had looked him in the eyes and promised him I would not climb alone. Somehow in my haze of determination, my fixation on summitting, I had completely forgotten that promise. Now seeing his face and realizing how much pain I must have put him through, it was all I could think of.

There were friends who had come at the same time as my parents. They had to wait outside, and my parents asked if I wanted to see them. I did want to see Izzy, but I definitely didn't want to see my guy friends just then. I felt like a horrible person because I knew they really cared and wanted to be supportive, but I was so desperately tired, and I just wanted to be with my family. I told my parents I didn't want to see anyone else.

Shelli

There was some banter between Mary and her sisters. Rachel and Ruth showed Mary the posters of her that they had made to hand out up at the Mount Hood Timberline Lodge area. Rachel said something like, "You owe me $50 bucks for the posters."

Mary half laughing and half serious said something like, "Argh! That backpack! Why? Of all the pictures!"

Bruce had given them the pictures to use for it. He told her, "It was because, when the police asked me what you were wearing, I told them, 'Not the backpack, but the clothes in this picture are probably pretty close to what she's wearing.'"

Mary admitted that the clothes had been very close to what she was wearing when she hiked Mount Hood—"but that backpack!?"

the infamous poster

Later, we joked that the real reason Mary "allowed" herself to be rescued when she did was that she didn't want anyone to see that poster. After the emphasis of all things as light weight as possible while hiking the PCT, the idea of being represented wearing this "big, bulky backpack" totally embarrassed her—even though she had been carrying the backpack for a friend when the photo was taken, and the main idea of using this photo was to find her.

Yes, we had our Mary back! I could hardly contain the joy of being reunited with her again. I was also immensely surprised and relieved she seemed to be in relatively good shape, though they weren't certain yet regarding the full extent of her injuries. She would end up being in the hospital for another twelve days and go through some painful rehabilitation and several surgeries, but we didn't know that—and wouldn't have cared. We were all just super glad she was alive and that we were back together again.

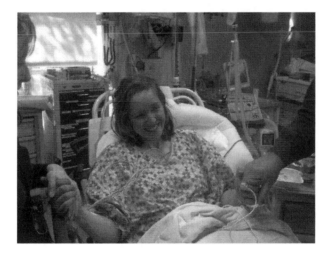

Mary in the E.R.

15

SATURDAY AT THE HOSPITAL

(SATURDAY, MARCH 30, 2013)

"Love is that condition
in which the happiness of another person
is essential to your own."

৵ ROBERT A. HEINLEIN, *STRANGER IN A STRANGE LAND* ৵

By the time Bruce and I, with Elijah, Izzy, and Mary's Portland friend, arrived at the hospital, the staff had deposited Mary's clothing, shoes, and other gear in a toxic waste bag. Since they were getting ready to move her to another room, this was one of the first things they handed us after our initial reunion with her in the Emergency Room. Later that night, when we were leaving the hospital, we took it home with us to see if we could salvage anything.

Later, dealing with Mary's clothes became a sensory glimpse for me into what she had gone through those six days on the mountain. Besides wearing the same clothes for six days straight, to conserve heat and energy, she had needed to urinate in her pants (not uncommon in extreme mountain climbing situations). But most noticeably, her clothes had absorbed what Bruce called the "death smell," a distinct smell from chemicals the body puts off when it is beginning to shut down.

One at a time, I gingerly lifted Mary's limp and badly soiled clothes out of the bag. I held onto as little of each article as I could to get it into the wash machine. Her leggings were already ruined from the gash she had received in her thigh when she fell, and from being cut by the paramedic. I returned them and the cut gaiter to the toxic waste bag almost as soon as I pulled them out.

Dealing with her clothing shook me up more than almost anything else during this whole incident. Every article of clothing, which I could hardly bear to see or touch, and which smelled abominably, pierced my heart all the way through; each item was a raw substantiation of her painful ordeal—intimate evidence of her distress and how very close she had come to death.

I put her socks, running shorts, tank top, "under armor," T-shirt, buff, beanie, North Face jacket, remaining gaiter, and gloves in the wash machine and ran them on the heavy-duty wash cycle with soap and treatments—over and over again. The terrible "death smell" that had seeped into all her clothes would not come out. Bruce finally said, "That's enough. We're going to have to throw them away."

I had set aside her shoes, the tarp, poncho, backpack, and even the nylon part of the climbing harness in another bag, which I later washed (and washed and washed) and tried to air out, too. As I remember, only the metal items (crampons and climbing harness hardware) ended up being salvageable.

Mary

In the E.R., the hospital staff put me in a wheelchair and wheeled me to a room with a huge bathtub. They were very considerate. They let my mom, instead of a nurse, help me take a bath. That bath hurt like the dickens. When things start to warm up after they've been numb for a really long time, it HURTS! My feet started to throb and throb and throb and throb. It felt like this five-hundred-pound gorilla was sitting on them, and that they were about to split open. But they didn't.

Shelli

Initially, they treated Mary's frostbite in the burn unit of the hospital. We learned that burns and frostbite are treated very similarly. Frostbite is some degree of tissue degradation (from partial to total) that happens when the body shunts blood away from the extremities to its core in survival mode. With severe frostbite the tissues begin to crystalize and cannot be restored. Dead or gangrenous digits have to be amputated.

To treat frostbite a *gradual* warming of the extremities is begun as soon as possible. The nurse instructed us beforehand that Mary's first bath, especially, had to be a little tepid, almost cold. Her swollen, dusty-looking, purple-almost-black toes and swollen, angry-red and purple fingers were extremely sensitive to even the barely warm water. Some of the pain probably had to do with damaged nerves re-awakening as the numbness faded.

She was so glad to be getting clean, even though the bath was more for soaking than cleaning, since we weren't to use soap and wash cloths. We were not to disturb the large pussy (infected) gash in her left upper, inner thigh. It took around an hour and a few tubs full of gradually warmer water, in the very large hospital tub, to start the process of warming her fingers and toes, and to get her soaked clean.

I was mainly there for moral support, but she did also need some assistance with getting in and out of the tub and with moving around. We had to be careful of her poor damaged body. Besides her throbbing extremities and the substantial gash in her left leg, both her legs were badly bruised, sore, and stiff, and her right leg from her knee down was nonfunctioning.

After the bath and drying off, she dressed in the clean hospital gowns she had been given (one covering front *and* one behind). Then, we settled her in the wheelchair for transport to her room in another wing of the hospital. She needed to use a wheelchair to get anywhere the first few days of her stay in the hospital. Eventually she worked into using only a walker to get around. And finally, the day before leaving the hospital she was able to stand and walk slowly on her own.

Mary

They finally got me into a very nice hospital room, and into one of those cutesy little hospital gowns. They gave me these gigantic fuzzy boot-socks for my badly frostbitten feet. The first sequence of hours when I was in the hospital are pretty foggy. I don't remember much except for my feet aching so badly, and my mom massaging them.

Shelli

Mary was given a relatively large room in the hospital, probably because of all the attention from family, friends, and the media she was already receiving. During her stay, I don't know how many times we commented to each other how grateful we were for the relatively large size of the room. As big as the room was compared to others in the same unit, it still often seemed too small with everything going on in there.

The nurse brought her what she promptly dubbed "moon boots" to wrap her feet in. They were fleece-lined, boot-like wraps that lightly, but fully encased her lower legs and feet, from her upper–mid calf down. They were for retaining warmth to help return and increase blood flow in her lower extremities. Good circulation facilitates the body's repair work. She was also instructed to keep her feet and fingers elevated as much as possible for this same reason. At every opportunity, we each took turns gently massaging her purple fingers and toes, again for the purpose of encouraging the return and increase of blood flow to her fingers and toes, to increase her chances of keeping them.

Mary

Once they got me to my room, they asked a number of times if I wanted to be on any pain medications. Although the pain in my feet was significant, I didn't feel like it was something that warranted drugs. The doctors and nurses seemed surprised that I wasn't experiencing more pain. I considered it a gift from God and an answer to the prayers so many were praying for me.

My first nurse had the word "Agape" tattooed on her forearm. The word was right in front of my eyes when she reached across me to put in a Saline IV. Her name was Charity. It was one of those moments when you just know God is grinning.

Shelli

Mary's doctor determined she needed surgery to clean up and close the six- to eight-inch gash in her left inner thigh and that she would possibly be able to go home in a day or two. Apparently, the puncture in that leg had been inflicted by a tree branch while she was "ping-ponging" down the mountain during her forty-foot fall. They started her on antibiotics to treat the infection in it.

Her right foot and ankle were both dysfunctional. She wasn't able to bend her toes or move them individually and she couldn't move her ankle. At first, hospital staff thought her leg might be broken. That was ruled out with an X-ray. Then they explored the possibility of it being severely sprained, which it was, but that was not the sole problem. It appeared she might have suffered some kind of nerve damage in the fall.

Family and friends wanted to know how she was doing, and so we told them as much as we understood at the time. Many who had previously been praying for her safe return voluntarily began interceding for her full recovery. Our hearts were overflowing with gratitude for this. It reinforced for Bruce and me what a huge blessing it is to be part of God's family—the body of Christ. To us, the continued prayers for her healing expressed another dimension of Jesus' love through His people—a love that doesn't stop because someone has done something stupid or that she shouldn't have done.

Izzy, Mary's roommate, was still there at the hospital waiting around. After Mary got cleaned up and somewhat situated, Izzy was finally able to visit her.

Mary's Portland friend eventually left since she wasn't up to seeing him. I also felt bad for another caring guy friend who drove a long way to the hospital just to be turned away. But I could also understand Mary's need for some space and time to adjust before seeing persons besides her immediate family and some of her closest female friends.

When two of Mary's best friends from childhood, Lacey and A.F., heard that she had been found alive, they headed north from the Rogue Valley in Southern Oregon to see her. It took nearly five hours for them to get to Portland, but they were determined to drive up, even though it was Easter weekend (with heavy traffic). When they arrived, there was another joyful, tearful reunion. Immediately after their visit, they had to return home to previous commitments.

Towards evening, two other close friends from GFU, Beth and Kaylena, who had received permission to visit Mary, came as well. Beth posted on social media:

> She once was lost and now SHES FOUND!!!

Izzy returned to Newberg with them after their visit.

Mary's being in the hospital was an adjustment for all of us. Especially for those of us in her immediate family.

Elijah

Everything that had happened that day seemed kind of surreal. *Okay, so this really happened.* The whole time Mary was in the hospital it felt unreal.

I remember before she was found, people processing with worried chatter, then after she was found with excited chatter. I didn't feel like there was much left to say.

Shelli

Jessika, Mary's oldest sister, could not join our family for our daily trips to the hospital during the almost two weeks Mary was there, but she did get a ride with a friend a couple of times to make shorter visits. She was extremely relieved when Mary was found, but at first, she was equally, if not more, upset with her for having jeopardized her own life in such a thoughtless, careless manner. Much later Jessika told me that she spent the first days after Mary's rescue in debilitating emotional distress.

I wish I had been more sensitive at the time to what Jessika and our other children were going through. Bruce and my attention was mainly focused on Mary during this time. All we knew was that Jessika didn't want to come with us to the hospital because she was (understandably) upset with Mary. At the time we believed we were giving her the time and space she needed so she could process everything. Eventually she took the initiative to come to the hospital to visit—though she still couldn't sustain the all-day or most-of-the-day visits we were making.

I think inadvertently, because of this, Jessika didn't see as much of Mary's changed attitude, or true sorrow for what she had done, or receive any of her direct apologies—which were all very real.

A few years later Mary made a lunch appointment with Jessika so they could be alone, just her and Jessika, where Mary apologized. All was forgiven.

Even though now Mary has been forgiven by all her siblings, to Jessika and Ruth, her actions were, and still are in some ways, bewildering. *How could anyone do such a heedless, careless thing? Especially to people one supposedly loves and cares about?* It seemed they could all relate to youthful, less harmful antics, but that they felt Mary's choice to try to climb Mount Hood alone, as she had done, was way over-the-top. Her misadventure still isn't something they like to revisit.

During Mary's hospital stay the general atmosphere of her room with each initial visit of family and friends would be tears of joy mixed with some amount of consternation as people would hug her, and reprimand her, and hug her again. *What HAD she been thinking to get herself into such a position!?! She could have died up there! She almost did! Had she learned anything from this? She'd better have!...* This was a repeated theme with each initial visit.

Mary, who had already been thoroughly humbled by her misadventure, and who was grateful to be alive, was humbled even more by the love and chastisement voiced by one person after another who came to visit, or who corresponded with her. She accepted it all as just desserts for how fool-hardy she had been, and she did not attempt to, or want to, represent what she had done in any other light, even to the media who were clamoring for her story.

During her hospital stay to the present time, I think she has felt more than any of us the Lord's mercies in preserving her life and in delivering her from the mountain. Her view of her part in relationships was markedly changed.

The first several nights Mary was in the hospital, she and we wanted someone in our immediate family to remain with her. We all needed that connection. However, we all needed to rest, too. Starting that first night, one family member, a different person each night, stayed with her in a reclining chair next to her hospital bed.

Rachel was the first to stay overnight with Mary.

Rachel

I wanted to stay with Mary while she was in the hospital as much as possible. I didn't want her to be alone after what she'd just been through, and personally I was greedy to soak up some sister time with her. I wanted to make sure she had the opportunity to "debrief" as it were, to talk about her experience at her own pace, or not talk at all if she needed.

Also, friends had told me what it was like being in the hospital for long stays. At first everyone is there and then everyone disappears and you're alone with the machines beeping the hours away. I really didn't want Mary to be alone. I told her I'd be with her, "haunting" her, unless she needed some personal time for a minute, I was going to be there.

16

RESURRECTION CELEBRATION

(SUNDAY, MARCH 31, 2013)

"A day without sunshine is like, you know, night."

❧ STEVE MARTIN ❧

Bruce

It was Sunday morning. Easter Sunday. And Mary was alive and recovering! I had slept well, with the burden of worry and uncertainty now lifted. And I woke up early, feeling joyful. This day I would celebrate the resurrection of Jesus with an exuberance and depth of gratitude I had never known before.

I went through my morning routine with anticipation. Enjoying the hot water of the shower, the tension of the last several days continued to ebb away. Stepping out of the shower, I looked in the mirror with the idea of shaving and cleaning up, to look my best, especially on this day.

I got out the shave cream and the razor. In the mirror I saw my now week-old beard. I thought of the previous few days and all that had happened. Words from a story in the Bible came into my head: "Then Samuel took a stone and set it up between Mizpah and Shen. He named it Ebenezer, saying, 'Thus far the LORD has helped us'" (1 Samuel 7:12). "Ebenezer" means rock of remembrance, or stone of help. When our children were young, we kept a book in which, each week, our family wrote ways that the Lord had helped us. As time went on, we would also read from it sometimes, remembering the things the Lord had done in our lives. How He had helped us. We called it our Ebenezer. I looked for a long moment into the mirror. Then I put my shaving things away. My beard would be my Ebenezer. My way to remember the great things God had done in the last few days. I also knew that Mary, who loved beards, would find this expression of gratitude particularly "joyful." I have not shaved off my beard since that time.

Shelli

That morning, we wanted to get back to the hospital as soon as we could. It was a drive of about an hour and a half on Highway 99 and Interstate 5. We had planned on holding our own Resurrection Day (Easter) service in Mary's room as a family.

When I called Jessika to invite her, she told me she was not emotionally up to going to the hospital with us, especially since it meant spending the whole day there and with a lot of people she didn't know. I tried to coax her—to explain how much it would mean to us (meaning her family) if she would come. But she was certain she was not up to going. Bruce and I were disappointed, and we knew Mary would be too, but I didn't want to pressure Jessika any more than I already had to join us. It did cause us to be concerned about how this whole incident might be affecting her, and it put a damper on everything, but not enough to keep the rest of us from returning to the hospital to celebrate this day.

I gathered up our traditional large, straw Easter basket decorated with flowers and filled with dozens of brightly colored plastic eggs. In each egg, along with chocolate and other candies, Bruce and I had placed a small strip of paper having a unique reference to a Bible verse or song about the resurrection printed on it. (A list of the verses we used is in Appendix A.)

When our children were younger, we hid the eggs all around the house before they woke up. Once they were all awake, full of anticipation, they hunted until each egg was found. We used to have other traditions as well, but the only tradition remaining was the one we were about to reenact at the hospital. Taking turns, each person would choose and open an egg from the basket, then read the slip of paper enclosed in the egg. If it was a reference to scripture verse(s), the person whose turn it was, would find it in the Bible and read it aloud to us. If it was a reference to a song, we would find it in our song books and sing it together.

Bruce and I were greatly anticipating the celebration of *this* Resurrection Day with our "resurrected" daughter—who had been lost to us, but who was now returned to us alive. Sometime before leaving for the hospital on this Sunday morning, Bruce shared some of what was in his mind and heart with friends and family on *Facebook*:

> HE IS RISEN!! The most glorious Easter morning ever!! He is alive and gives life and saves life. I am overwhelmed with the gifts of God.

Deana S.: ♥

Jerry K. (Bruce's friend from high school): He is risen indeed!

Christopher C.: Thanks be unto our God and Father for his bountiful gifts and blessings.

Janet S.: He has power over sin, hell and the grave! So thankful for a Risen Savior!

Bob Gilmore: Amen!

That Easter Sunday morning when Bruce and I and Elijah arrived at Mary's hospital room, a surprise was awaiting us. Everyone who knew Mary, also knew she *never* wore make-up. But there she was, all made-up and looking very good for someone who had so recently been hammered by a mountain!

Rachel was a professional photographer and sometimes she helped clients with their make-up as part of her job. She had an exceptional eye for enhancing natural beauty. Maybe it was her leaning towards the "natural" that helped convince Mary to let her apply a little make-up for the coming news interviews that morning. Whatever rationale was behind it, Mary did look very nice for those interviews.

But she also got to put up with a lot of ribbing for the rest of the day. Not only was make-up unusual for her, but also the difference between how she looked on her arrival at the hospital the day before and her appearance Sunday was remarkable—and it was repeatedly noted.

I thought it was very appropriate she looked like new on that Easter Day, after her own rescue from death. Later, I posted the following on *Facebook*:

> Cleaned up by her sisters for interviews. Who says you can't be beautiful even after getting beat up by a mountain? Though I opine that most of the beauty is insid'er.

Mary "cleaned up"

Besides our large, decorated Easter basket full of brightly colored eggs, we had also brought our Bibles, and song books. (Mary's guitar wouldn't have fit anywhere in the room.) We were ready to celebrate—with overflowing joy—the resurrection of Jesus, as we often had before—but unlike we ever had before—together on that day.

For Christians, Jesus' bodily resurrection from the dead was a turning point in history. The celebration of Easter, which commemorates this miraculous event two thousand years ago, is one of the two most significant Christian holidays. (Christmas, the celebration of Jesus' birth, is the other.) Jesus promised, and His Spirit with us affirms His promise: "I am the resurrection and the life. The one who believes in me will live, even though they die; and whoever lives by believing in me will never die" (John 11:25-27). And he promised: "Because I live, you also will live" (John 14:19b). Because of the Lord's Spirit with and in us, we believe Him. We believe Jesus came to restore us to life, peace, love, and joy—reunited with God and loved ones for eternity.

As we arrived at Mary's room, one news crew was finishing up, and the last of the several crews that were given permission to interview her was still hovering nearby. I think it was our large Easter basket, decorated with flowers, and full of colorful eggs, that grabbed the attention of one of the remaining news reporters.

When he saw us arrive with our basket and books, the reporter asked us if he could also take some footage of our Easter celebration after his interview with Mary. Bruce said, "No, thanks." At first, I was a little dismayed by Bruce's immediate answer. But after hearing the questions the reporter asked Mary and observing his off-the-mark interpretations of her answers, I was glad Bruce had refused permission, and I didn't pursue anything different. This reporter was friendly enough, and seemed genuinely curious, but in the end, I was glad he wouldn't be interviewing us or sharing his view, unrelated to us or what we meant by it, of our Resurrection Day celebration with the world.

When all the reporters were gone, we closed the door to Mary's room for privacy and so as not to disturb the other patients or hospital staff. We were finally free to celebrate the day with family members, a few friends, and Mary's nurse Charity, who joined with us in singing while she was in the room.

C.S. Lewis expressed it well in his book entitled *Miracles,* when he said: "Death and resurrection are what the story is about and had we but eyes to see it, this has been hinted on every page, met us, in some disguise, at every turn..." This Easter, made so poignant by Mary's rescue, gave a strong foretaste—like no Easter we had celebrated before—of the future, pure joy of being reunited with God, our Father, and loved ones forever because of the Lord's mercies and deliverance made possible and available to us through Jesus.

Mary ⸻

That morning, opening the Easter Eggs with my family, I was filled with so many emotions. Celebrating Resurrection Day with the words still ringing inside me, "You're Alive!" My heart was still caught up in the absolute clarity and vivid sensory affirmation of that moment on the mountain when God spoke to me again. At the same time, going through the simple tradition of opening the eggs together, I felt deeply the reality that I had almost taken that away from my family, that this and so much more would have changed if God had not been so merciful. Singing song after song about life, about death, about the power of God to save, every time my eyes would meet someone else's, there would be tears and laughing.

Shelli

Ever since she was very young Mary has liked poetry, music, and doodling. She learned to play acoustic guitar in her teens. These have been outlets for expressing her thoughts and feelings. In 2009, for Easter, she wrote a poem and put it to music. From then on, we have included it in our annual Resurrection Day celebration. It is a beautiful song that continues to have deep significance for Bruce and me on many levels. As we all sang the words of this song in the hospital room it seemed like some of the most beautiful music on earth. No eyes were dry as we sang the words:

> *Oh my Father, Oh my God,*
> *My soul is trembling.*
> *Lost in the flood of a Sovereign's love,*
> *My God, how can it be?*
>
> *King of Glory,*
> *Do You wash my dirty feet?*
> *Holy One,*
> *Can you bear the touch*
> *Of such a one as me?*
> *Worthy of all glory,*
> *Yet You chose my shame,*
> *A King becomes a servant,*
> *So an orphan finds a name.*

Oh my Father, Oh my God,
I'm falling on my knees,
Washed by the blood of Righteousness,
My God has ransomed me!

Blessed Jesus,
Show once more Your bloody scars.
Broken One,
Teach my soul to run nearer to Your heart.
Print upon my memory
What You bore that day.
The breaking of Your body,
For the breaking of my chains.

Risen Savior, Glorious One,
I stand in You redeemed,
Made perfect by the perfect Son,
My Shield and Covering.
The Master kneels,
A slave is freed.
The precious blood and offering,
Accepted by the Father.
In Your sacrifice complete,
Completely Free.

Oh my Father, Oh my God,
How can I help but sing?
Swept up in tides of fiercest joy,
My life to You I bring!

(Mary Owen, "New Song"[22])

Because we didn't generally sing this song the rest of the year, we relied on Mary to help us remember the tune. That year when this song came up in our celebration, we realized how close we had come not only to losing the melody, but also Mary for the rest of our lives. Many little realizations like that came up several times a day for a long while after she was rescued.

What the Lord had done for us in preserving Mary's life was a powerful picture for all of us of what the Easter season is all about and what God is all about. It was the most memorable Resurrection Sunday we and many others had ever experienced. The Lord amplified for us what we had only vaguely understood before.

Though this incident had been almost overwhelming, and we knew it wasn't over yet, the most important thing—that Mary had been found alive—was a heady thing. We were aware that others were perceiving this story very differently than we were, but despite this, our gladness couldn't be dampened. It kept rising to the surface, and we did not hold it back. It was a time for rejoicing.

Jon W. (Portland area, family friend): What a praise report, I woke up to on this Easter morning. It was poetic to wake up to find out a friend isn't dead but alive.

Beth W.

Happy to Celebrate Resurrection Sunday with family knowing Mary IS ALIVE and recovering!!!

Mary, I have come to tears many moments today with that recurring thought of doing life without you (I'll try not to be too feely, but I can't entirely help myself). Your friendship means more to me than I could ever express to you. Your beauty, courage, and faith are an example to all who know you. Love, love, LOVE you!

Megan A.

This Easter, as I celebrate the resurrection of Jesus, I am also celebrating the relief of Mary being found.

M.R.M.

A favorite, for you, Mary.

[Shared a link to Keith Green's "Easter Song":]

Hooray for Easter!

https://www.youtube.com/watch?v=aHRpRXs6E2w

Larry C.

This Easter weekend I have witnessed the Lord work a miracle!

#tearsofjoy #praisekingjesus

————————————————

Bob Gilmore to Bruce

Mary's Miracle

Lost and alone in freezing cold

But Jesus was there, too

No human helping hand in sight

Her life could have been through

With thousands praying fervently

That she would soon be found

The outcome would be guaranteed

She'd soon be homeward-bound

God heard and answered all our prayers

Her precious life was saved

It happened on a glorious day

When weathermen behaved

Have faith and never doubt God's power

He raised Christ from the tomb

And brought our friend down from Mt Hood

Safe from a frozen doom

Bob Gilmore

3-30-13

The next day a dear friend, who has since passed into the arms of Jesus, released from her cancer forever, sent this email about their celebration of Resurrection Sunday (Easter).

4/1/13

Dear Friends,

How's the patient doing today? How are the parents doing today? We celebrated along with you on Resurrection Sunday—and just as you said, a better understanding of being lost, being found, being rescued, being saved—and praising God for saving all of us and bringing us into the love and safety of His family. What a great God we serve!

We pray Mary is recovering quickly...

We just want to let you know we are still thanking God along with you and so happy Mary is home safe. Please give her our greetings and our love.

Have you gotten a good night's rest yet? When will you be normal again? Ha ha! 😄

Love you guys,

Holly

A few years after this incident, Mary's friend Sue wrote the following reflection on what that Easter was like for her.

I first met Mary at a wedding.

She approached me at the reception, after some dancing. She had,

of course, no shoes on. We had both been hearing about each other

for quite some time. She said something like, "I've been told I should

meet you." We had maybe fifty friends in common but had never met.

I invited her to come help me in my home-based bakery during the

Christmas season. My daughters had grown up working with me in the

bakery, but now they were both launched, and I had not made the

transition to hiring outside help. I thought this would be a good

chance to get to know Mary and get some experience in having new

hands to help.

Oh my.

It was more than just help—so much more. Mary calls us kindred

spirits. I remember asking her how she got there on one of the days

she arrived to help. She said she walked. From her house. Which was

at least six miles away. And she was happy. And you know, I could

totally relate—I walked everywhere—often barefoot—as a late

teenager. Across town to work, to the beach, backpacking. Kindred

spirits indeed.

And the work time flew by—somehow the cookies got baked and wrapped

and the dishes washed in record time, and we hardly noticed because

the conversation was such an adventure—God and theology (which are

two different things, you know), favorite and not so favorite books,

missions, and what matters in life. Relationships and how to navigate

them, what is church all about. Such rich conversations. How I

loved them.

She often helped at my bagel stand at the local Grower's Market over

the next few years, and the relationship continued and

deepened—ultimately she and her family moved up to Newberg, where

she enrolled at George Fox University.

Fast forward to the week before Easter, 2013.

It's Saturday morning.

I am set up at the Grower's Market with my crew,

We have known for several days that Mary is lost on Mt Hood.

We have no idea what is going to happen—she has not been found,

even after intensive searching.

We have hope—but it is waning. It is starting to seem as though we may have to accept a terrible thing—that we have lost her. I remember facing into that searing pain. It is a fearful thing. Early in the day, two of Mary's friends come to the stand, seeking me out. They are distraught. We duck behind the sun screen I have hanging behind one of the tables, and we all break down together. We pray together. We acknowledge that we may have lost our Mary. But we also still have hope.

The morning passes in sober hope—and then, the news reaches us! Mary has been found! She is alive! The joy and relief flood our hearts! The wonder and the remarkable timing of it all. I don't even know all the details at this point, but I know this: Mary is alive! Her life has been spared!

The next morning is Easter Sunday. The story details are filtering in. But the details, really, are not what holds my attention. Instead I am pondering Christ's resurrection from the dead, its enormous significance—and Mary's return to us from being lost. It still makes me ponder to this day. Wiser writers than I could probably put words to it—but my prayer is that the story causes you, too, to ponder. It sounds like something I'd like to talk over (again) with Mary. How grateful I am that I can still do that!

Mary

C.S. Lewis uses the term "a severe mercy."* This is what I felt my experience on Mount Hood was. I believe God was mercifully but sternly disciplining me for my careless approach to the life He had given me. Think, if you will, of a child who is put in time-out for poor behavior in order to give them an opportunity to reassess their actions. At the same time, He gave me a tremendous gift. He allowed me to physically walk through death and resurrection, to meet Christ in the great chasm that necessitated His coming.

What I experienced has changed my relationship to Jesus and to missions. In the days that I was held in silence on the mountain, every fiber of my being cried out, "My God, my God, why have you forsaken me?"

I met my Savior in His suffering, and I glimpsed the dreadful urgency of His mission of love. The silence and death that I sat face-to-face with for days on end is the same that every soul stands in peril of. It is the chasm that formed when man rejected his Creator. Jesus suffered the silence, the pain, and the betrayal of the world in order to heal it. His love alone is deep enough to fill that chasm. His desire alone is strong enough to bridge it. Only the Son of God could enter into death itself and shatter it to pieces.

When I heard Him speak, when He shattered the silence with His Presence and His Word, I knew with every fiber of my being that He is Alive. Until then, I had only brushed the surface of the Truth and Power of the Resurrection. Now I cannot sing of it without weeping. I cannot do less than dedicate my life to inviting others to embrace this good and powerful Savior.

> *"In Christ alone my hope is found;*
> *He is my light, my strength, my song.*
> *This cornerstone, this solid ground,*
> *Firm through the fiercest drought and storm.*
> *What heights of love, what depths of peace,*
> *When fears are stilled, when strivings cease,*
> *My comforter, my all in all,*
> *Here, in the love of Christ, I stand.*

---

* In Sheldon Vanauken's autobiographical book, "A Severe Mercy," he shares letters he received from C.S. Lewis. In one letter Lewis identifies the circumstance before the death of Sheldon's wife, as "a severe mercy." They were circumstances—which in answer to his wife's prayers—ultimately resulted in Sheldon becoming a believer in Christ.

"In Christ alone, who took on flesh,
Fullness of God in helpless babe.
This gift of love and righteousness,
Scorned by the ones he came to save.
'Til on that cross, as Jesus died,
The wrath of God was satisfied,
For every sin, on him, was laid,
Here, in the death of Christ, I live.

"There in the ground, his body lay,
Light of the world, by darkness, slain.
Then bursting forth in glorious day,
Up from the grave, he rose again.
And as he stands in victory,
Sin's curse has lost its grip on me,
For I am his and he is mine,
Bought with the precious blood of Christ.

"No guilt in life, no fear in death,
This is the power of Christ in me.
From life's first cry to final breath,
Jesus commands my destiny.
No power of hell, no scheme of man,
Could ever pluck me from his hand,
'Til he returns or calls me home,
Here, in the power of Christ, I stand."

∽ Keith Getty and Stuart Townend, *"In Christ Alone"*

17

AWE AND GRATITUDE

"Whether you can observe a thing or not depends on the theory which you use.
It is the theory which decides what can be observed."

⧼ ALBERT EINSTEIN ⧽

There are some things that the scientific method and natural laws cannot explain, and to which they cannot be applied. Many of the things we experienced in the course of this incident were outside the material realm. They are in the classification of things that cannot be measured, calculated, studied, or understood materially.

Faith, by its very nature, is based on something that cannot be proven or disproven by material means. Faith in God "…is the substance of things hoped for, the evidence of things not seen" (Heb. 11:1, NKJV). Faith is not necessarily "blind" or without evidence. Though the evidence for God is not material but spiritual, character-based, and relational, it is based on the reliability of His character and word (including His promises). All of us in this world take many things on faith every day, even in science. (Unseen elements, laws, and theorems are trusted as the basis for forming hypotheses and for material experimentation.) All the time, for survival and sometimes for enjoyment, we humans live our lives trusting in love, loyalty, relationships, the character or soundness of people, institutions, ideas, and so on—sometimes of individuals or entities who or which we have never seen or that are generally not seen by us, except by their "fruits" over time.

From the beginning to the end of this incident, unexpected revelations of the Lords hand at work "behind the scenes" were opened to our eyes. When we were able to see or recognize them, they gave us reason to pause and ultimately to be filled with amazement and gratitude to God. As we spent time with Mary in the hospital and heard her story repeated many times over, things began to appear that we couldn't have seen from any other view. Things which also caused our awe of and gratitude to the Lord to become our fixed attitude for days, weeks, months, and years! And we hope forever. (Help us, Lord, not to humanly "forget"!)

The most obvious thing that *everyone* was seeing was that our ill-equipped daughter had been found, and was still alive, after being injured and stranded for six days on a glacier on Mount Hood.

Very soon after Mary was settled in her room in the hospital, some good friends of our family's came to visit, bringing a whole basket of home-cooked and baked goodies. They also shared something noticed by all the members of their family that jolted me hard.

For a very long time they had lived in a home in the hills near Gresham, essentially in the foothills of Mount Hood. Year after year they had all observed the increase of fatalities on Mount Hood during spring break. They attributed this to there being more people on the mountain during that time, but also to the inevitable springtime weather on the mountain.

What they shared with me was that in all the years they had lived in that area, they had *never* seen such an extended period of clear, mild weather on Mount Hood during spring break as there had been this year while Mary was stranded on the mountain.

As they were sharing this with me, I had a visceral reaction of chills like electricity all over my body. I had grown up near the Colorado Rockies. I knew what springtime can be like even on the plains just below the mountains. I had also lived in Germany through several winters. I had spent many days skiing at Timberline ski park on Mount Hood in the spring. It was deeply imbedded in my experience that springtime is when higher elevations get most of their snowfall and storms. I knew that even the very normal rainy spring weather in lower elevations in Oregon can translate into severe snowstorms on the mountain. I also knew well that expected storms could turn the mountain (if even the plains) into a hellacious wintery beast bent on removing or devouring all living things.

When our friends shared their observation with me, I knew they weren't exaggerating. After my initial reaction of terrible alarm, I was filled with a profound, enormous, overwhelming gratitude directed again to God.

The weather had been so nice that previous week where we lived, I hadn't really thought about it. I knew that the weather the mountain itself had generated had been miserable enough for Mary; but before talking with our friends, I hadn't considered what it was *usually* like in the springtime up there. A six-day stretch of mild weather at that time of the year was not only unprecedented, it was an unlooked-for miracle! Mary's body would not have survived exposure to the usual weather, stranded as she was. This was **no small detail**. But it was not the first.

When we had arrived at the hospital right after Mary's rescue, a remarkable phenomenon had become apparent. The sheriff, who was interviewing Mary in the E.R., kept insisting that she had summited Mount Hood, but she knew she hadn't. She had turned to head back down the mountain at the base of a rock cliff, which she believed was more than a thousand feet below the summit.

We knew why the sheriff kept insisting that she had summited. The helicopter crew, on their test run reported what appeared to be a sleeping bag imprint on the *summit* of Mount Hood with tracks leading from it, down the mountain. The helicopter crew followed these tracks over to Reid Glacier and then directly on down to Mary. But she did *not* summit the mountain, and she did *not* have a sleeping bag. The main reason she had not been able to find her way back down the mountain in the first place was because her own tracks had been filled up and covered over by snow. She also slid a fair way on her bum as she was heading down the slope initially (no footprints there).

When Bruce and I heard about this dialogue between Mary and the sheriff and understood the discrepancy between these two accounts, we immediately recognized that these tracks—*however they were made or revealed*—were a **direct** answer to our **specific** requests that the Lord would send an "angel" to lead SAR directly to Mary that Saturday. We were immediately filled again with joy and awe and overflowing gratitude to the Lord for how He had managed another very straightforward and HUGE answer to our prayers.

Others had also voiced this specific prayer, independent of us and our request; they also recognized the Lord's hand in this arrangement of tracks. My sister Celeste, who I quoted earlier, later also shared:

> . . . I continued in prayer, and then I heard about Mary being rescued on Saturday morning. I heard that the helicopter crew... started from the top and they were shown footprints in the snow.... Those prints led directly to Mary's location.... There is no doubt in my mind at all God sent one of His messengers to show the way.
>
> I thank the S&R teams that looked for Mary, and especially those in the crew that were able to follow the path that God's messenger left that led to her rescue. I am so grateful that God, in his mercy, listened to me and others to safely bring Mary home alive. God is Great! God is true and loving. He will guide us if we ask and open our hearts and will to Him.

To us, SAR finding Mary right as we had arrived on the mountain had been more than enough of a miracle and answer to our prayers; sufficient to satisfy us for the rest of our lives. Now, here was another leading up to it! From then on, we called the tracks, Mary's and otherwise, that the helicopter crew had followed directly to her, "angel tracks."

A couple of months later, when we got to speak with the helicopter crew about Mary's rescue, they told us just how unprecedented it was. They had never experienced anything like it. They were able to fly to Mount Hood, to the summit, follow Mary's tracks, pick her up, take her to the hospital, and return to their base in Salem on one tank of gas. The directness in finding her was unheard of on any missions they had flown or heard of.

What our friends had observed about the weather amazed us even more. We were already like kites soaring as high as they could go on their strings. Yet this was not to be the end of it!

Each time we heard Mary tell her story, initially to us, then for friends and for media, new details surfaced. We began to see a pattern that indicated to us clearly that an unseen Providence had been with her protecting her despite her willfulness and confusion due to hypothermia, and independent of her perception that God was not with her.

For example: things she had learned previously were brought back to her mind *at just the right time* and helped to preserve her life over and over again, in impossible circumstances, including severe hypothermia, when people's thinking usually becomes too foggy to preserve themselves.

There was *the warning in her mind* (notwithstanding her simultaneous attitude of willfulness) that kept her away from the potentially deadly fumaroles when she wanted to warm her frozen hands on her way up the mountain; *the sense* not to try to use her climbing gear to scale a rock face in the dark when she was dead tired, even when the rock face confirmed she was "only" around a thousand feet from the summit (this might sound like common sense unless you knew Mary then); the crevasse she missed plunging into because *she had just barely reconsidered* her tactic of descent-by-sliding, a few feet from it on her way down the mountain; protection from falling through snow over the running water she could hear growing in volume under her because of *remembering a story* she had read earlier in her life; *protection from avalanche* despite all her rough attempts at climbing up the side of the mountain, herself falling, and her being in a prime spot for one; the fact *her fall was stopped at forty feet* or so and did not continue on down the steep, icy terrain, especially since she had lost her ice axe as a means for arresting her descent; the ankle injury on top of the leg injury *that kept her from moving around* more than she did, which alone could have saved her life (you'll see why later); the *clarity of mind* to sit on her climbing gear, which kept her up off the snow and helped to preserve sufficient body heat for survival; the *inspiration through the "paper cat"* to move in among the trees when she was up on the ridge, which also preserved body heat amidst an icy glacier; the *recall of the outdoor skills she had learned* so she was able to start a fire to temporarily warm herself, to ration her food, to insulate her body with the insufficient gear she had, and to obtain water to drink; *the confidence* that kept her from fear and panic, which also can end up killing people when they make irrational and poor decisions. She survived through all this, despite being in absolute misery because of the cold and firmly in the clutches of hypothermia.

After hearing Mary's retelling of her story many times, our understanding gradually opened to the realization that she had **never** been alone on the mountain. God had truly been actively watching over, protecting, and giving her inspiration—bringing things to her mind in a timely manner—the whole while she was up there. Against all odds, she did not die on that rugged, unforgiving mountain. What could we feel but even greater amazement and gratitude to the Lord with each of these realizations?!

Once the door of gratitude had been opened, more and more and more entered our hearts. Gratitude is not only a response; it's also an attitude that greatly increases one's vision of good things everywhere. Ours was directed to God, who was revealing (showing us) His help and Presence had been with Mary, reminding us that He is always present; He is with us all—always, even when we don't *feel* that He is. I believe prayer, or looking to the Lord, helped to open our eyes so we could see these things.

Going forward, our awe and gratitude continued to grow until it all but overwhelmed us. Mary's frostbite could have been so much worse than it was because of where she was situated on the mountain—high elevation, in the snow, on a glacier—and her injuries more severe because of the length and force of her fall. If she had moved around much more, as we learned later, it could have easily precipitated her quickly bleeding to death. Any one of her injuries could have turned into a life-long disability. Instead, she was in an excellent hospital served by highly competent staff, on her way to a relatively full and rapid recovery! This wasn't what we expected. This wasn't anything any of us basically "deserved." We had been so glad, alone, in Mary being found alive and that she was with us!

It was a huge mercy to Mary and to us that the Lord had placed it so strongly on so many hearts to be praying for her and for us. I don't believe we humans generally have a natural urge to pray for people who aren't part of our family. God gives people this kind of love and desire. Then, in answer to people's prayers, He worked and orchestrated and did the behind-the-scenes things that only He could do.

Yet another mercy we came to recognize was that of our learning Mary was missing in time for SAR to be in place and for her to be rescued alive. And it appeared that several times the Lord had softened hearts and worked on the minds of SAR personnel helping them be willing to do "impossible" searches for someone, and for someone who in their experience, was probably frozen to death.

An extra blessing (good thing) we also eventually saw was how the Lord had simultaneously used this experience to teach Mary important lessons about her mortality, how her decisions affect others, and how interwoven her life is with others. She did learn a healthy fear on that mountain. We never would have imagined our earlier prayers being answered in this way, but God doesn't waste anything. He used her willfulness and folly to discipline and instruct her in the consequences of careless endangerment of one's own life. And He did this without stripping her of her love for the outdoors or adventure. In this, too, we saw that nothing regarding our eternal souls is too big or small for Him. The Lord's good and merciful use of something that could have turned out so badly, His timing and His transforming work in Mary was absolutely **no small thing**—it was towards her life, her eternal life, with Him.

What we saw the Lord do, He did despite how Mary had exercised her will in direct defiance of Him, how she had broken the promise she made to her dad, and how she had gone contrary to safety and sanity in order to have her own way. In the end, the undeserved, unchanging, gracious mercy, and love God showed to her and to us who love her, seemed like the greatest wonder of all. Only God could have taken something that began so disastrously, and intricately recreate it into something so incredibly wonderful for all (who were/are willing) to see.

Timing is everything, and the Lord's timing was (and is) perfect. Not "just" in what He did for Mary, our family, friends, and communities in preserving and delivering Mary from the mountain; He also allowed the whole world, those who would or could, to see that His providence and Presence is with us and at work in the world.

I don't think the timing of Mary's rescue was an accident. We noticed reporters being sensitive to the significance Easter has for many people. So—extraordinarily—much more reporting of "God things" in relation to her rescue was included than is generally tolerated in the media, mainly because of *when* she was rescued. Quite a few reporters gave us a fair hearing and representation from our Christian perspective. We believe the Lord intentionally orchestrated this, too, to reach out beyond our circle to individuals who were looking, listening, or hoping for Him to be there.

Because Mary's rescue was one day before Easter, more people than usual were already thinking about the Lord and their relationship with Him. Many people, who generally weren't attuned to thinking about God, were paying attention to what He did for Mary and us in her rescue. We saw the Lord show many people we knew, or came to know about later, that He was/is "there," not only for Mary but for them as well. The revelation of His Presence to various individuals—to draw them closer to Himself through what He did for Mary—was one of the sweetest, most beautiful things we got to witness through this incident. It was yet one more thing that was wonderful to behold. We were overwhelmed with awe only seeing this small glimpse of His great love for the souls of all humankind.

It seemed the Lord had arranged many things to preserve Mary's life and return her to us safe and sound. This and the healing He gave afterward, and other mercies tied to this incident were some of the most abundant and direct answers to prayer many of us had ever experienced. Yet at the same time, we were still very aware that sometimes the Lord answers our requests in ways that run counter to our hopes or expectations.

A GFU professor wrote an eloquent blog touching on Mary's preservation and rescue, which she posted just after Easter. It, along with its following comments, reminded us of a common conundrum. (See Appendix B, "Holy Doubt," by Abigail.) This blog stirred my thoughts for a long time afterward for other reasons as well (another book!).

Before this event, even though we had entreated the Lord, Bruce and I and beloved family and friends had suffered the loss of family members through disease, car accident, suicide, and mishaps on outdoor adventures. We and people we love had also endured other kinds of loss, due to disabilities, mental disorders, divorce, and other not-going-to-be-named-here difficulties. Often in the midst of our distresses it had seemed like God was not listening at all. In most of these instances the Lord had not answered our appeals to Him in the way we hoped He would. (In some instances, He still hasn't.) But overall, He *had* shown up, and was still showing up, in other ways to comfort and help us get through these hard things and learn valuable lessons as a result.

Hard things were still happening even while we were celebrating Mary's deliverance. We learned that the same day Mary was rescued, a young man, Russell Tiffany, died on Mount Hood. Being intoxicated, he had skied off on his own into an out-of-bounds ski area and had fallen headfirst into a hidden stream after punching through the snow above it.

Later we learned that many of the mountain climbers mentioned in the chapter on Mount Hood—the staff and students from the Portland Episcopal high school, Kelly James, Luke Gullberg, Anthony Vietti, and Katie Nolan—were Christians, and many people had been pleading with God for them as well, but they still perished on Mount Hood.

In the summer after Mary's rescue, news stations tried to contact her in hopes she might be able to somehow comfort the family of a beloved Salem dentist and avid mountain climber, Kinley Adam's, who had disappeared on Mount Hood. Later Adam's body was found on a perch at the top of Sandy Glacier. It appeared he had fallen 1000 feet to his death. There had been people praying for him as well after he didn't return as scheduled.

What do we do when awe and gratitude are the opposite of what we are feeling? When we know with our mind that God is supposed to be good, while we're not seeing it or feeling convinced, because of what we're presently experiencing? When the Lord isn't answering or doesn't answer prayers we are praying as we'd hoped or expected Him to? When the stark reality of a situation causes us to have serious doubts about God?

❧

According to *Merriam-Webster* the noun phrase, "the benefit of the doubt," means: "The state of accepting something/someone as honest or deserving of trust even though there are doubts."

Bruce and my joy in what the Lord had done and was doing for Mary was not a blind kind of joy. But our joy was overflowing and allowed to run free as a result of a choice each of us had made in situations prior to this, and in this situation as well, to give God the benefit of the doubt. Faith requires trust in God's character. Trust according to His revelation of Himself through creation, the Bible testaments, and His Spirit. We had chosen over and over again, despite our difficulties, to believe in His goodness, eternal wisdom, and faithfulness—His word and promises, independent of our own current understanding or feelings.

As David Cook is credited for teaching in the book *Everyday Supernatural*, "A life of faith isn't one free from all doubt, it's one where we keep expecting God to be faithful in the midst of our questions." Eventually, in each situation in which we have chosen to trust in God's justness and love, in His much greater, overarching perspective, and in His much higher purposes for our eternal souls, we have not been disappointed. With time, we have found that He has been more than faithful—He has not only been absolutely reliable, but also, He has been exceedingly merciful, generous, and kind to us. He has blessed us beyond measure!

Giving things time and trusting God no matter how things appear is described in the Bible as "waiting on the Lord."* This is something that is very difficult, if not impossible at times, for us to do humanly. But God will also help us with this, even, when we honestly, humbly ask it of Him.

If it is true, as we believe and see evidenced throughout the known universe, that God created and sustains this world through His wisdom, power, and foresight—then something far more amazing than what He did for us is that He generally restrains Himself from "helping" us when it would in fact hurt us. Sometimes what we are asking for would hurt us or others, but without full, clear hindsight or foresight we can't know it. Sometimes we just need to wait (even though it is hard). I believe all the Lord's answers in His timing are in keeping with His character, including His respect to the agency (choice or "free will") He's given us for the sake of love.

Looking back at this and other times of crisis makes me believe that sometimes, in the Lord's pursuit of us, He allows difficult and painful things to come into our lives if it might cause us to look to Him and trust Him more, to draw us closer to Him and away from our sinful (wrong) inner beliefs, desires, ambitions, obsessions, and thoughts that most often manifest in dishonest, hurtful speech, actions, and habits of living. William Nicholson, discussing C. S. Lewis's book, *Shadowlands*, about the death of a beloved wife, notes Lewis's conjecture that, "…Pain is God's megaphone to rouse a deaf world. Why must it be pain? Why can't he rouse us more gently, with violins or laughter? Because the dream from which we must be wakened is the dream that all is well."

Reflecting on Mary's experience, her grandpa (my father) shared the following thoughts:

> … Mary had filed a hiking plan and expected that they would start looking for her Monday. She had this empty feeling that no one was looking for her or praying for her all day Monday, Tuesday, Wednesday, and Thursday, and that was really hard on her—given

---

* See: Psalm 27:14; Isaiah 25:9; Lamentations 3:26 (https://www.biblegateway.com/)

that she is a very spiritually sensitive person. Friday morning, she woke up and felt peace and that she would be found that day. She saw search planes but could not catch their attention, but she then knew she would be found, that God had a work for her to do yet on this earth. Her feelings corresponded exactly with the prayer requests that went out.

One may ask, "Couldn't the Lord have answered her prayers earlier in the week without the rest of us praying?" Certainly, He could. She is full of faith. But praying for one another is one of the main ways we reach out in love to one another, and this was a great opportunity for the Lord to teach this principle to a large number of people. I am sure that Mary having to suffer those six days and nights alone without help is a price she does not regret paying, seeing so many people touched for good through her ordeal. The faith that was developed, the love that was felt, and the heart-felt prayers offered in our family were deeply touching to my soul...

So, prayer is our great opportunity to grow in love and to be filled with His love. So, we have a great witness in her ordeal of the great purpose and power in prayer. It is our shield against the adversary and our way to show our love to the Lord and for His children. Ultimately, this is the ideal society, where we all love one another.

These three things: prayer, the decision to trust, and gratitude seemed to open our eyes so we could see God's love for and pursuit of us to a degree far beyond anything we had previously imagined.

It didn't disturb us at all that some of the things God orchestrated, He did through other human beings and the use or arrangement of existing circumstances. Even though God is the God of the universe and could unravel and compel us with grand demonstrations of His power, we had seen many times that He generally works in much subtler, quieter ways. Following Mary's incident and inspired by it, a GFU alumna, Sara Kelm, wrote a blog, "Missing Miracles," regarding her own faith, which spoke exceedingly well on this subject. Barbi D., a GFU employee, forwarded a link for it to Bruce at work. You can read it in Appendix B. Bruce commented on Sara's blog after reading it, sharing with her our story about the lost boys and the "angel tracks." (The story which inspired our prayers that God would send an "angel" to lead SAR directly to Mary.)

I believe God most often uses "natural" means so that faith remains a choice—so we are never compelled to believe or to *love* God. We have to choose to believe in what is unseen, what we cannot see through blatant or obvious, tangible evidence. Our faith must be based on God, His character and word. And though He and much of what He does is unseen or intangible, He is still very real in that other, unseen dimension—the dimension that only the inner soul or spirit of a person can experience or "see." Though the Lord most often works through "natural" means, in this instance with Mary and us, He arranged everything so extraordinarily that anyone who might have had an inkling to be looking could see Him at work—and learn He *is* "there" for them and for us all.

We also saw through this experience how things in the Lord's economy, multiple things, are interwoven and considered by Him all at once. During and after Mary's hospital stay, and for months afterward, we were in an almost constant state of awe and thanksgiving, especially once we realized we were surely only seeing a *minuscule* part of what God must be doing or desiring to do every day, all over the world in individual lives. As G. K. Chesterton once said, "The whole order of things is as outrageous as any miracle which could presume to violate it."

18

PUBLIC OPINION
AND OUR RESPONSE

"This year, or this month, or, more likely, this very day,
we have failed to practise ourselves
the kind of behaviour we expect from other people."

➦ C. S. LEWIS, *MERE CHRISTIANITY* ➧

O f course, not everyone saw Mary's ordeal just as we did. There was a large and mixed, world-wide public response. Most public comments following the news reports were from people in the greater Portland metro area, but there were also people commenting from all over the US, the UK, Australia, Europe, and Asia. Many people were kind, gracious, understanding, and forgiving of Mary's youth and indiscretion. Others were not. The majority of the comments made in connection with online news stories covering Mary's incident are no longer available. Overall, this is probably not a great loss—in my opinion—except as a study in human nature.

Most of the news coverage came out the first few days Mary was in the hospital. She was almost constantly visiting with people, receiving medical care, or sleeping. She didn't seem to have much time for paying attention to the news stories about her, let alone for reading all the comments.

I wasn't paying much attention to them either at first. But Bruce was. He brought to my attention several things people were saying in response to the news about Mary's incident, that in some instances made me crazy with frustration or anger. *This person must be someone with little practical experience of how life and relationships actually work. This person has either forgotten or never noticed the effects of their own thoughtless behaviors…* I had plenty more, and less generous thoughts of my own in turn.

Unfortunately, it's easy and quite natural to get defensive and let emotions carry one away into judging others. This is something I'm as prone to as anyone else. But the Lord and Bruce helped me consider things like: *Do I want to be just like this person who seemed to have jumped to their conclusion and thoughtlessly blathered their hasty opinion with no knowledge or care at all?* Even we, who essentially had front row seats, didn't get Mary's story right at first; in fact, things about her incident were still unfolding. We also knew the circumstances of these commenters even less than they did ours.

At one point, I too went back and started reading some of the news stories and comments for myself. This was a mistake. Immediately, I wanted to answer every "unfair" or "wrong-headed" comment. I remember starting to answer one especially outrageous comment, but then realizing this person, if they really thought this way, wasn't going to "hear" a word of what I was writing—if they read it, which they probably wouldn't. Writing back to every comment was impossible and addressing the especially thoughtless or rabid comments would truly be a huge waste of time and energy. It did make me very grateful for all the kind or at least "fair" responses. They really stood out in contrast to some of the really horrible expressions that seemed to me like manifestations of total indifference, lack of feeling, or blatant hatred.

It helped me a lot to discuss some of these comments and the whole phenomenon of ready public opinion with Bruce. I'm so glad we were able to face and discuss almost every aspect of this whole incident together. Certainly, this experience with public opinion of Mary's highly publicized rescue gave Bruce and me a close-up view of human nature. Incidents like Mary's apparently bring out "publicly," into the open, what is sometimes "secretly" already in people's hearts.

There were quite a few kind-hearted people who extended grace to Mary for what she did—people who seemed able to empathize with her, who apparently had not forgotten their own past mistakes or follies. Some expressed gratitude for how others gave them grace in their craziness. And some who didn't receive this grace wanted to give better to others than what was done to them. Many balanced their views by acknowledging, yes, it was a very careless thing she did, but they could also empathize with her youth and humanness, and they were glad she was found alive and relatively well despite what she did.

Some seemed to be overly preoccupied with "fairness," which was a little ironic since that used to be Mary's own strong tendency. These folks had different takes on the price they thought she should have had to pay. Some were determined she should have had to pay back every cent that was spent on her rescue and recovery.

The truth is, we could have never repaid all we would have owed to the police, to SAR, to the National Guard or anyone else involved. That's *why* these things become a public service or volunteer service or both—of which we became aware and so grateful for. This was a fact quite a few other people brought out, while mentioning other public services provided such as firefighters, coast guard, military, hazard clean-up, and so on that most if not all people benefit from at one time or another in their lives. And that unless there is malicious intent or forethought to do harm behind something, we don't generally expect people to pay for these kinds of services.

A few dark souls even seemed to think it would have been better or pure justice if Mary had lost her life. To me, this was a really, deeply sad commentary on the extent of the disturbance in and depravity of that person's own soul. We were all aware this was what she deserved. In truth, all humans are ultimately and justly (compared to perfection) sentenced to die. However, can anyone with any empathy blame us if we were grateful this did not end up being Mary's sentence just yet? I think one has to forget their own failings first in order to be so unsympathetic and unforgiving of other's misdeeds or "debts."[23]

Apparently, there are also always a few rabid individuals who troll the internet, to intentionally exaggerate the obvious, attack others in the cruelest way possible, and who seem to derive great pleasure from hurting or denigrating others. And they do this no matter the extent of the obvious price that has already been paid. Bruce and I concluded that our best response to these trolls was to pray for them. So, we did. We prayed that instead of their lashing out and seeking attention in this de-humanizing way, God might lead them to find help and healing for what must be deep, painful brokenness, and that they might ultimately learn to have empathy and compassion for their fellow human beings.

Overall, Bruce paid much more attention to people's responses and opinions than I did. He's generally the front man in our relationship when it comes to news and media. But even he had to stop paying attention after a while. Dealing with all these opinions on top of everything else we were trying to process was just too much for us to handle. Both of us learned to have more empathy for others, and that we should dig deeper before commenting or sharing an opinion. These words of Jesus came forcefully home to us: "Be merciful, just as your Father is merciful. Do not judge, and you will not be judged. Do not condemn, and you will not be condemned. Forgive, and you will be forgiven" (Luke 6:36-37).

After reading the many comments and responses, we knew we could never respond to them all individually, and we especially knew it was better not to respond at all to commenters who were just picking a fight. We still felt we needed to respond in some general way, so each of us did.

On Friday, April 5th, 2013—six days after Mary was rescued—Bruce wrote an email to the *Mark and Dave Show* (now "Portland's Mark Mason Show"), a radio program which airs in the greater Portland area. The hosts gave him airtime to read it during their show:

> I am the father of Mary Owen, the hiker that was rescued off of Mt Hood last Saturday after six days on the mountain. I just wanted to say thanks to everyone who had a hand in Mary's rescue. The gratitude of our family is something that seems to have missed the cut in many of the news reports that have been in the press.

I was hoping that by sending this to Mark and Dave, the biggest, most heard voices in the Portland area, we might be able to get that message out that we are so grateful to the Newberg Police Department, the Clackamas Sheriff's Office, the Oregon National Guard, Mountain Wave Emergency Communications, Portland Mountain Rescue, Eugene Mountain Rescue, Corvallis Mountain Rescue, Hood River Crag Rats, American Medical Response, the Hood River County Sheriff's Office, and the US Air Force Pararescue Specialists, all of whom responded to the call and came to save our daughter. They will all be heroes to us forever.

Literally thousands prayed for Mary, and many offered to help in whatever other way they could. We are so thankful to all of these people as well. Many people have contacted us since Mary's rescue to wish her a speedy recovery from her injuries. Again, we are thankful.

I know there has also been criticism of Mary's actions and the cost to the community to mount such an effort. Our whole family, including Mary, recognize that those criticisms are valid. If Mary had acted with better judgement, such a rescue would not have been required. Mary has many times, in many interviews now, publicly apologized for acting so foolishly and is so thankful that no one else was hurt in the rescue effort. The true cost in dollars and cents is a debt I can never repay. Could you have paid that cost out of your own pocket if it had been your son or daughter out there? Very few in our society could afford to mount such an effort with their own resources. I will tell you that I will contribute to Search and Rescue for the rest of my life in gratitude and will encourage others to do the same.

I must say that I am so grateful to live in a community that still believes that one life is still worth being saved, if possible, even if that person acted foolishly in getting into the situation they were in.

Our thanks, again, from a grateful father and a grateful family,

Bruce Owen

After the show, Mark and Dave sent an email in response thanking Bruce for the story and expressing their hope that no one would be critical of Mary, since we have all done things we question later.

A day later, I finished something I wrote to send to the *Newberg Graphic*, a local newspaper. Tyler Francke, an affiliated reporter, published my letter in his *News Blog*.

April 6, 2013, Tyler Francke

Message from hiker Mary Owen's mom

On Friday, The *Newberg Graphic* received an emailed statement from Shelli Owen, a local resident and also the mother of Mary Owen, **the 23-year-old hiker who spent a grueling six days on Mount Hood before being rescued**. The Graphic declined to publish Shelli Owen's statement due to length, but I don't have any space considerations here. Her message appears below in unedited form.

Thank you to all the people who prayed with us for Mary to be found alive and well, and to those who have continued to pray for her; also, for all the well wishes that have been sent to her and to us. Thank you also to those who have been praying for us, her family; her friends; and for her and our other needs which have arisen. We have been inexpressibly blessed by God through His overflowing answers to your prayers!

Thank you to the Newberg/Dundee police department for the diligence and skill which they faithfully and patiently applied to quickly determine Mary's general whereabouts. Thank you to Search and Rescue and the National Guard and other volunteers who gave, or who were willing to give, of themselves and their resources to find and rescue our daughter/sister/friend!

Thank you to the skilled and kindly hospital staff at Legacy Emanuel Hospital who have taken such excellent care of Mary and so patiently dealt with us, her family and friends; and to Kaiser Permanente for their speed and personal help in replacing Mary's eyeglasses, etc.

Thank you to those individuals with the media/press who represented us initially in trying to find Mary, and to those who made an honest effort to accurately share her meaning and the different aspects of her story which they covered. Not all the media/press has taken that care. We have shared some good laughs as well as some consternation at some of the "stories" that have been fabricated (for lack of a better word) around her true story and interviews.

Thank you to friends and family who have been such a wonderful mortal (and moral) and emotional support in both tangible and intangible ways! Mary and everyone involved with her have been hugely blessed by the outpouring of your love to her and to us.

Most of all, thank you, God, for your particular answers to our prayers, and for the grace and mercy You showed to Mary and to us in allowing us to pin-point her on that incredibly vast mountain, and for her rescue and healing, and so much more which we cannot share here.

Some things happen to people by accident, but what happened to Mary was more a result of willful decisions. She has since acknowledged over and over to us and to others that she was being wrongfully head-strong and prideful to try to climb Mt. Hood alone and in failing to tell any of her friends or family that she was going to attempt it, so someone would know where she was and when she should be expected back. She understands now why no one knew to look for her sooner. While she was on the mountain, I believe she came to fully realize these things, and that they could cost her life and leave those who love her with unimaginable pain and grief. The first thing she said to her dad and then to me after we arrived at the ER was, "I'm so sorry..." She has since been repeatedly apologizing to us and to others. This is a learning experience that will not be wasted.

Some people have been commenting on social media about how stupid or costly this was; and, yes, they are right; but they are also wrong. In failing to give her (and others?) any mercy or grace, they are failing to acknowledge their own human failings and those of us all. Mary's failings in this instance might be far less stupid or costly to others in the long run, than the daily thoughtlessness, carelessness, arrogance, and selfishness that sometimes or often takes over in our own lives. These "little" things eventually add up to the equivalent of a mountain in the lives of the people who love us and/or who live the closest to us each day. We are grateful for God's grace and mercy in bringing Mary back to us. May each one of us also extend grace and mercy (but not excuses) to those whose failings are exposed to us – just as we would like our own failings to be treated.

Even after this experience, Mary will probably never grow tired of seeking novelty, adventure, challenge, and even danger, and in a way, we wouldn't want her to. This is part of who Mary is. But we are relieved by how she has internalized this experience and expressed the desire to never again intentionally allow this desire to eclipse her submission to God's leading or warnings or to doing what is right by the people in her life. She has expressed the realization that we are all attached to one another in the tapestry of life. She has experienced now how what one person does affects EVERYONE else. Through this experience, she seems to have encountered that this is both a fearful and a wonderful thing. It has become a powerful reason to her for looking to God for His wisdom and love, for direction in her daily walk, and in her relations with others.

The timeless wisdom in the following verse has new meaning in the light of Mary's experiences, not just for her, but if we will take it to heart, for the rest of us as well:

"Trust in the LORD with all your heart; do not depend on your own understanding. Seek his will in all you do, and he will show you which path to take. Don't be impressed with your own wisdom. Instead, fear the LORD and turn away from evil" (Prov. 3:5-7 [NLT]).

These were Bruce's and my responses to public commentary about Mary's incident. Even though Mary hadn't seen much of what was being said publicly, many visiting friends and family, as well as people she had been corresponding with through other means (phone calls, email, social media), had reprimanded her for what she had done. After Bruce and I had shared our thoughts publicly, I think Mary felt like she, too, should offer a statement to her communities of family and friends. She shared her reflections as a "Note" on *Facebook*. Since quite a few of our family friends and relatives were not using *Facebook*, we also shared what she had written through email. Here is what she wrote:

Mountain Time-out

by Mary Owen on Sunday, April 7, 2013

It's been over a week since they pulled me off the mountain, and I know I haven't written much as far as updates on here. Part of it has been that there is so much to write. Part of it has been trying to figure out how to say what needs to be said. I've stayed away from a lot of the negative coverage of my own story. I've never believed in living a life in regret. But one of the most cutting comments has been the simple question from a much-loved friend, "Well, did you learn anything?"

And my answer is, 'Yes. Yes, I have.'

This experience for me has been first and foremost a very stern, though gracious, rebuke from God. I feel as though I was put in timeout for four days. The other day I was reading Isaiah 30 and it is basically the story of my "accident." It begins, "'Ah, stubborn children,' declares the Lord, 'who carry out a plan, but not mine...'" (Isa. 30:1a, ESV)

Looking back at my own behavior on Sunday, preparing to go up the mountain, I made one bad decision after another. I feel as though God purposefully removed His Spirit from my reason. Without Him I am just a dumb blond who stubbornly walks up a mountain after several warnings not to (two from experienced mountaineers); carries a GPS but doesn't use it; has the opportunity to turn back but doesn't take it. God never removed His hand of protection from me. Believe me, during the whiteout I was literally walking through a graveyard - places where others more experienced than I have died on that mountain. But I do believe He allowed me to end up where I did on Monday morning, curled up in the snow with one leg torn open and the other foot sprained, unable to just get myself out of the situation.

"...therefore I have called her, 'Rahab who sits still'" (Isaiah 30:7, ESV).

On Monday I noticed that God wasn't talking to me, and it scared me a lot. I don't believe in fear. I wasn't afraid of death, or the elements, or whatever I would experience out there, but I've learned now that there is one fear that I must believe in—I WILL FEAR GOD.

Sitting out there with nothing else to do, I began to realize how very carelessly I've carried my own life, treating death as though it was just between myself and God. The immenseness of this foolishness hit me on Monday. You may think that your life doesn't count, that it's not a big deal if you disappear—or like myself—that you know where you're going when you die—life security—Jesus and I are buddies. You are wrong. I was wrong. Your life is inextricably tied to the lives of millions of other people. There is no one-person who can be removed from the tapestry of life without leaving a gaping hole behind; such a momentous decision—to remove a life—does and must belong solely to God. I realized while I was out there that the way I carried my own life, with such carelessness and so little regard for those who loved me, was equivalent to committing suicide.

So, to all of my dear friends and family, I am truly sorry.

God cut me off from His own voice and from the intercessory prayers of others including my own mother. He didn't talk to me again until Good Friday morning, when I woke with a verse in my mind:

"Do not be anxious, saying 'What shall we eat?' or 'What shall we drink?' or 'What shall we wear?' ... your heavenly Father knows that you need them all. But seek first the Kingdom of God and His righteousness, and all these things will be added to you" (Matthew 6:31-33, ESV).

I also woke with the overwhelming knowledge that thousands and thousands and thousands of people were praying for me.

"And though the Lord give you the bread of adversity and the water of affliction, yet your Teacher will not hide himself anymore. But your eyes shall see your Teacher. And your ears shall hear a word behind you saying, 'This is the way, walk in it'" (Isaiah 30:20-21, ESV).

This is the way, walk in it: If you call yourself a Christian, it is more than life security; it is more than a nice relationship that you can depend on to make you feel better when you're feeling discouraged or threatened. If you call yourself a Christian, your identity is now in Christ. You have been crucified, buried, and resurrected with the Living Savior and your life no longer belongs to you! You and I no longer have the freedom to walk in our own will and according to our own desires and understanding. This is the God of the Universe who has purchased your life with His own Blood! It is not a thing to be taken lightly or frivolously. You are now a part of the Kingdom Mission—Reconciling the World to the God who Loves it.

It is hard to believe, looking back, that I almost gave up everything that God has planned for my life and all of the precious relationships that He has given me for the foolish pride of standing on a mountain peak and saying I had summitted.

God is good. So good. That is my conclusion to every message, every conversation. He graciously protected and provided for me while I was out on that mountain. He sternly corrected my foolish and careless attitude towards the Life that He has given to me. He has given me another chance to be a part of His Kingdom work; I will take it with joy, a new humility, and a greater fear of the Lord.

To all of you who prayed and hoped and waited, thank you!

And to the search and rescue teams and Blackhawk crew who risked their own lives to find me, thank you!

And to all who are praying for my recovery, thank you!

I am stuck in the hospital for a while longer - the doctors are being very careful with the wound in my left leg—it is humbling to be here, but I'm not complaining. I know that God truly does work all things together for the good of those He loves and for the good work of the Kingdom.

If you do not yet know that God loves you, believe me, HE DOES! And He will shake the world and move mountains to bring you to Himself—to bring you to wholeness and freedom.

If you claim the title "Christian" but live as though your life belonged to you, STOP. You have no idea what you are messing with. This is the Holy One, the God of the Universe, and if you give your life to Him, you had better be prepared for Him to take it—ALL OF IT.

I am blessed that I still get to be a part of Kingdom work. I am blessed that I still get to live in a relationship with each of you who are reading this post. I am blessed to be alive and to be a servant of the King. And if my life does not show it, please, please remind me of what He has brought me through, saved me from, and purchased me for.

"The grace of the Lord Jesus Christ be with your spirit" (Phil. 4:23, ESV).

My God is good. So good.

I love you all.

Mary Owen

We observed a sweet, humble peace with Mary after her sincere apologies and "repentance"—her whole-hearted acknowledgment of her folly and remorse for the actual and potential distress and expenditure her actions had and could have exacted from others. Those who loved her, even those who had been especially stretched by what she had done, seemed to accept her expression of self-reproach as genuine, and her determination to not shift the blame or make excuses for what she had done as a sign she had owned what she had done and would not repeat it, and they forgave her too. This included Bruce and me as soon as she apologized to us in the ER.

Mary *did* learn many important lessons, yet we saw at the same time that our Father, *God* was not overly harsh or judgmental with her. The lessons she needed to learn did *not* have to come through His hands with a huge or devastating price, which she was bound to pay for the rest of her life. No one has been better or more merciful to us than God (who IS perfect)!

19

OUR HEROES

"We rise by lifting others."

❧ Robert G. Ingersoll ❧

Another kind of attention Mary's misadventure received was that of going down in history as an *infamous* climbing accident. Not long afterward, her experience was included in various reports about how to avoid what had happened to her. Reports like these can be a helpful service to rescue workers and mountain climbers alike—when people pay attention to these publications. We have come to appreciate these documentations and are grateful to those who make them, for how they're used to aid rescuers workers in preparing for future incidents, and for how (in this instance) they can help climbers and mountaineers avoid similar incidents themselves. Most of all, we were and continue to be grateful for how rescue workers put into practice what *they* had learned so they were able to find and rescue Mary.

As long as *Wikipedia* is around, Mary's particular incident will be remembered among other "Mount Hood Climbing Accidents," as follows:

> On Sunday, March 24, 2013, college student Mary Owen set out in the early morning hours to complete a solo climb. She was supposed to be a part of a group climb, but when the leader of her group canceled the climb due to what he thought would be bad weather, Owen decided to climb alone. As she climbed higher, whiteout conditions set in, and approximately 1000 vertical feet from the summit she decided to turn back. Disoriented due to the conditions she became lost and, attempting to climb out of the canyon, she slipped and fell about 40 feet, severely spraining her right ankle and suffering a puncture wound to her inner left thigh. Unable to walk, she was stranded on the mountain for six nights, surviving on one day's worth of snacks. Though she registered to climb, some mishap caused her information to be lost and she was not reported missing until Thursday, March 28. She was found alive on Saturday, March 30, by an Oregon Army National Guard Blackhawk helicopter rescue crew and flown directly to a hospital. Aside from her ankle injuries, she suffered frostbite in her feet and toes, but recovered fully.[24]

Mary's mishap gave us a major, new awareness of, and appreciation for, public servants. Individuals who, whether paid professionals or volunteers, put their lives on the line almost daily to help and protect others, including those who at times behave recklessly, like Mary had.

These public servants help generate and instigate the precautions and warnings that actions like Mary's precipitate. They sometimes share their research, reports, and training between agencies (police, SAR, mountaineering groups, ski patrol and instructors) and the public (mainly through websites or blogs). The purpose for this is to educate and equip others with the knowledge and skills to avoid similar calamities, as well as providing themselves greater awareness of how people become enmeshed in various difficulties, and how to best help them. This is how basic safety rules or policies often come about.

Sometimes there will be small discrepancies between reports, even though generally there has been an effort to represent things as close as possible to how they happened. Varying points of view, slight errors, and the omission of some material should be allowed for and expected. Overall, a compilation of reports can help give a pretty clear picture of an event. Following is a fairly comprehensive report taken from the PMR website ("Portland Mountain Rescue: Saving lives through rescue and mountain safety education"):

Lost Mt. Hood Climber

March 29-30, 2013

The subject, a 23-year-old woman who is a student at George Fox University, set out alone on Sunday March 24, 2013 at around 11:00 a.m. to climb Mt. Hood. She apparently did not leave a clear itinerary with friends who only knew that she might be spending a portion of her spring break hiking and climbing on Mt. Hood. She was wearing trail shoes and had only a plastic poncho for protection against wind and rain. She was not prepared to stay out overnight. She ascended into deteriorating conditions above the Palmer Lift, apparently became disoriented, and strayed far off course on the descent. She fell and hurt her leg that night and was unable to continue traveling the next day. She survived on snack food and water collected in her poncho until she was rescued on Saturday March 30, 2013.

Friends or family reported her missing on Thursday, March 28 and the Clackamas County Sherriff's Office located her automobile in the Timberline Lodge parking lot that evening. The sheriff requested assistance from Portland Mountain Rescue the next morning, Friday, March 29.

That day, a team of six PMR rescuers swept the Zig Zag Glacier below 8500 feet and cut for sign in Little Zig Zag Canyon and Sand Canyon. A team from Pacific NW Search and Rescue (PNWSAR) searched the Timberline Trail south and east to the White River Snopark. A fixed wing aircraft from the Hood River County Sherriff's Office conducted an aerial search and spotted possible tracks on the Reid Glacier that could be searched the following day. Search efforts were suspended shortly after dark on the 29th.

Four PMR rescuers were back in the field around 4:00 a.m. Saturday morning. A snow cat carried them to the top of the Palmer Lift. From there, they headed toward the summit to search the upper south side climbing routes. By 7:00 a.m., eight more PMR rescuers along with rescuers from the PNWSAR [Pacific Northwest SAR], [Hood River] Crag Rats, American Medical Response, US Air Force Para-jumpers, Corvallis Mountain Rescue, and Eugene Mountain Rescue joined the search. Teams were dispatched to check the upper, lower and the western areas of White River Canyon, Illumination Saddle, terrain west of Mississippi Head down to Paradise Park and sections of the Timberline Trail.

Around 9:00 a.m., an Air National Guard Blackhawk helicopter arrived. After a quick briefing, the helicopter headed directly to the [summit then to] Reid Glacier to investigate the tracks spotted on Friday. They followed the tracks down the mountain below tree line where they spotted the subject at around 4800 feet elevation (marked on the map [on their website]). They hoisted her into the helicopter and transported her to Legacy Emanuel Medical Center in Portland. In television interviews, the subject reported that she suffered frost bite to her feet and had deep lacerations on one leg.

During this mission, the media reported that the Clackamas County Sheriff's Office was unable to locate a climber's registration form that the subject completed and filed in the climbers' registry at the Timberline Day Lodge. Apparently, the US Forest Service Ranger responsible for the climber's registry removed out-of-date forms (including the subject's) from the file earlier in the week. Although climbers are asked to return to the registry to check out after their climb, few do. Therefore, the rangers assume that the many older registration forms that accumulate at the registry are for folks who made it home, but did not check in. These forms are filed for later compilation of statistics on mountain use. After this mission was over, the Forest Service located the subject's registration.

Also, the subject reported that she was surprised that no one started searching for her when she did not return at the time she estimated on her registration form. As posted in the climber's registry, no one monitors these forms, and there is no system to identify over-due climbers or to trigger a rescue. All back country users should leave an itinerary with a responsible adult. This subject survived six nights in rough, snow-covered terrain. Fortunately, weather was unseasonably mild that week. PMR urges back country travelers to carry equipment appropriate for the conditions and their objective and to build appropriate skills before climbing in technical terrain.

© 2001- 2013 Portland Mountain Rescue. Public Information used with permission.

Next is an excerpt highlighting Mary's hindsight advice, taken from the nearly hour-long report Mary gave to the officer from the Clackamas County Sheriff's department, Saturday, March 30, 2013, when he interviewed her in the Emergency Room right after she was rescued. This interview or debriefing was part of protocol to account for Clackamas County and SAR involvement in her rescue and for future training. It was important to them to learn what had happened to her, but more specifically how she ended up stranded on the mountain. The interview was later edited and posted by the Clackamas County Sheriff's Office (CCSO) on *YouTube* and made available to the public. (To see the complete transcription of the edited *YouTube* report and/or the *CCSO News Releases* visit: https://www.mountainrescue.online/official-reports.)

"Words of Wisdom from Mary Owen"

Well, first of all, don't go up alone in the snow. Generally, I wouldn't say don't ever go hiking alone, but I would say unless you're confident in your own abilities don't go hiking alone, and don't go hiking alone in the snow even if you are confident in your ability, because that's a whole different picture there.

I actually had a GPS on me, but the batteries were low, and I hadn't been using it on the mountain. I was stupid. And at that point..., I know not everyone believes in God, but I do, and I believe that His Spirit is able to enlighten our reason and able to help us to reason and I think that sometimes when we make decisions, when I make decisions that are completely out of His will, He'll take His Spirit away from my reason and then I'm just a "dumb" [person] who walks up a mountain with a GPS and doesn't use it, basically.

...And something that I'm pretty convinced of is that fear plays a huge role in the reasons why accidents turn into death. Is that something happens to you, and you get hurt and you're in a compromised, vulnerable position, and people get afraid. And they freak out and their mind and their body start going downhill from that point onward.

Mary's incident provoked a fair amount of chatter back and forth on various hiking and climbing websites and blogs. I noticed that these platforms sometimes shared the kinds of reports mentioned and shown above, or pertinent information from them, on their platforms. One piece of considerably basic and useful advice, which could have possibly made a big difference for Mary, was offered by J. E., someone who "is not a hiker, but plays one on TV." He commented on a "Back Packing Light" blog, Apr 1, 2013:

> I heard she was found near Sandy Glacier. That's over Yocum Ridge and down. Wrong direction all together. Sounds like that snowboarder from the east coast that got lost a year or two back. He descended into one of the canyon areas and became lost.
>
> Simple **compass** would have helped.
>
> Not trying to be an ass, I'm just trying to learn from other's mistakes. Note to self: In a whiteout, pull out the compass sooner than later.

It's true, if Mary had carried this one small item, it might have spared her and others a great deal of trouble. We had a couple of good compasses at home, either of which she could have used. Another simple, often-recommended item Mary could have carried, but didn't, which might have helped her to be found sooner, is a whistle. These two items are generally inexpensive, small, and relatively light weight. Someone else's "twenty-twenty hindsight" can be useful for others going forward.

Besides their helpful documentation of events that happen on their watch, we were even more impressed by the professionals themselves. When the search escalated and the Newberg-Dundee Police Department became involved, they gave full and thorough attention to our report of Mary being missing—as if it were their own family member who was missing. Each person who worked with us was professional, kind, and considerate. At least one individual on the force was always working on Mary's 'case' from the time we submitted our report until the time the truck she had borrowed was found at Timberline Lodge, even after the main investigation was turned over to the Sherriff of Clackamas County and Search and Rescue. Later, we learned there were even some individuals on the police force who began to pray for her to be found as soon as they learned she was missing.

The search and rescue effort was also top-notch. We learned while we were on Mount Hood the day Mary was found that many of those involved in SAR participate because they, themselves, have been rescued at some time, or because they have family or friends who were rescued by SAR. Others become rescue workers because of their interests and skills and love of the outdoors, and this was their chosen way of earning a living and/or serving the greater community. Most of them are unpaid volunteers. It's a wonderful way of giving back or giving to the community while adventuring in the outdoors—something they love. All of them have gone through the specialized training required. Putting their own lives on the line to rescue others is their common fare.

The PMR report above listed some of the organizations represented at Mount Hood the Saturday Mary was found, who contributed to the search, including the US Air Force Pararescue Specialists (Oregon National Guard helicopter crew and support), who found and rescued Mary. Others who were present that day on the mountain were personnel with their equipment from the Clackamas County Sherriff's Office, Mountain Wave Emergency Communications, SAR from Clackamas County, and the Hood River County Sheriff's Office. We were (are) grateful to each SAR person who was involved in the search for Mary, especially those who came voluntarily that day and/or including those who we never got to thank in person! We will be forever indebted to each one.

In Mary's initial interview or debriefing with the Clackamas County Sheriff, she expressed her deep gratitude for those who helped search for and rescue her:

> ...I'm just very, very thankful for everybody who came forward, for all of the Search and Rescue teams. Really for the hope of everybody who was involved—that people didn't give up hoping. That the Search and Rescue team wasn't without hope that they would find me. And that the helicopter crew wasn't without hope. I think that hope is the life of our humanity—and when we have that, we are alive. And it makes the difference between life and death.

> Definitely, I want to thank the crew on the Black Hawk helicopter. Thank you especially to the medic who came down off of the chopper and pulled me back up and took care of my feet and everything. Also, to everybody, all the volunteers, all the search and rescue team. It's such an incredible thing to me that people would be willing to go out and look for somebody who'd been gone for six days that they'd be enthusiastic about that, and [willing] to risk their own lives for something that looks so impossible. So, I really do just want to thank everyone from the Newberg police department to the Search and Rescue people to the Black Hawk crew... I've been really blessed by the work and the kindness and..., just the belief of other people that I would be found, that I was still alive, that I was still out there.

We were super excited when sometime later, the US Air Force Pararescue Specialists with the Oregon National Guard allowed Bruce, Mary, and me to go to their facility to meet and thank the helicopter crew who rescued Mary from the mountain. They even brought around the same helicopter they had used to rescue and transport Mary to the hospital. This memorable meeting was recorded and later reported by the Guard's own news team. As soon as pictures were made available (May 10, 2013),

Bruce immediately shared them on *Facebook*. Below photographs, captions, and descriptions are from the Oregon National Guard and their news team.

Chief Warrant Officer 3, Wickenhagen; Capt. Edgecomb;
Mary Owen; Sgt. Buchan; and Sgt. Cleveland

Oregon National Guard

130509-Z-OT568-038

Mary Owen (center), 23 of Newberg, Ore., poses for a photo with her rescuers, Oregon Army National Guard soldiers with Charlie Company, 7-158 Aviation, at the Army Aviation Support Facility in Salem, Ore., May 9, in front of the Blackhawk helicopter that hoisted her off of Mount Hood. Owen was injured and stranded for six days when the helicopter crew located and rescued her on March 30. Owen and her family visited the flight facility to thank the soldiers for saving her life (Photo by Staff Sgt. April Davis, Oregon Military Department Public Affairs).

Bruce Owen *with* Mary Owen.

May 10, 2013

On the Blackhawk with Sgt Dan Cleveland... under way better circumstances than the last time. 😊

Mary, Bruce, and Sgt. Cleaveland

Oregon National Guard

130509-Z-OT568-101

Mary...and her father...receive a tour of the Blackhawk helicopter that hoisted her off of Mount Hood from the Oregon Army National Guard flight medic who helped rescue her... (Photo by Staff Sgt. April Davis, Oregon Military Department Public Affairs).

Shelli Owen *at* Oregon National Guard - Oregon Military Department

[Shared Bruce's below photo].

The seat/anchor that was lowered 100 or so feet to lift Mary and one of her rescuers up to the helicopter.

Sgt. Buchan; Mary; and Chief Warrant Officer 3, Wickenhagen

Oregon National Guard
130509-Z-OT568-073
(Photo by Staff Sgt. April Davis, Oregon Military Department Public Affairs).

Whenever we look back at these pictures and that time, our gratitude soars again for these individuals who conscientiously invested the time and effort to train for what they did, and who did it so well.

We cannot release all the names of the police officers, SAR personnel and volunteers, and everyone who invested their time, energy, and skills in the search for our daughter Mary, but you know who you are. We will never be able to thank you enough, and we will ever be grateful you were there, and that you were each so dedicated to your work. Bruce and I continue to remember and pray for you—some by name. May the Lord ever bless you and keep you in His care! You'll always be heroes in our eyes.

Bruce and I and Mary would like to end this chapter with a thank you to *all* the honest and caring first responders *everywhere* who give their best, sometimes their lives, to what they do for their communities.

HOSPITAL, SURGERIES, AND RECOVERY

"Christ's miracles were not the suspension of the natural order
but the restoration of the natural order.
They were a reminder of what once was prior to the fall
and a preview of what will eventually be a universal reality once again
— a world of peace and justice, without death, disease, or conflict."

&ra; TIM KELLER &la;

Following in the course of this whole incident, the care Mary received at Legacy Emanuel was amazing. In regard to our daughter's physical healing, out of all the hospitals in the Portland area, Legacy Emanuel Hospital, with the staff and equipment that were there, ended up being the optimal place for the treatment of her specific injuries. It was exactly what she needed.

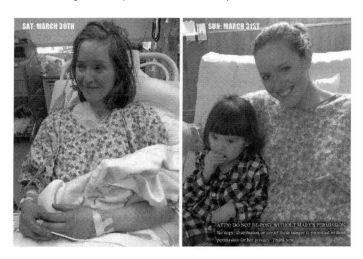

Mary on arrival vs one day later

When she first arrived at the hospital, she was in pretty bad shape. She had severe frostbite, especially on her toes. At first, caregivers weren't sure whether she would be able to keep all of her digits. She also had an eight-inch long by three-quarters of an inch wide gash on the inner part of her upper left thigh, and it appeared to be infected. She had quite a few major bruises on her legs. Her right leg was basically immobile from the calf down; she couldn't move her right ankle, foot, or toes.

Before more was learned about all the injuries she had sustained, the doctor thought she would only need to be in the hospital for a few days. It appeared the gash would just need to be stitched up, and that the break or sprain on her right lower leg would probably receive a cast or bandages, but not be a reason to keep her in the hospital. We thought that the frostbite could also be treated at home. However, as the full extent of her injuries became more apparent, we understood she might have to stay a bit longer. As Mary spent more time in the hospital, we were more and more glad for all the arrangements there.

Even the smallest things can make a big difference. The hospital had a well-maintained, relatively large garden in an open courtyard within its precincts, which was made available to hospital patients. It had a few picnic tables under a pagoda, a water feature, blooming flowers and shrubs, trees, and benches. It also featured some whimsical and humorous art forms throughout, including replicas of frogs, turtles, butterflies, and birds in different poses. Mary's window looked out on this garden. After a few days in the hospital, she and her visitors were able to spend a lot of the time out there. This was an unlooked-for and much welcomed assist for the recovery of an out-of-doors spirit like hers.

After a week or so in the hospital, and the almost continual social interaction, it began to get a little overwhelming for Mary to be with people *all the time*. For this reason, she also came to appreciate the hospital chapel, which afforded her a place of quiet reprieve, not only from constant interaction with people, but also from the regular hospital noise and routine. She began to need and want a place to be alone with God. There is no doubt these details of the hospital's design also lent themselves to her recovery.

Mary, occupied with correspondence via her computer

Mary

Initially in the rare moments I was alone, I would try to sleep. I tried to journal some, but I had difficulty putting what I had experienced into words. As I began to heal and grow more mobile (and more stir crazy), I would leave my room sometimes and wander out into the garden to play my guitar. I found the small hospital chapel, and when there was no one in there I would go in and sing hymns.

I explored the different floors of the building I was in. I must have made a strange sight – a young, healthy-looking woman using a walker with a strange machine hooked up to it, aimlessly wandering the halls.

One day I ventured farther than ever along a walkway connecting to one of the other buildings. I ended up in the children's hospital. It didn't strike me until I was there how much I had missed seeing little children around. It was sunny, open, and colorful. I stayed for a good long while just enjoying the sounds and atmosphere.

On my way back to my room, a woman coming in the other direction stopped me and asked if I was the person who had gotten rescued off Mount Hood. Despite all the media attention, it still felt odd and special to me to be recognized by a complete stranger.

Shelli

The hospital staff was generally professional and kind. Mary's main doctor was personable and clear in his communications with us, and each of her nurses was competent, caring, and kind when giving treatments. Mary enjoyed getting to know them as opportunities for conversation arose.

Mary seemed to connect especially well with a nurse named Chris, and with Charity—the nurse with the word "agape" tattooed on her arm. Agape is a Greek word that was used to refer to the Lord's unconditional love. It seemed that Charity was not only a good nurse but also a Christian sister and friend who ministered to Mary's spirit as well as to her body.

There was also a kindred spirit in a gentle, insightful man on the janitorial staff, who had the schooling and training and opportunity to do other work, but who had chosen to do just what he was doing. Mary described him as a caring person, invested in the relationships in his life, and an out-of-the-box thinker. She expressed enjoyment in the conversations she had with him while he worked. I don't think it's presumptuous to say, the positive interactions with these kind and caring souls also surely contributed to the forward momentum of her healing process.

In answer to our prayers, because of the expertise, skill, and excellent care of the staff under the doctors there, Mary was able to keep all her toes. All her digits returned to normal or near-normal function. The "moon boots" they gave her to improve circulation and the frequent massaging of her toes and fingers by visiting family and friends, which was also encouraged, made a huge difference. Because of the frostbite, she'll always be especially sensitive to cold in her extremities—this is a normal consequence that will never go away. She can no longer go barefoot in the snow, but this was a very minor set-back compared to what could have been.

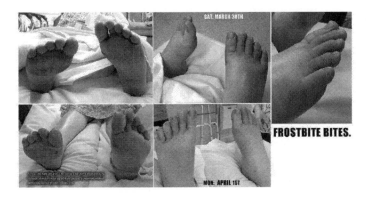

Mary's toes "before" and "after"

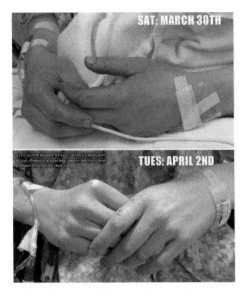

Mary's fingers "before" and "after"

A few people contacted Mary wanting to share their own stories and experiences of frostbite in empathy with her. These individuals knew first-hand what frostbite is like and how agonizing it can be, sometimes long-term. They shared what had helped them and let her know she wasn't alone in her pain. She appreciated these people who reached out to her.

Mary ended up having several surgeries. The first one, Sunday, March 31st, exposed what a mercy it was that she hadn't been able to move around on that mountain much and that she didn't move around more than she did. We didn't know how deep the gash actually was until the surgery. It is amazing that it didn't bleed profusely right after her leg was torn by the tree branch during her fall. All we can figure is that the fat and tissue of the inner thigh must have immediately closed back in on itself. We also had no idea there was a large splinter (3 cm / 1 ¼ inches) and other debris embedded in the gash as well. The doctors removed all they could see, including one wood splinter that they said was only a millimeter or two from her femoral artery! She would have bled out immediately had that artery been punctured.

Once they had removed all the visible debris, they inserted a sponge and vacuum into the wound to clean and drain infection from it. They wanted to do another surgery and more probable clean up once the swelling went down.

We and the doctors took pre-, mid-, and post-surgery *photos* of the leg wound, leg bruises, and the relatively large splinter. Since these may be upsetting or cause trauma to some people, they've been relegated to Appendix C to be viewed at the reader's discretion.

After the surgery, Bruce posted the following update:

March 31, 2013

Mary is doing so much better today as you can tell by the interviews. The surgery on her leg went well. She is, however, likely to be in the hospital until at least next Wednesday. We found out today that the wound to her leg was really a puncture wound from a tree branch. They had to open it up and remove wood and bark. The doctor found a [1 ¼] inch splinter that was very close to her femoral artery. If this had been severed, she would have bled to death in minutes. We are thanking God again for yet another miracle. We still covet your prayers as Mary recovers. The doctor is still somewhat concerned about possible ligament damage in her ankle even though there was no break. The doctor did say that her feet seem to be recovering from the frostbite pretty well. We would ask for your continued prayers for this also.

Thank you all so much for your prayer and support. We have been truly blessed by this outpouring of prayer and compassion for our daughter.

The next day, Monday, April 1, Elijah posted:

> The surgery on Mary's leg went very well yesterday. They are gonna do another surgery on Tuesday. She's doing great! 😊 It's so good to see her smiling face. Thank you guys, for all of your prayers and encouragement. God is good!

In the second surgery on Tuesday, April 2nd, doctors again cleaned out more debris, and since the swelling hadn't gone down all the way, they decided they needed to do at least one more cleanse (in surgery) to make sure they had gotten everything.

I sent out an update by email after this surgery in reply to a friend's inquiry about how Mary was doing, and whether she was home from the hospital yet.

> 4/4/13
>
> Hi Geri Ann,
>
> Please thank everyone for their prayers!
>
> Mary is not home yet, but we hope today or tomorrow. She is doing very well; it looks like she'll get to keep all her toes. Her sprained or strained ankle will take a little more time. The swelling has gone down significantly, and she is getting a little more movement and feeling in it and in her toes each day. The 8" gash in her upper inner thigh went down into the muscle…. They were going to stitch it up Wednesday but have decided it needs to heal from the inside a little more before/if they sew it up. She is now walking around without the walker and wheelchair. If she is discharged, she'll still have to continue with the vacuum/sponge and foot braces, etc… for some time until things fully heal.
>
> We are all so happy to have our Mary back! Things are gradually getting back to 'normal' and we're catching up with sleep little by little. Also, by God's grace, we all have been able to keep healthy. Again, thank you and everyone so much for your prayers (and love and e-hugs)! …
>
> Love and blessings,
>
> Shelli

4/4/13

We'll continue praying for Mary as she receives further medical treatment...and for your family as you support her and try to find balance again in your daily tasks and try to rest and stay healthy and so on. What a time for your family. Thank you for sharing with us so we can pray for you.

Jerrie L. (Portland area, family friends)

———————————————

Thanks for the update. E-hugs back! ☺

-Nate (Shelli's brother)

———————————————

So glad to hear this, Shelli! I continue to pray for you all!

Lori S. (Rogue Valley, close family friend)

———————————————

Thanks for this update, Shelli! We're so happy to hear Mary's health is getting better every day... though we know it's not a "cake walk"! ☺

Mike and I really enjoyed talking to her on the phone a couple of days ago. She sounded very good and positive.

Love and hugs to you and all!

Nancy O. (Mary's Aunt)

———————————————

Hi Shelli Sister!

It is so awesome how well Mary is doing considering her injuries. God is GOOD!

And I am glad that you are keeping healthy through all of this. Another of God's blessing raining down on all of us!

We love you guys sooooooo much!

Barb (Rogue Valley, like-family friend)

———————————————

Shelli

...I am so glad that she is getting better and that she'll get to go home very soon.

We will keep praying for her healing. We prayed last night at church for all of you...her for healing and the rest of you for recovery from the trauma.

Blessings.

Geri Ann H. (Portland area, homeschool friend)

_____

4/5/13

Thanks for the update. It sure sounds like a nasty leg wound. Tell Mary there are probably easier ways to become famous. ☺

Blessings,

Laurie C. (Rogue Valley, close family friend)

_____

4/6/13

Dear Shelli,

Thank you for the update on Mary. I am so glad to hear she is healing well and will keep her toes.

We would very much like to visit, at her convenience, of course.

So happy for you all! Keep the news coming!

Love,

Ann P. (Rogue Valley, family friend)

While the large splinter and other debris were cleared from the wound during the first and second surgery, the doctors were not satisfied that they had been able to clean everything out. Treating the infection in this wound was now a *major* concern. The doctors were being very careful. They wanted to make sure the wound was completely free of infection before they closed it up—before she left the hospital.

At first it was a little frustrating to us all that she wasn't able to go home after the first surgery, as the doctor had originally anticipated. However, we understood much better after Bruce's brother, Mike, shared some details about something that had happened in the past to one of Mary's cousins, Matthew. His leg had also become severely infected, in his case after multiple fractures; but in his situation, the infection went into the bone tissue. This resulted in a life-threatening condition that required almost a year of rehabilitation to heal. We hadn't realized that all the complications he had faced were due to the infection getting so out of hand.

What Mike shared with us overcame our temporary short-sightedness, which was replaced with another wave of gratitude to the Lord for providing this hospital and these doctors for Mary at this particular time. Doctors who were apparently very aware of the dangers of such a deep and large area of infection.

As the swelling (from infection) decreased, the doctors were able to get more debris out of the wound in a third and fourth surgery. After the fourth surgery, the doctor was finally satisfied the wound would heal cleanly and could probably be stitched closed. He wanted to do one final surgery to check, before, presumably in the same surgery, removing the vacuum and stitching it closed.

As things unfolded, we began to see that the excellent care the Lord was providing through these specific doctors and this particular hospital as another direct answer to prayer. Our gratitude for the support, especially in prayer, of family and friends also increased with this realization. The Lord was answering our prayers. Eventually our ever-increasing gratitude included thanks to God for the competent hospital staff and His provision through them for the complete healing of this infection.

I don't think that God only uses Christians or believers to do His work. I don't think we always know when God has us in a specific place at a specific time to help or bless people in answer to prayers. But I do believe He knows the past, present, and future and ". . . that in all things [He] works for the good of all those who love Him . . . " (Rom. 8:28) or who turn to Him with their whole soul (Joel 2:32a).

Following is an email update we sent to family and friends who were concerned and praying with us:

4/7/13

We have been so blessed and encouraged by the outpouring of love we have felt through your prayers and kindnesses to Mary and to our family. God has truly blessed us with the people He's placed in our lives (each one of YOU!).

Mary is still in the hospital. The greatest concern is the gash/puncture wound in her left, inner thigh. She's had four surgeries now. They're still putting her fully under for them. In the one they did yesterday, they removed some more splinters of wood.

The antibiotics course they have her on (which they've been giving I.V.), does not finish until Tuesday. The sponge/vacuum apparatus that sucks the fluids away from the wound is still in place (Mary calls it the "Jelly Maker"). The sponge is in her wound and there is tubing attached to it and then to a vacuum machine that sucks the nasty fluids out, away from the wound.

Mary is understanding and appreciative of the doctor's concern and care because a few years ago, one of her cousins had some very serious complications—including major surgeries and a great deal of time in recovery and therapy to help save his leg and the function in it—after his [bone] tissue became infected. We are hoping and praying that her leg wound will in fact heal properly and that no complications arise.

She still has limited movement in her right ankle. Though there is still some swelling, it has gone down significantly. She is doing some exercises to help remind it of its function, including walking around a little. She's been given a brace and some shoes (her "cow shoes") to protect her toes so that she can walk around without her "moon boots" (the fleece-lined boots that help blood circulation in her feet and lower legs). Her toes are looking soooo much better. They almost look normal again, except in a couple of places, and more feeling is coming back each day.

We thank you again for your prayers for her (and for us). We are also seeking with you, to turning our concerns and anxious thoughts into prayers whenever they arise. God has been so faithful in His care of us all. His answers usually don't come in just exactly the way we have prayed or expected, but His ways and timing are always PERFECT and GOOD—in fact the BEST in the long run. The final outcome, the salvation and sanctification of our souls is His priority. His love is over all. We can rest in this if we will.

We love you, and pray God's blessings to be upon each of you,

Bruce & Shelli

4/7/13

Thanks for the update...

Steve and Anna H. (Rogue Valley, NCFCA, family friends)

Dear Bruce and Shelli,

Thank you for sending this encouragement and update...

So, so grateful for all of you.

Love,

Robin M. (Rogue Valley, close family friend)

Thank you for update. Will continue prayers for blessed recovery.

Much love,

Wendy T. (Utah, long-time family friend)

4/8/13

Bruce and Shelli,

We read both your email and the email with Mary's Facebook post. Thank you for keeping us up to date. We will keep praying for the leg wound to heal completely. If you have time for a lunch conversation again in the next week or two (or three) let me know, Bruce.

Jerrie L.

Bruce and Shelli –

Thanks so much for the update...I know she's certainly going through a lot and not quite out of the woods.

Overall, it sounds like she's healing well, so we're happy to hear that. I'm sure she's anxious to get out of the hospital and return to some normalcy. ☺ She must miss her own bed!...

We continue to think of all of you daily.

Love,

Nancy O. (Mary's Aunt)

In the treatment of Mary's other leg, her right leg, after x-rays and various examinations, hospital staff first ruled out a break, then a serious sprain, and then ligament damage. They were unable to figure out definitively what kind of injury she had sustained in that leg. It acted the most like an injury sometimes seen in ballet caused by the constant jarring of ankles and toes, so that's how they finally treated it.

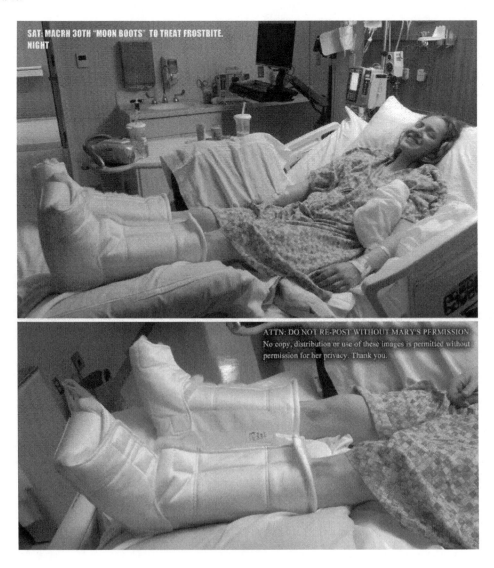

Mary's "moon boots"

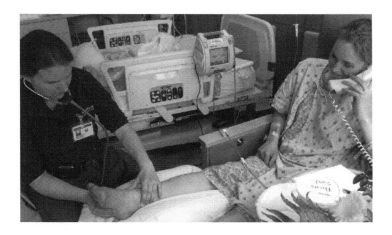

physical therapy

Initially, a therapist would get Mary positioned her in her bed, then her in-room physical therapy would consist of the therapist and nurses moving and exercising her right ankle and foot and her toes for her. Eventually they were able to provoke some independent cooperative movement in her right ankle and toes by having her move her left ankle and toes in the same motions at the same time. Through this means, she began making progress towards the full restoration of thought-induced movement in her right leg, independent of what her left leg was doing.

She had to continue these exercises for months after she left the hospital. It took almost half a year before she regained full movement and feeling in that ankle and foot and in all her toes again. But she did. The therapy and exercises the hospital staff gave her put her on the path to full recovery.

Meanwhile, concerning her left leg, because of the splinters found in the wound on the fourth surgery, Mary ended up having a fifth (March 10th) and a sixth (March 12th) surgery. This is described in an email update I sent on March 11th to family and friends.

Dear Family & Friends,

Your prayers continue to be felt! And because of them, we have good reason to hope that this will be the last update with Mary still in the hospital.

Yesterday the doctors stitched a lower layer of tissue together inside the wound on Mary's thigh, and replaced the sponge-vac on top of that. They're planning to remove the sponge/vac and staple the top layer of the wound shut on Friday and send her home! Again, this is our hope!!! ☺

Also, yesterday an X-ray was taken on her knee, in case damage there might be what is causing lack of nerve / messages to her strained ankle, which still has limited movement but no pain. They didn't see any damaged bones there, so are just going to continue to give that more time (nerve and tissue damage take longer to heal apparently).

Her toes are doing great. Only two still have no feeling, but they have good circulation. The nerves will hopefully eventually wake up again in those two toes and in her foot to do their jobs. God is such an incredible engineer/designer and healer!

Her health is good, and her spirits are up; though she is getting more and more anxious to be out of the hospital.

May God bless each of you with more of His love, peace and joy this day and always,

Shelli (for the family)

4/11/13

This is so great to hear. I hope everything goes as planned and she can get out of the hospital tomorrow....

Love to all,

Jeannette

Another significant thing we watched the Lord do, and another great mercy, was how He worked in people's hearts to provide financially for Mary's hospital stay. An inevitable aspect of any hospitalization is how it will be paid for. And even good insurance coverage—if one is "lucky" enough to have it—can sometimes be a headache to navigate. After being scooped off Mount Hood in fairly rough condition, Mary was flown directly to Legacy Emanuel because it was the best available trauma hospital, and potentially offered the kind of care she might need. We didn't even think about which hospital they were taking her to at the time, but Legacy wasn't Mary's insurance provider, Kaiser was. Nevertheless, Kaiser was very accommodating.

Not only did Kaiser cover the bulk of the cost of her stay at a non-Kaiser hospital and the procedures done there, but they responded beyond obligation. When Mary needed to replace the glasses she lost while she was on the mountain, friends helped pay for them, and a staff person from Kaiser delivered the replacement pair in person, directly to Mary's room in the hospital!

We wouldn't have had insurance coverage if Bruce hadn't been working at GFU—where enrollment in an insurance plan was required and facilitated. We hadn't been able to afford insurance most of our married life. And of course, without insurance, it would have taken Mary or us the rest of our lives to pay off Mary's stay and treatments at the hospital.

Also, GFU graciously covered the bulk of Mary's insurance co-pay—which would have been a substantial amount for her to have to repay at that time. This is an email Mary sent to Bruce:

4/8/13

Hey Dad,

Toni sent this to me this morning. God's a few steps ahead of us. ☺

Love you.

Mary O

---------- Forwarded message ----------

From: Toni S.
Date: Mon, Apr 8, 2013 at 10:26 a.m.
Subject: Med Bill Help
To: Mary Owen

Hey Mary,

I've been thinking of ways to help your family out, and I know medical bills are probably going to be pretty daunting. Fox has a Student Emergency Fund that someone outside of your family can apply for to have money given from the Fund toward medical expenses. I have the form that I'm ready to fill out, and I've talked to Brad L. and he said that once your medical bills come in, if I have a copy of a specific bill that your family's insurance does not cover to a certain extent, I can apply for up to $XXX from that fund to go to your family for that bill.

If you could tell your dad that I'm wanting to turn in this form for you guys I'd appreciate it. I can meet up with him and get a copy of a specific medical bill that you guys need help with, and I'll fill out the form for whatever is needed, up to $XXX, and turn that hardcopy into Brad L.

I hope this can help you guys. Love you.

Toni S.

Outreach Ministries Director & Little Bruins Coordinator

George Fox University

If you have ever had a loved one that has needed hospital care or have needed it yourself for an extended period of time, you can understand very well the depth of our gratitude for these additional mercies and what a big blessing we viewed this financial help to be.

The only shadow over Mary's hospital stay for Bruce and I was in the second week, when the hospital staff asked for permission to do a psychiatric evaluation because of Mary's "over-bright aspect." Bruce and I were both well aware of how significant mental illness manifests (another story). When we learned of this request, we both felt that this was an uncalled-for measure and expense, but Mary had already agreed to be evaluated.

To our view, Mary had not manifest behavioral signs—any *major* imbalance—that would indicate to Bruce or me, or most others who knew her then, that we should be concerned about her mental health. We understood that fearlessness at her age was not uncommon. According to different articles we'd read (and research still shows),[25] a young adult's brain doesn't become fully developed until around the age of twenty-five, and until then, they aren't generally able to think the same as a mature adult might.

I knew that when Mary first entered the hospital, she was overjoyed just to be alive and to be with people she loved. The rest of the time, she was holding up admirably in a state of transition, in the unnatural state of hospital life. Neither Bruce nor I, who cared for her more than anyone else but the Lord, saw anything in her behavior that warranted the extra cost or hassle of a psychiatric evaluation.

Nevertheless, Mary allowed the evaluation, which required Bruce and my cooperation as well. Even though I wasn't convinced it was necessary, I answered the questions about her that the staff asked me. Of course, no conclusive diagnosis could be given based on only one evaluation, but she and we, her parents, were cautioned to keep an eye on her behavior. Her more recent cycles of great and prolonged energy with small need of sleep followed by days of discouragement suggested to the psychiatrist that she might have very mild, but highly manageable, bi-polar tendencies.

Mary was counselled to get adequate sleep and keep a little more balance in her life. We all agreed with this, but I also thought, this is also something many college students have been counselled to do, for the same reasons, often to no avail—until they're done with college. And if we are honest, all of us could probably find some aspect of ourselves in the ever-growing "Diagnostic and Statistical Manual of Mental Disorders," a volume used for Psychiatric evaluation and diagnosis (and already one of, if not THE, biggest and most expensive books in the world). My guess is that everyone on earth could be evaluated and found to have some degree of some kind of "mental illness"—including all the psychiatrists who have contributed to this hefty publication. My firm belief is that of all the humans who have ever lived, only Jesus was wholly sane and sound.

Aside from this evaluation, the hospital care Mary received could hardly have been better. And considering the injuries she sustained, she ended up being in the hospital for a relatively short time—just 13 days in all. She was well on track to a complete recovery from all her injuries before she was released. After Mary's release from the hospital, she only needed to wear the prescription protective boots she was given until she had all the feeling back in her toes, left ankle and foot, and to do the exercises she had been given—which she did.

Things could have turned out so differently. Again, we saw all these things that helped to bring about her full healing as sweet, gracious answers to prayer; definite mercies and provision from the Lord—things we could never have humanly orchestrated ahead of time or afterward. Our awe and gratitude towards God continued to deepen and grow; we were so thankful for all the people who continued to give their love and support, especially through prayer, even after Mary's rescue, throughout her stay in the hospital, and beyond.

MEDIA ATTENTION

"I think all good reporting is the same thing—
the best attainable version of the truth."

❧ CARL BERNSTEIN ❧

Bruce and I realized that even we, Mary's family, who were with her almost constantly after she was rescued, weren't able to understand the story of Mary's incident on Mount Hood with total accuracy, especially at first, even after hearing it repeated by her several times. We could certainly understand how news reporters might not be able to get a story straight based on just one interview. However, some journalists were noticeably better than others at practicing their art with skill and integrity despite human limitations, deadlines, and the temptation towards bias or sensationalism.

From our perspective, reporting by Tyler Franke of the *Newberg Graphic* was exceptional (see author's website: https://www.mountainrescue.online/), and the *The Oregonian/ OregonLive.com* (Portland, OR daily newspaper) staff provided consistently objective and mainly accurate reports. Mary, Bruce and I thought two articles published online by them were especially well-written. One covering the time just after Mary was found entitled, "Family of missing hiker, 23, overjoyed she's found after week alone on Mount Hood," written by Lynne Terry, was also published on the front page of the Easter Sunday issue of *The Oregonian*, under the heading, "Mountain hiker found and family exhales." * The other article, "6 days stranded on Mount Hood leave hiker Mary Owen with frostbite, new outlook on life," was a write-up from an interview with Mary while she was recovering in the hospital, which was done by Emily Fuggetta, which also appeared in *The Oregonian* paper under the heading, "Rescued hiker felt the prayers of 'thousands,'" on Monday, 1 April, 2013.** After Bruce posted a link to this last article on *Facebook* a friend commented:

---

* http://www.oregonlive.com/pacific-northwest-news/index.ssf/2013/03/family_of_missing_hiker_23_ove.html or see author's website: https://www.mountainrescue.online/media-news.

** http://www.oregonlive.com/portland/index.ssf/2013/03/6_days_stranded_on_mount_hood.html or see author's website: https://www.mountainrescue.online/media-news.

<u>Laurene W.</u>: Very cool article. Thanks for sharing!... I've shared this article a couple of times now. I saw another one by a different journalism site, but I like this one better. I like that they shared her views on prayer. That really impacted me. Prayer matters.

While Mary was in the hospital, a Public Relations (PR) staff person for Legacy Emanuel, Meagan, was assigned to work with us. Meagan was well-suited for the responsibility of managing in-hospital interactions between us and the media. She did her job with skill and tact. She had to juggle the hospital's concerns, other patient's privacy concerns, Mary's care needs and privacy, as well as our family's needs and privacy, while still allowing the news media access to Mary. She accomplished all this with grace and relatively few complications. I'm guessing she had to work some strange, long hours sometimes to do this. Though this may have been common in her job, we were sincerely grateful for her professional assistance to us from beginning to end.

Before Meagan came on the job, some of our family members were reprimanded by hospital staff for pictures they took of Mary in the hospital, which they immediately shared on *Facebook*, without realizing they needed hospital permission first. The reason for this became apparent when news teams immediately began seeking hospital permission to use the pictures. Of course, the staff at the hospital has plenty of responsibilities for patient care already, without adding into the mix having to deal with the media. None of our family realized all this, including that the news media would have access to pictures some of us were posting on social media, until we were asked to stop posting.

Since the news teams were not initially allowed in the hospital all day Saturday, the day Mary was rescued, Bruce went out to give interviews at the park where we had seen all the news vans before we had entered the hospital. He did this only after first spending some good time with Mary, and while she was getting a bath and situated in her room. One news team had posted the following request on his *Facebook* timeline:

News Desk *to* **Bruce Owen**

Bruce, Great news. Can we use your picture of Mary in the hospital? We have had so many people wondering about her. Also, could we use the message you sent that she had been found. This truly is a great Easter for your family... And when you and/or Mary are up for it we would love to talk with you both about this. Not every one of these stories has had such a great ending.

S—— /*XXX* <u>News Desk</u>

Bruce gave this and other information to Meagan, who made the arrangements between Mary and news reporters for interviews in Mary's hospital room for Sunday morning (Easter) and from then on.

The makeup Rachel applied was the only physical preparation Mary had for the in-hospital interviews. Mary's past training in impromptu speaking (through our homeschool speech and debate club) stood her in good stead while she was being interviewed. There wasn't more preparation than that, on her part, for the interviews she gave.

Mary

I vaguely remember someone telling me about Dad giving interviews to the press the day they took me into the hospital. I understood that they had helped to broadcast the news of me being missing.

On Sunday morning, Easter, I was more than a little annoyed with the news reporter who pushed his way into our family gathering, stuck a mic in my face, and tried to induce me to say something thrilling about how "terrified" I was to be lost out there. But as I shared the story, I glanced past the reporter and caught the look on the camera man's face. He was tearing up, and there was something in his eyes that said that he needed to hear this. I realized that it wasn't about what I wanted or how I felt about media coverage. I had done something stupid. God had done something amazing. What He had done for me was for other people too, and for so many reasons that only He knew. After that, I didn't feel like I could turn down an interview. It was a penance of sorts, to continually tell this story—my failure, my recklessness, my pain—and tell again of God's voice, God's power.

Shelli

While in the hospital, Mary was interviewed by *The Oregonian/OregonLive*, "Good Morning America" (*ABCNews/CNN*), *KGW8, FOX12, KOIN6, KATU,* and others. Of all the live or video interviews of Mary that were aired and then posted on the internet, the live coverage we appreciated the most was done by the *KGW8 News* team. They not only summarized her story the most accurately, but they also posted a link to the entire, unedited, interview in three segments on their website. We felt these three interviews best caught the essence of Mary's story. Sadly, these segments are no longer available. (Learn from us—keep or make recordings!)

On Tuesday, April 2nd, "Starting Point" (the *Good Morning America* show, with *CNN*) interviewed Mary live from NYC.* I think because of the earliness of the hour in Oregon, and because of all the

---

* https://abcnews.go.com/blogs/headlines/2013/04/hiker-survived-6-days-in-mt-hood-snow-cave/

equipment the news team needed to set up in advance for this interview—since it was live—Meagan had to arrange for a larger room, away from other patients' rooms, in the hospital. As I remember, the only other people present in the room besides Mary and the news crew were Bruce, Meagan, and I. We had to be in the room with Mary set up and ready for the interview by 4:00 or 5:00 AM, PST (our time).

Mary

Rachel fixed up my hair and put make up on me before we headed over. I remember the interview went by so quickly; I really didn't get to share much at all. It was rather anticlimactic after all the fuss building up to it.

Shelli

I thought the interview went okay, but it wasn't one of the better interviews in my opinion. Maybe I felt this way because of the early hour (none of us was very awake), or maybe it was the kinds of leading questions Mary was asked. What I mean by leading questions is: questions asked that expect presupposed or desired answers. This was a little disappointing to me due to the larger audience it had. But even so, I thought Mary was still able to express herself well—much better than I could have done. Following is a photo we took that morning, which I later posted on *Facebook*:

[Mary] in the lights (LIVE, but not all the way awake, on CNN early in the morning)

Mary in the lights

Coverage of Mary's incident spread worldwide in English-speaking locations, including to the UK and Australia. Comments came from all over the globe.

Ruth

It was good to have the press involved to help find Mary, but it was kind of frustrating for them to be involved after that. It felt very intrusive into our privacy and like they were making her a celebrity for something she did that was really careless of the people who love her. I think a lot of our existence is being there for other people, and it seemed like she forgot that when she decided to climb Mount Hood—how important her existence was to other people.

Shelli

We learned later on that Ruth was not the only one of Mary's siblings to feel this way. Jessika expressed something similar to me as well. I don't know if we (Mary or Bruce or I) would have done differently had we known, but it would have been good to know how they felt. We didn't think to ask any of them at the time.

For a while after Mary had been found and rescued, the media coverage didn't stop. Later, mainly through Bruce, she was contacted and asked to do interviews for platforms including the *Katie* Couric show (June 27, 2013); producers of a documentary for a British TV station (February 6, 2014); and an episode for Roma Downey's "Answered Prayers" series (August 16, 2015).

Being involved with the *Katie* Couric show was both a positive and negative experience for our family. A representative told us they'd pay expenses for travel and accommodations for Mary and two family members if she would travel to New York City to be part of an episode. This episode was to feature people who had miraculously survived "impossible" circumstances. At first Mary was reluctant because she was pretty certain her story would be misrepresented in this venue, but in the end she, Bruce, and Rachel all decided to make the trip.

At first everyone expected that I would go with Mary and Bruce; but in my estimation, Rachel—our city girl, photographer, designer, and sometimes make-up artist—was a much better candidate for joining them on this venture. She had been to NYC before and loved it (she now lives there). I'd never had even the tiniest desire to go there. I knew Rachel wouldn't argue with me about going in my place, and she didn't.

Bruce, Mary, and Rachel on NYC public transport

As anticipated, they all enjoyed the experience of going to NYC together. They got to do a small amount of sight-seeing the morning before the show—a trip out to Battery Point, Time Square, and back to their hotel. Someone on public transport, who Rachel had struck up a conversation with, remembered seeing Mary's story on the news and recognized her, which surprised them all.

The producers of the show had put them up at the Beacon Hotel, a really nice hotel on Broadway, and they were being transported where they needed to go in a black Cadillac Escalade. For the production, they were taken to the studio, first to the "green room," which was not green, but had concrete gray floors, walls, and ceiling with couches, chairs, and tables around an area rug. This was the room where guests on the show waited for their turn to go on. The guests chatted back and forth. There was a snack table, and they could watch the show from a large monitor on the wall while they were waiting. Each guest, including Mary and Bruce who were going to be on camera, was taken upstairs to rooms where their make-up was applied. After this, and just before Mary's turn to go on, they were taken backstage where Mary and Bruce were fitted with wireless mics. Bruce and Rachel were then escorted around to seats in the front, middle section of the "audience."

The episode in which Mary was included also featured a man who had been sucked up into a tornado while in his truck and somehow survived, a woman and her child who were miraculously rescued after a car accident that left them hanging precariously by a wheel of their car from a high suspension bridge, and a couple of men who had survived a plane crash. Mary, Bruce, and Rachel got to hear these amazing stories as each person in turn was taped for the show.

Before Mary went on, they played the recording from her phone. It was the recording she had made for Bruce and I when she was on the mountain and first realized she was stuck and thought she would likely die there. Bruce and I knew of this recording, but neither of us had heard it. We hadn't wanted to because we didn't think we could take it emotionally. Bruce didn't realize they were going to play this recording; it took him off-guard. It was extremely difficult for him to hear—and in that setting especially. If he had been free from the constraints of a public show and makeup, he would have broken down sobbing.

After that, they had Mary walk onto the talk-show stage and Katie Couric began her interview. Towards the end of the interview, Bruce (in the audience) was asked a few questions as well.

The last guest on the show was a survival expert who talked about what to do, or not do, in a life-threatening situation. After the show was over Mary, Bruce, and Rachel were taken straight to the airport. Coincidentally, this was the day of the Boston Marathon bombing and their flight home was delayed for hours. They were very glad to finally get home.

Sadly, as Mary (and we) had mostly anticipated, mentions of prayer and God's part in helping each person—an integral component of each of these stories—were mostly cut, with very few exceptions, from all the stories. It seemed false and highly misrepresentative to us that for the final cut, the producers would not acknowledge the aspect of these stories (God's intervention) that the survivors obviously considered the most important to their survival. I guess they strive to give the public what they think it wants—usually not the whole truth about anything, especially having to do with people believing in God. Censorship is especially heavy on that topic. This seemed to be a growing trend.

My own view of the media, as a whole, had been colored long before this by one thing after another beginning with the initially isolated, and obviously sensationalized, reporting of the 1989 San Francisco/Loma Prieta earthquake up to the present, sometimes very inaccurate, reporting of Mary's misadventure. I had seen a general track record that suggested "objective" reporting is indeed an exceptionally rare thing. Bruce and I prized honest reporting when we saw it. The *Katie* Couric show was a letdown.

Another disappointment with the *Katie* Couric production was that they never sent the promised copy of this episode, not the uncut, original taping of the show, nor the final cut version. They also moved the date of the airing of the show and didn't notify us of the change, so none of us even saw the show when it finally aired.

However, the trip was memorable for Mary, Bruce, and Rachel; they had a pleasant time together. It was exciting for them to be part of the taping of this production and moving to hear the stories of the other people who were featured in the same episode. And there were people who were positively impacted by Mary's unedited story. So despite the end product, the trip was not a failure by any means.

After Mary, Bruce, and Rachel returned home, all we heard from the producers, weeks later, was that they weren't sure whether or not they were even going to air the episode featuring Mary's and the other survival stories. Bruce later posted on *Facebook*:

June 30, 2013

So, for those of you who may have wondered [along with us] whatever happened to Mary being in the *Katie* Couric show, well, the episode finally aired on June 27. Mary's segment is posted below. I must say that the show was heavily edited, and all of Mary's references to God's miraculous provision are gone. Somehow, they did allow my mention that we asked friends and family to pray for her to make it into the final cut. I am at least glad they did not scrap the show altogether.

[Shared the below, now-unavailable link:]

"I Survived: The Ultimate Survival Guide!

The ultimate survival guide! How ready are you for an emergency or disaster? Hear extraordinary survival stories from people who came face-to-face with death and lived to talk about it. What you need to know to survive a car crash or hiking accident...." (katiecouric.com).

Producers from the UK, doing a documentary on surviving snow entrapment for *Channel 5 Broadcasting*, a British television station, asked for permission to interview Mary. She agreed to give interviews at our home, and they ended up being the most extensive and thorough of any that were done on her misadventure. The production staff were amiable and easy to talk with. It was a pleasure having them in our home. Bruce was also asked to participate in some of the interviews, which he gladly did. They also honored my initial request not to be included in any interviews, and they put no pressure on me whatsoever to change my mind. I appreciated this a lot.

They set up screens that went behind Mary and Bruce and adjusted the screens and their lighting equipment and Mary and Bruce's positions on a stool until they had them just the way they wanted them. No makeup was applied on either of them. I think they simply adjusted the lighting so they wouldn't be washed out.

Of all those who presented Mary's story in an expanded form, Bruce and I thought these producers were among the most respectful and representative of her perspective. Even though Mary's story comprised a relatively short portion of the final production, the producers did include references she and Bruce made to God's part in the story, including the "angel tracks." The full documentary was produced by Leopard Films and entitled "Snowtrapped." It aired in the UK on 6 February 2014. Following is *Channel 5 Broadcasting's* summary of their documentary:

This is the documentary that brings to life unbelievable stories of ordinary people trapped in the snow. For days, weeks, sometimes even months on end. In SNOWTRAPPED, we're going to tell their astonishing stories. How they survived against the odds, and against the elements. How they were found, despite having no means of communicating with the outside world. And how they were rescued, often in high-stakes missions that put their rescuers in extreme danger too. Using unique and visceral user-generated content and archive footage, along with interviews with key protagonists, in SNOWTRAPPED we'll find out how our cast of survivors made it out of the snow (sometimes others with them weren't so lucky) and hear the heart-stopping stories of their ordeal. Featuring stories of some of the worst things that can happen to you in the snow—from avalanches to in-car burials to icy plane crashes—this documentary will take the viewer into the heart of the story, as we experience just how petrifying it is to be trapped deep under the snow.[26]

Bruce posted a link to this documentary after it came out on *YouTube*:

March 24, 2014

A British television station did a documentary on snowbound survival stories. They did a segment on Mary. Her story begins at the 28:48 mark. All of the stories are amazing.

[Shared the now-unavailable link to:]

Snowtrapped (2014) Full Documentary

I wish we would have also taped the interviews these producers did with Mary and Bruce, because they were so thorough and reflective of her and our experiences (and would have made the writing of this book easier!). However, we did not, and we failed to ask for a copy of the interviews as well.

a photo of "Barefoot Mary" (having very dirty feet), for a GFU magazine featuring Mary's story

A year or so after Mary's incident, a team from LightWorkers Media contacted her. They wanted her story to be part of an episode for the actress and producer Roma Downey's "Answered Prayers" series. They worked together with Mary while she was in the midst of her master's program at Trinity Western University. Doing these interviews was challenging at times; finding a time they could meet and a place for taping was difficult.

Mary

After extensive interviews over the phone, the film team ended up coming out to meet me in Bellingham, WA. They did my make-up and film interviewed me in a conference room in a hotel. The person interviewing me took reams of notes. The full recording must have been several hours long.

After that we went walking out at Whatcom Falls Park for an hour, and they filmed me "hiking" from various angles. For all of their thoroughness, I was disappointed in the end result when we finally received a DVD with the episode I was in. This was the last time I agreed to do an interview on my experience on Mount Hood.

Shelli

In the production itself, a few liberties were taken with the story to facilitate a portion of Mary's misadventure being acted out by a professional actress. In the final cut, the professional acting was sandwiched between some of Mary's narrations combined with photographs from Mary's incident. The scene about Mary's incident was about 20-minutes in total length.

GFU staff posted this announcement on their *Facebook* page before the show aired:

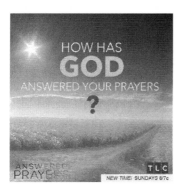

announcement for "Answered Prayers" episode featuring Mary's incident

George Fox University

August 11, 2015

This Sunday at 8 p.m. TLC's new show "Answered Prayers" will feature the story of George Fox alumna Mary Owen, who in March of 2013 was injured and stranded alone on Mt. Hood for six days before a miraculous rescue.

It aired on cable TV (TLC) August 16th of 2015. We did not have a subscription to the channel it was on, and we were not able to find anyone who did, so we didn't get to watch it live. However, Roma Downey very graciously sent us a disk copy of this episode afterward with a note written and signed by herself. That was a personal touch we did not expect, and which we appreciated.

By this time, Mary was completely preoccupied with other things. However, her story continued to be on Bruce and my mind and heart quite often. Reminders would pop up all the time, sometimes from unexpected places. It seems to have stayed on other people's minds as well. Not long after the "Answered Prayers" episode aired, we were taken by surprise by another apparent reference to it.

A few weeks after the 2015 fall term at GFU had started, Alin, a Chinese student who previously had stayed with us in our home during GFU orientation week, was watching the show *Agents of SHIELD*. Alin was aware of Mary's story and thought she recognized a reference to it when one of the characters apparently used Mary's example to encourage another character to persevere. Alin messaged Bruce on *Facebook*, indicating to him the scene and reference.

Alin W • October 27, 2015

Watching the *Agents of SHIELD*, season 3, E4... and I think he is talking about Mary!!!

Megan A.: What?! So cool!

Celeste L. (Shelli's sister): I will have to check it out.

Bob Gilmore: Bruce, why not? She is a marvel.

Vicki O. (Bruce's sister): Wow! Interesting...

Kenny R. (Elijah's best friend): That's crazy. lol

Bruce • October 28, 2015

[Shared Alin's post]

Apparently, the rescue of our daughter Mary off of Mt Hood was referenced in the latest episode of Agents of S.H.I.E.L.D.. How crazy is that? It is in season 3 episode 4 at about the 14:10 mark in the show.

McKaylee A. (Shelli's sister): You're an inspiration still! [emoji: kiss]

Roy N Hollie S. (Portland area, close family friends): Just watched it! Definitely about her! How cool is that! "Her faith saved her...she never gave up hope!" Mary Anne quote: "That is so freaking cool!"

Bruce: I think my reaction was the same as Mary Anne's! ☺

As far as I can tell, this possible reference to Mary's story on *Agents of SHIELD* probably came from the *Good Morning America* show, recorded live April 2, 2013, while she was in the hospital; or from an *ABC News* blog written by Neal Karlinsky,[27] reporting on it; or from a write-up in the *Huffington Post*.[28]

Other media groups than those we have mentioned also invited Mary to be on their shows or to do prerecorded interviews in the months and even years following her misadventure. But to her it was becoming more and more apparent the Lord had a different call on her life. It didn't seem to her to be worth the effort or how she wanted to be spending her already very stretched time. She was now fully invested in preparing to serve on a Christian mission, and she wanted to give her full attention to what she felt God was calling her to do in her present circumstances.

Mary --

It was only as the requests kept coming, and as I had the opportunity to read or watch how my words were spun out, that I began to feel the weight of my doubts bear down. Out of how many interviews, news articles, and shows had anyone attempted to be true to the actual story of God's discipline of me and His miraculous intervention? Maybe two news articles. There were so many misquotes, misrepresentations, errors, embellishments, and omissions in what was being churned out. I found that almost everyone who had interviewed me filtered and crafted my story through their own lens, with their own preconceptions and purposes overshadowing what had actually happened.

I slowly gave way to cynicism. I grew more reluctant to give interviews, still feeling like I had an obligation to do so. Finally, I did say no and started saying no more frequently.

I hate to feel so jaded, but I now read every news article I come across with a large dose of skepticism, knowing how even the most straightforward facts can get skewed, from experiencing how biased many of the news agencies are. I do believe that God used the media for His own purposes, despite their reluctance to mention Him. It's hard to avoid God when you're reporting on a miraculous survival story on Easter weekend.

HOME AGAIN!

(FRIDAY, APRIL 12, 2013)

"Where we love is home —
home that our feet may leave, but not our hearts."

❧ OLIVER WENDELL HOLMES, SR. ❦

Finally, the day arrived! Friday, April 12th. Our whole family got to the hospital as early as we could. Bruce and I were invited to watch the final surgery that morning. While we watched, the doctors closed Mary's leg wound with stitches, after the sponge and tubes belonging to the vacuum were removed from the wound. Mary was then cleared to leave the hospital (at approximately 11:00 AM).

Finally, she could put on normal clothes again and once more go about without having to seek permission. We were all overjoyed, but no one more than she was. As superb as the staff and facility had been, Mary was very ready and excited to go home. "Real food" and uninterrupted sleep were among the things she had begun to long for. And now, she was finally returning "home" to us and to her roommates and to the world at large, to go on living her life.

We gathered Mary's belongings from her hospital room and transported them, with everyone's help, to the van, parked as near the hospital as possible. Once her room was cleared, she could be signed out of the hospital. The sign-out desk was our final stop before leaving the hospital.

A little before noon, with hugs and kisses all around we said good-bye to Ruth and Rachel, who were returning to their home in Portland. Bruce, Elijah, and I, with Mary, headed towards McMinnville, towards home.

Elijah

April 12, 2013

Mary is coming home today!! ☺ God is good!

We stopped at GFU for a while on our way through Newberg so Mary could take care of some loose ends there. She was between jobs at the time, so that wasn't an issue, but she needed to get her course work for the two weeks of school she had missed and take care of some other things regarding her work with Urban Services.

Mary

The day I was released was almost dream-like. The question hung in the air the day before and that morning. Was I really going home? Checking out, receiving my papers, walking through the big double-doored entrance and out into the world, it all went like a dream. For six days I had been surrounded by Mount Hood's canyon walls; for thirteen days I was surrounded by hospital walls. My life had been so abnormal for so long that doing something so normal as walking down the sidewalk to the car felt surreal.

When I returned to campus on Friday, I felt at once connected to all things and places. I was clumping around in my special protective shoes, moving sluggishly, my body not yet recovered from the drain on its energies. Everything glowed with meaning and life, the trees, the flowers, the blades of grass. Most of all, I had a different sense for the people around me. I could almost see the massive shapes of their presence and potential, their glory, hovering over them like giants. This sense gradually faded away as the days went on and life returned to "normal." The memory lingers though, the glimpse into a reality of purpose and love, greater than our imagining.

Shelli

There can be no adequate description of our feelings as we drove the rest of the way to our home in the hills outside McMinnville. It wasn't because of returning to the house we lived in. Mary would stay in the spare room that weekend. It was probably the cleanest room in the house. We had been in something like crisis mode ever since Mary had turned up missing, so keeping up with normal household chores had been put on the back burner. But none of us were concerned about the tidiness of our house. We weren't mainly looking forward to a return to the house itself—but to being together in it.

Once we arrived home, I began fixing a simple but favorite meal at our home: spaghetti, French bread, and salad. Mary had especially been looking forward to a home-cooked meal. That evening it was a joy to fix a dinner that I knew everyone was looking forward to, especially to a meal we would share *together* in our home. It seemed like it had been a really long time since we had had a meal together, so much had happened since the last time. A "permanent" separation had nearly happened.

While the family was waiting for me to complete the finishing touches on dinner, with his heart overflowing (again) and tears rolling down his face, Bruce wrote to friends and family:

> So tonight, after a week lost on Mount Hood, and two weeks in the hospital after her rescue, Mary is home. She is just sitting on the couch talking with us and emailing friends. In a few minutes we will gather at the table for dinner and give thanks.

Mary (with Shelli) is HOME!

A deep, quiet joy, and an all-encompassing sense of God's love saturated the atmosphere in our home that evening. Each of us continued to be a little amazed, after all that had happened, that we were in fact, in reality, all together again in our home.

Bruce continued his post:

> So much to be thankful for, for all of you who prayed that Mary would be found alive, for a God who hears and answers prayers and is so good. We will also be thankful for Search and Rescue workers who answered the call and brought Mary home to us, and local police who

worked so hard to find out she was on the mountain in the first place. This could get long....
Thanks again.

Beth W.: Teared up reading this!! Happy, happy day!!!!

Janet S.: Just rest in His great joy and peace and all His goodness, too! So very happy for you
all!

Bob Gilmore: All praise to God, and thanks to her rescuers! Welcome home, Mary!

Laurene W.: Praise the Lord! Thanks for the reminder that God does answer prayers. I've
been feeling like God has been silent lately. I really needed to hear this. Thanks for posting.
And yes, I was one of the people praying for her. When bad things happen, I sometimes
forget the good things that have happened. I need lots of reminders apparently.

Scott W.: I am so happy for Mary and for your whole family, Bruce! Praise the Lord, for His
Love endures forever! We will continue to pray and praise the Lord!

Jackie E. (Portland area, close family friend): So glad Mary is home!!!!!!!

James D. (Rogue Valley, our former pastor and friend): Mercy and grace overflows with
gratitude.

Christine C.: Rejoicing in the Lord from thankful hearts with you, Brother! MUCH love to the
whole fam! ♥

McKaylee A. (Shelli's sister): Thank you for keeping us updated so we know how she is. So
blessed to have such an incredible family! So blessed that God heard our prayers and so
blessed that Mary is home! XOXOXOXO to you all. Love you guys bunches.

Karie C. (Shelli's sister): L O V E

Mike O. (Bruce's brother): We're all so happy she's on the mend!!!

Mary

I don't actually remember what we ate that first night. I do remember a poignant moment of silence as
I sat with Mom and Dad and Elijah at the table and all of us felt the weight of the loss that could have

been. The house itself had little sentimental hold on me, as my parents had moved there while I was working elsewhere, and then I had been going to college and rarely slept at "home."

Sitting around the table though. That table has been a fixture wherever we have lived throughout my entire life, and it is where many of my memories of "home" were anchored—Thanksgiving meals, doing schoolwork across from my siblings, family time playing board games, friends coming over for a meal together, reading morning devotions before dad went to work, building gingerbread houses, laying out an art project with my mom, learning how to make bread with my dad. The memories go on and on. I think that's why that moment, almost like grief—the sense of barely averted disaster and gratitude that it has passed us by—happened when we finally sat down together again at the table.

That night at my parent's home there would be moments so overwhelming that we would cease talking or laughing and sit in silence, each of us tearing up. It came in waves, aftershock from the tremendous grief that had been mercifully averted.

Shelli

Our hearts were very full; quite a few times our hearts overflowed into tears of gladness. We couldn't stop hugging and holding each other.

It was like, but even better than, the day of Mary's birth because we already knew and had grown to love each other—and then Mary was gone—and then we had her again. It was a type of "re-birth-day" for Mary and our family. It was definitely a new beginning, the start of a new and phase in our lives. It was a post, what-almost-happened-to-Mary-but-didn't day, and week, and month, and months, and year, and years….

Of course, life continued on after that with its usual demands, never slowing, never stopping, even for such an occasion.

To keep family and friends updated, the next morning we posted on *Facebook* and sent out an email to our family to our family and friends who weren't on *Facebook*.

Saturday, April 13, 2013

Mary is HOME!!!

They put her under yesterday (Friday, Apr. 12th) and stapled her leg wound closed; she has to leave it untouched under the bandage until the 15th, and then have the stitches removed after the 19th, if all goes well and it remains uninfected, etc. They let her go around lunch time. She was able to walk—though slowly—out to our car in the hospital parking garage (no wheelchair for the distance).

She has to wear an ankle brace and shoes that protect her toes from getting damaged while she still is getting feeling back in them. The toe guards look like a cow nose, so "moo-shoes." They asked her about pain. She said, "no pain."

They said, "miraculously no pain?"

She said, "yes, no pain," and the reason being that so many people are praying for her!

With grateful hearts for your prayers, love, and encouragement; and prayers that God will richly bless you for your goodness to us, and just because He is good and loves to bless those who pursue Him,

Bruce & Shelli

4/13/13

Yahoooo! Thanks for the good news, Shelli and Bruce. We are all really happy for Mary and you! I know how stressful the past few weeks have been on all of you, so hopefully now you can all start to relax a little more and enjoy this time together.

Love to all!

Nancy and family XOXO (Mary's aunt)

———————————

Thank you for the update, Shelli. We are rejoicing with you! Enjoy your time with your sweet daughter.

We are praying for complete healing, and hope to visit soon.[emoji: hug]

Love to all of you,

Ann P. (Rogue Valley, family friend)

———————————

So glad with you!

The H——'s

[Steve and Anna H. (Rogue Valley, NCFCA, family friends)]

———————————

Praise the Lord!! ☺ This is very good news. We rejoice with the Owen family.

Blessings

CHERISH (homeschool group)

———————————

Praising God for you all that this miracle happened for you all.

The fine line between a positive and a negative outcome is very thin, and I am so glad the Lord gave you a positive outcome....an outcome of life and limbs for Mary.

So many reasons to give God the GLORY!

Blessings.

Geri Ann H. (Portland area, homeschool friend)

———————————

Thank you for the updates...we are so happy for Mary and for all of you. God is good!

Jerrie L. (Portland area, family friends)

———————————

Hi Shelli,

Our whole fellowship and everyone down here was praying! What a relief to hear she was alive!

Steve H. (Rogue Valley, NCFCA, family friends)

Holly A., a close family friend who was battling cancer, and is now resting with Jesus, replied:

Dear friends,

We can only imagine the peace and the grace and the gratefulness that must fill your hearts to overflowing! He is a mighty and loving God, One who is able to speak life into existence and yet One who is constantly listening for our prayers. His miracles surround us every day. Mary was never lost from Him – only from us. His care for her while she was on the mountain, watching over her, providing for her, as well as lovingly teaching her—WOW! These are things a loving father here on earth would do, but never done so perfectly as it was by the Holy Spirit who ministered to Mary while she lay helpless on the mountain.

As your family *basks* in the greatest love there is, our hearts are full of joy and hope and praise. We love that you love God and are giving Him the praise and the glory and the honor that is His.

Mary, thank you for sharing what you learned on the mountain. Your realizations are thought-provoking and bold . . . truths we don't like to admit or acknowledge in our human condition. We pray you will continue to heal quickly and that your life will be even more effectively used by Him because of this experience.

Bruce and Shelli, thank you for never wavering from your trust in God and for your powerful testimony throughout this trial.

We love you all so much and are rejoicing with you, sometimes still with tears.

Holly

Christopher C.: May the God of grace and mercy fill you to overflowing.

Mary was "home," but our lives would never be the same. Mary's life would never be the same. Our connection with her and with others was forever altered. All of our relationships seemed so much more important—so much more real, especially our individual relationships with the Lord.

After Mary's spring break ordeal and roughly two weeks in the hospital, she returned to school full-time on Monday, April 15th. After being able to soak in time with her over the weekend, it was strangely easier than I had anticipated to watch her go back out into the world. Our hearts were full, but life must go on.

After this, for quite some time, friends and family continued checking up on Mary.

April 22, 2013

Jackie E. (Portland area, close family friend): How is she doing?

Bruce: She is doing well, Jackie. She is back [to going] barefoot but walkin' kinda slow these days. Frostbite recovery still in process...

April 24, 2013

Karen B.: How is Mary doing now?

Shelli: Hi Karen! She's doing relatively well. The leg wound in her left inner thigh seems to be healing nicely; the doctor allowed her to take her own staples and stitches out at her request Tuesday. They're wanting her to schedule a test to find out what is going on with her muscle/nerve in her right leg/ankle that was sprained. She still has restricted movement and feeling there.

She's still supposed to be wearing shoes that protect her toes (until full sensation is back) and an ankle brace to support her bad ankle. She has been wrapping her right foot to help prevent swelling there as well.

Other than that, she's trying to catch up in all her classes before finals next week, so she doesn't have to do an extension in any of them but is still trying to keep up all her other activities/ministries and part-time work at the same time.

She and Bruce and Rachel also got to fly to NY last week to be taped in front of a live audience for the *Katie* Couric show, a show featuring miraculous survival stories.

She's busy! So that's way more than you wanted to know even if it is the brief run-down. ☺

The day after I shared the above update through email, Mary responded, and added a correction:

4/25/13

Just FYI, I'm only trying to avoid taking out an extension in one class. The other four I'm applying for incompletes - meaning I'll finish them over the summer. Just thinking, I know I'm stubborn and over ambitious, but I have gained a little wisdom in all of this. I hope. I'm doing my best to pace myself.

Many of Mary's friends and their relationships were also changed by what had happened to her.

Beth W. *with* Mary and others.

May 2, 2013 · Newberg, OR

Fire. Foods. Friends. And the Mountain story. God is so, so, SO good!

Mary with friends around a campfire

Emails:

4/16/13

Thank you for the update, Shelli... We'll be praying for her, specifically with her studies and continued healing.

The LORD bless you, Shelli. Say hi to all your family for all of us.

Jerrie L.

_____

God bless you all and complete healing for Mary! Thanks for keeping us informed.

L.M. (California friend)

_____

You have all been in our thoughts and prayers, and I want to thank you for all the updates and insights.

"Phone hugs" to all!!

Love,

Neil and Cole (Rogue Valley, family friend)

Some years later, Lacey, one of Mary's long-time best friends from the Rogue Valley in Southern Oregon, shared the following thoughtful response when I asked her (for this book) about the impact Mary's experience had had on her.

The truth is, I really didn't understand the severity of Mary's situation until right before she was found. I remember Bruce had messaged me asking if I had heard from her or knew where she might be, but I never gave it a second thought that something might be seriously wrong. Seemed like pretty typical Mary behavior to fall off the grid for a few days! It was Saturday morning by the time I started getting concerned, but she ended up being found just a few hours later. It feels strange to think back on my lack of awareness of how bad the situation was. I see a lot of the same "invincibility" thinking in myself as Mary had during that time. Seemed at the time like truly tragic things only happened to other people. The naivety of young adulthood, I suppose?

With everything I've been through since losing Colin [a younger brother], I've realized much more how fragile life is and how dependent we are on God's perfect plan to give and take regardless of how we think things "should" be. Unfortunately, I think some of the reality of loss doesn't sink in until you've encountered it yourself. I believe you [Bruce and Shelli] and my parents had a better grasp of what could have happened to Mary and our ultimate dependence on God's will to save or spare her.

Haley, a still-close friend of Mary's who was also her roommate their senior year at GFU (2013-2014), was also willing to share some of her reflections. She shared the following June 4, 2016, three years after Mary's incident:

The first time that I met Mary I knew we'd be friends. We were both participating in a college volunteering event and were assigned to a park building project that required a short drive in a school bus. Mary and I happened to sit next to each other, and I noticed she wasn't wearing shoes—something I deeply appreciated because I don't much like to wear them either. We spent the whole bus drive postulating whether we could climb out of the bus while it was in motion, and by the time we reached our destination we had built up some strong opinions on the matter. Of course, after arriving at the park construction site, Mary was asked to kindly remove herself from the premises and join a different volunteer group as she was shoeless, but by then it had already been established that we would make great adventure buddies. And so we have.

Mary is a very dear friend to me, as dear a friend as a sister, and I can't imagine what my life would be without her in it. I know that it would certainly be a more boring and less thoughtful one. We have weathered many things together (figuratively and literally) and through these years I have come to admire and respect her for her courage, physical and mental strength, her wilderness skills, her love of mountains and stars, her striking intelligence, her compassion, her indefatigable pursuit of bringing the scripture to Papua New Guinea, and her faith in the salvation of Jesus Christ. But there is another side of Mary, one that I find lovably endearing though, at times, infuriating.

Mary is not the best at communicating plans. Yes, she has come a long, long way in the past year or two, but when we were in college, no one ever really knew where Mary was. Ever. I heard rumors that she lived under a desk in the Urban Outreach office where she ran a ministry to help the homeless in downtown Portland. I also heard rumors that she did own a cell phone, though email was a better way to get a hold of her (kind of). At one point I knew she kept a bedroll in our friends' tiny apartment above a burrito shop, but no one really expected her to be there. If one was to look for Mary on any given weekday, it made the most sense to check the free coffee station in the Religious Studies office, or the college ceramics shop. But most often she would just appear, and those appearances would be sure to be the bright spot of the day.

Mary spent her free time adventuring, which, when you live in a small Quaker town, means climbing buildings, climbing onto trains, and long walks in the starry dark. In those circumstances, Spring Break is a windfall, a whole week of adventures outside of town, maybe even a trip up to the mountains. That particular Spring Break Mary had wanted to summit Mt. Hood. She brought it up in several conversations with me and asked me to come with her. I am never one to shy away from adventure, and I love mountains, but I knew that summiting Mt. Hood would be hard and technical. I ended up opting out.

I didn't realize Mary was missing until our friend Izzy called me on Wednesday of that week and told me she hadn't heard from her. Izzy asked me whether she should call [Mary's folks and the police] or wait. I thought about this, and assured Izzy that Mary was probably fine and that we should wait a little longer before calling. In retrospect, that was dumb. But at the time, considering Mary's lifestyle, I thought that it might be a little overkill to call in the troops. I figured that she'd decided to do some hiking on Hood, or maybe had mixed up the plans we'd made to hike when she got back.

Eventually, thanks be to God, [the police, then] search and rescue [were] called and the search for Mary became a full-blown operation. When the vehicle she borrowed to drive up the mountain was found parked near the trailhead with her pack still inside, I knew she was in trouble. I never once doubted Mary's survival and mountaineering skills, but I did at times doubt her judgment. I was aware of Mary's ability and experience, but I was equally aware of her tenacity and over optimism in regard to potential danger.

Strangely enough, though my heart wished to know where she was, I wasn't exactly in a panic of worry. I knew that she wasn't going to die. I don't know how to explain that—but I simply knew that she'd be found and make a recovery if she was hurt. It was risky to trust that; I'd been tragically wrong before in a similar situation. I was well aware that peace, which did waver from time to time, could either have been denial, or the peace of God which surpasses all understanding.

I felt a bit guilty about that peace when I knew the anguish Momma and Papa Owen must have been in, but there was nothing that I could do by worrying. I also was riddled with guilt for suggesting that Izzy not call [her folks or the police], and even at first for not going with Mary. Maybe she would have been more cautious with a greenhorn in tow. I could only trust that God knew where my friend was, and that He was doing a great work for His glory through the situation. I spent much of that week in prayer and wonder.

The night before Mary was found I had wandered into the woods to pray and was filled again with the spirit of peace. Looking up from my place of worship I was taken in by the coalescence of green that can only be found in the western Oregon woods at springtime. I saw the first trillium of the year there, and I was reminded that life is fragile, and it is delicate. It is easy to ignore this when distracted by the perceived safety of daily life. It is easy to pretend that by wearing a seatbelt, washing produce before eating it, riding a bike with a helmet, and filing your taxes on time (these are all good things by the way), we will keep catastrophe from entering into daily life—but we all know that calamity will come to us all. Danger is everywhere because we are mortal. We will all die.

Many people found it easy to judge Mary as a reckless adventurer, looking for trouble by climbing a mountain in bad weather (trust me, we've all given her a hard time about that). But we are all reckless. Maybe your recklessness is in safety—perhaps you are recklessly squandering the minutes of your precious life by planning your days around the TV schedule because you have lied to yourself enough to be convinced that thing called death is a far-off shadow....

God was using the time on Mount Hood to teach my friend, and though it may seem crazy to say, I believe He was teaching her in a loving way and preparing her for the struggles she has and will face in the future. God is a relational God, He knows His children, and He speaks to us as individuals. It is telling of Mary's character and personality that God chose to speak to Mary through 6 days of dying on the side of a mountain—that's just the kind of gal she is.

The first time I saw her after her rescue, I was crammed in a hospital room—crammed not because the room was small, but because there were so many people there—and, true to her natural self, Mary was ministering to *us*. Surrounded by her sisters, parents, and homeless friends from URBAN, she read from Isaiah 30:

"Ah stubborn children," declares the Lord, "who carry out a plan but not Mine and who make an alliance, but not of My spirit, that they might add sin to sin: who set out to go down to Egypt, without asking My direction. . ." Therefore the Lord waits to be gracious to you, and therefore He exalts Himself to show mercy to you. For the Lord is a God of justice; blessed are those who wait for Him."

Don't go down to Egypt. Don't trust in the perceived safety of your own plans, schemes, and abilities. Trust in Jehovah God. This is faith. Mary has said that her attempt to summit was prideful, and that God composed that chapter of her life to teach her to trust in Him rather than herself, but we all learned from God that week. We all were able to experience the mystery and power of answered prayer, and we were all forced to rely on God's providence. We were all helpless in the situation and had to trust that she was in God's hands.

I don't like to think of how miserable it was for my friend to be stranded in a mountain canyon, freezing cold, totally aware of her location but unable to communicate with those looking for her, unable to extract herself because of the gnarly, life threatening gash in her thigh. I feel for her, being completely humbled as a mountaineer before news audiences by her miscalculation (one any of us could have made), and the fact that all the news broadcasts were showing an old picture of her hiking around with a late '70s external frame pack—trust me, as an adventurer *that* is more than embarrassing. I am furious at the hateful comments of passersby who didn't bother to read the facts of her experience before savagely criticizing her intelligence and her mistake. But I do like telling this story of God's miraculous redemption, His infinite mercy, His answer to prayer, and even His humor in this situation.

After many conversations with my friend about her ordeal on Mt. Hood, I am convinced that the only logical explanation for her survival is that God chose to save her. God chose to orchestrate the miraculous so that there can be no doubt in His omnipotence, and His mercy, and His glory. There is no doubt in my mind that it was more than merely coincidence that Mary was found alive the day before Easter Sunday and brought to the Emanuel hospital where she was nursed back to health by a woman named Charity with *Agape* tattooed on her forearm. There is no doubt in my mind that as harrowing an experience as this was, God was lovingly disciplining and preparing my friend for a future full of adventure and work for the Kingdom. I am grateful that God answered the prayers of hundreds of my brothers and sisters in Christ, and that He saved my friend.

A more recent reflection, that also stood out to me when it was posted on *Facebook*, was one shared in May 2018. It was in response to a prayer request concerning Mary, who at the time was living in PNG and was in severe, long-enduring, ongoing distress with her first bout of malaria. The post was written by Lauren, who had been the director of GFU's Christian Services Leadership Charter while Mary was attending GFU. Through their work together they had become (and still are) good friends.

There is a woman who went alone to a mountain and was lost there for days. Her greatest revelation was that no one was looking for her until the morning she awoke and could feel the prayers of so many people. She spoke this truth to the nation through social media and national television and reminded the hearts of many of the power of prayer and the truth that in Christ we are all connected and never truly alone....

This was an unforgettable episode in all our lives.

Mary did a willful thing.... We all can be willful about certain things at certain times.

She was independently alone and was injured in her attempts to get herself out of a bad place all by herself.... We make disasters in our life worse when we value our independence above all things and try to do life and fix our problems on our own.

She felt like God was not with her, but He was watching over her all the time, even when He wasn't letting her sense His Presence and wasn't directly talking to her.... We are often in this same space, believing God isn't there, because we have rebelled and chosen what *we* wanted. He gives us time to consider the consequences in cold and lonely places, even while he is watching over us and keeping us from even worse things.

She was stranded on the side of a huge mountain, like a needle in a haystack, in a place no one could find her in time without some general indication of where to look; but no mountain is too big for God, and no one can ever be too lost for Him to rescue…. Whatever mountains we face, and in whatever ways we're lost, God knows exactly where we are and can send whatever, or whoever, is needed for our rescue or deliverance—ultimately Jesus.

God has given us to one another to be family, to be there for one another. The first and best way we can support each other is to begin by calling on the Lord for one another. Then by this means, God will work in and through us and other people to do what only He, who knows all things from beginning to end, can orchestrate. But He doesn't work against our will or without an invitation.

We will all die in the end—death is the sentence we all (except Jesus) deserve, and will suffer, for our willful, rebellious, sometimes-just-ignorant choices that hurt or harm ourselves or others; but God has a rescue prepared for us. For this life and/or the next, instead of *everlasting* misery and death "everyone who calls on the name of the Lord will be saved…" (Joel 2:32) for *eternal life.*

If we trust God with the weaving of our stories, He'll make them more beautiful and lasting than anything we could ever imagine. And in the end, He'll bring us Home, to live with Him and a family of those who will love us with Him forever. "For God so loved the world that he gave his one and only Son, that whoever believes in him shall not perish but have eternal life. For God did not send his Son into the world to condemn the world, but to save the world through him" (John 3:16-17). The ultimate truth is, "…[Jesus Christ] the Son of Man came to seek and to save the lost" (Luke 19:10).

AFTERWORD

"Try to exclude the possibility of suffering
which the order of nature and the existence of free-wills involve,
and you find that you have excluded life itself."

∽ C. S. Lewis, *The Problem of Pain* ≋

This story wouldn't be complete without answering a couple more of the questions Bruce and I get asked a lot: "Did Mary ever summit Mount Hood?" and "What is she doing now?" The last threads of this tapestry will be our and Mary's own final reflections.

Mary wrote the below account in July 2019, more than six years after her misadventure, and more than four years after the event she describes here:

Climbing Mt. Hood with Ben

By Mary

My recovery continued long after leaving the hospital. One starlit night, sitting in the back of a truck with friends, I looked up to see an airplane pass overhead and a shudder ran through my body. For a moment I was back in the cold and silence, desperately aware of the life I was cut-off from. Some days the scar on my leg would tug at me with a sudden stab of pain. For many months my right leg from the knee down had no feeling. One cold night, walking with my friend and roommate, Izzy, I was suddenly close to panic, filled with the urgent need to get somewhere warm. There was a day with friends at the coast, several months after the accident, when I discovered with delight that I could run again. That summer (2013) my grandfather and I hiked 20 miles round trip to summit Mount Tallac near Tahoe. It was a shared triumph for both of us.

That same summer, I met the man who is now my husband. I was working night shift and he was day shift lead at a group care facility for teens who were not doing well in the Foster Care program. For our first wedding anniversary (May 4, 2015), we climbed and summitted Mount Hood. The day before, we prayed together, asking for God's blessing. We started the ascent at 2:00 AM under a clear sky. We didn't need our headlamps. The snow glowed so brightly with reflected moonlight. We moved steadily upward, following the same path I had taken in 2013. We stopped for a snack at the snowcat shed. We crossed over the ice field with the boulder formations. We skirted Hell's Kitchen, smelling the sulfur coming off the rocks. We crossed the glacier to the Hog's Back and I could see straight up the glacier to the great, black wall of rock and ice that had halted my previous ascent. It was strange to move over the same places under a clear sky. To see it all without the external and internal fog that had pervaded my first attempt. This time there was a sense of clarity and rightness to each stage of the journey.

We traversed a second glacier, praying for God's protection as ice skittered all around us. I looked down into the bowl and the outlet chute that I had navigated so recklessly before. Then we were making the steep final ascent, clinging to the icy wall of snow, placing our feet into the holds cut by previous climbers. We reached the summit ridge as the dawn's approach imbued the horizon with a rainbow light.

In the semi-darkness, the wind whipping round us, we huddled together under the poncho that had helped to save my life and savored the exhilarating views in every direction. This was more than what I had desired. I had wanted to conquer the mountain, to be able to say that I had done it. I had wanted it only for myself. Now as I sat on the summit next to my husband (a fact which was in itself a product of miraculous intervention), I felt a triumphant peace and Presence, permeated with joyful permission and great blessing, of the mountain beneath me and the God who orders my steps.

For this climb, Mary had gathered all the appropriate equipment needed to ascend and descend safely. She let Bruce and me and others know the day and time they were planning on making the ascent. She kept an eye on the weather and made sure the conditions were right. She and Ben made the climb with our full knowledge and blessing (and prayers!).

Eight years after her Mount Hood incident, Mary and her husband Ben, along with their three children now live in Papua New Guinea as Christian missionaries. Mary is a "Translation/Literary Consultant," and Ben is the "PNG Field Director" for *Word Made Flesh*, their sending organization. They were invited to PNG by five affiliated villages. These same tribes built them a hut-on-stilts in the village of Baku.

tribal dress in Baku, PNG

the hut the tribes built for the Grimms

PNG is a land blighted by malaria, tuberculosis, and various other diseases, where Mary and Ben daily put their lives on the line to help the people there. The expressed needs of the villagers include not only their first priority, Bible translation and interpretation, but also daily access to clean water, sanitation, language development (learning to read and write and express their stories in their own language), disease prevention (versus traditional superstitions that precipitate harm and death), knowledge of basic first aid and nutrition, general education, agricultural and natural resource protection and development, and so on. Mary and Ben have dedicated their lives to serving the Lord wherever He locates them. Currently He has given them this specific kind of "search and rescue" (For more information or to donate visit: https://wordmadeflesh.org/about/staff/papua-new-guinea-staff/).

Benjamin, Mary, Adira, Joya, and Isaac in PNG

Mary doesn't only avoid telling her Mount Hood story, but she's also been very busy since the incident, finishing her schooling and graduating from GFU, getting married, attending graduate school in Canada, beginning a family, moving to PNG to start a new phase in her life as a Christian missionary and community developer with her husband Benjamin, and the list continues.

Now that Mary is no longer living on the North American continent and is so much engaged with her own family and the people and work in PNG (and rarely has internet connection), it has been more difficult than ever to secure her assistance in writing this book. But she's done the best she can because, with us, she understands that this story is fundamentally not about her. It is about the Lord, our God and how He loves and reaches out, generally through whatever means are available, to encourage, help, and rescue people anywhere and everywhere, regardless of circumstances.

⚘

Our family has been asked how this experience changed us and what we learned from it. As a whole, our family dynamics have changed considerably since this incident, but not necessarily because of this event—though I'm sure it's had its influence. One thing that doesn't seem to be changing over the long run, after this event, is how much we value each other's existence.

How did this ordeal change our personal lives going forward? Here are some reflections family members have shared regarding the effect this incident has had on them individually. Mary's reflections are last.

Rachel's Reflections

Family members are easy to take for granted. One of my fears has always been of losing someone that I haven't taken time to appreciate and talk to recently. I don't want to regret missing out on conversations I could have had with them, or things I should have said to them or simply wish I'd known them better. It really hits you when it's not theoretical, when you're staring down the barrel of the gun—which is what it was like when Mary went missing. It is more important than ever to me now to spend time with people and be there for them, and for them to know I care about them.

Shelli's Reflections

I tend to be a task-oriented person and an introvert, but after this "event" I'm (still) becoming a lot more present with people when I'm with them. I value the time I spend with people a lot more.

Another change is that I've become a lot more intentional in my personal prayer life about calling on the Lord for other people besides my own family members and extended family. And this practice has continued to grow more outward. In the last couple of years Bruce and I helped start a prayer ministry at our church—including members who are disabled, homebound, or elderly who have a hard time getting around, who want to serve and participate as part of the "body of Christ" (the church) by praying for people—which ministry I believe might be the most important in the church, since God's people will not act as His people unless they are first seeking His will and obeying Him through His Spirit.

Living in awe and gratitude has become an almost constant attitude in my life since then, and it has changed my life—a lot. It is probably the most effective "tool" the Lord has given me for maintaining victory over the tendency I have had towards depression. Practicing remembrance of who God is and what He has done elicits awe and gratitude—and refreshes my memory when my focus has gone awry, also helping me see even more of God's goodness and love at work everywhere, including in other people and in myself.

This incident has also pushed me a lot further towards making trust in and submission to the Lord's will and timing for things, a way of life. Trusting God, rather than worrying so much, as I have in the past, about things I cannot change is life-changing in itself. In a way, what happened on the mountain and afterward was preparation for learning to deal with Mary and her family being half a world away in PNG with the related concerns this has caused—including the day to day adventures this family lives. It's also helped me deal with other real concerns regarding our other now-adult children and other people I love, as different issues arise.

Surrendering to God, in turn, has required that I practice living one day, one step, one moment at a time, relying on Him to guide me. Besides the people and circumstances He's given me (put in my life), He brings to mind (mainly when I'm in prayer and paying attention) people to pray for and/or sometimes how to pray for them. He also guides me in who I might spend time with or be in contact with, and/or in what to do and where I'm to go (if its somewhere else) for the present, next step in my life. I've been learning and seeing that if I just take the next step the Lord has opened to me, He'll then open the one after that, and after that.

Of course, there's been the process of birthing this book, which has included going back to school so I could improve my writing skills. I could go on, and on…. Mary's Mount Hood incident has most certainly continued to have a major impact on my personal life since it happened.

Bruce's Reflections

I reflect on Mary's ordeal and rescue often. And every time I do, I'm overwhelmed with gratitude that brings me to tears. Even now, as I write this, I do it with tears running down my cheeks. I cannot help it, I cannot change it, I don't want to.

I'm grateful, of course, to all the people involved directly in her rescue. This includes Mary's friends and roommates who called us worried about her, law enforcement who acted so quickly and energetically upon our reporting her missing, and all the search and rescue personnel who physically went to look for her, knowing that after six days and nights, the probability that she would be found alive was very low. Though I know that this last group would never accept the title of "heroes"— what other word is appropriate for those who, repeatedly, answer the call, gear up, and go in search of the lost, even when experience has taught them their efforts will likely end in sorrow?

I'm also grateful to the thousands of people, family, friends and so many we do not even know and never will, who lifted us up and encouraged us and prayed for Mary's safe return. A literal army of people who believed in the possibility of miracles, and the God who can make miracles happen.

I'm most grateful for the God who did make miracles happen. And because of those miracles, Mary is still alive and well today.

All of this comes flooding over me every time I revisit the events of those days.

I have been asked how this experience has changed me. The truth is, this experience, as difficult as it was, was one link in a long chain of experiences. And they continue to teach me, over and over again, to trust the Lord, and surrender to His will. The Bible uses the words "His good and perfect will" (Romans 12:2).

Surrender. This is a word that I know makes most people wince. It makes me wince. In the storms of life, I often have a difficult time accepting God's will, or believing that His will is always "good and perfect." I guess that is why it is a lesson I must learn again and again.

At some point in my life, I came to the realization that I needed Jesus, and I surrendered my life to Him. I put Him in charge of it. And ever since then I have spent a good deal of my time telling Him, *yes, of course I'm grateful for salvation and for the forgiving of my sins, and of course you are "in charge" of my life, but "I got this." Really, I can handle it. I will let you know if I need you.* And so often, I have had to relearn the truth that Jesus is not an AAA card I keep in my wallet, only to be used when my life breaks down and I can't get it started again myself. He IS the way. Jesus said it himself, "I am the way the truth and the life" (John 14:6). So that is what I have learned, yet again, through this experience. Surrendering to that truth is the only way I have any true peace in this life, especially in the middle of the storms.

It is naïve to believe that, by believing in Jesus, nothing we do not want to happen will ever happen. I'm grateful that, in this case, Mary did not die, that she was not taken from us. I know full well though, that sometimes, events do not unfold in the way we would want them to. In the hours before Mary was found, when the outcome was still very much in doubt, I was encouraged by the faith of a person I knew had faced incredible sorrow and loss. This person's words helped me to hope, but also to surrender to God's will. I knew that Mary's heart belonged to God, and that there is so much more to God's plans than this mortal life.

I have found that there really is an incomprehensible peace that comes from Jesus in difficult times. "In this world you will have trouble. But take heart! I have overcome the world" (John 16:33).

Mary's Reflections

...What [did] I [bring] away from my time on the mountain and all the experiences surrounding it? I learned that every life is deeply interwoven with the lives of those around it. No person can cease to exist on this sphere and not leave a ripple effect. I glimpsed the powerful force that we know as the spark of life, and I found that [its best if] God...determine[s] when that spark will be extinguished. For some weeks after my time on the mountain, I had a sort of double vision where I could see people as everyone else saw them, but I could also see their essence or the potential of their glory like great shimmering giants walking around. I've never forgotten that.

I've also been deeply changed by the sheer fact of surviving when others have not. People would call me up when another climber went missing on the mountain, or they'd ask me what I had done that helped me to survive. I've had to repeat more times than I can count that it was God who saved my life despite my recklessness and the mistakes I made. What I did, sitting there waiting for rescuers for five days, is not worthy of retelling were it not for God's intervention.

I struggled with and avoided telling my survival story for years after a dear friend of mine died in a terrible accident. Grieving with his family and realizing the enormity of what my own family would have suffered had I died tore me up. I felt that I deserved to die for my foolishness, while my friend was such a light and joy to those around him, he had done nothing to warrant such an abrupt and terrible end. Ultimately, I had to wrestle with my faith in the goodness of God and come to a place of submission. [I am leaving it] in His hands to give and to take life according to His perfect understanding of how all of our lives work together within His will.

My experience on Mount Hood refocused my daily life. I now see every soul I encounter as astoundingly precious to God. Every day I've been blessed with is a gift from Him, not to be taken lightly. Where before I had been careless, even reckless, with my ties and responsibilities to others, I now see them as a profound privilege. While I had known God before my mountain rescue, I had not *known* Jesus. Now I do.

Perhaps the most effective result of my experience was a deep sense of the truth and urgency of God's mission to save people and restore them to right relationship with Him. Encountering death face to face in that terrible silence, I encountered the truth of Jesus' death. And in being restored to God's Presence and voice, I encountered the truth of Jesus' resurrection. This is what He did to bring us back to Him. All of history and all of the natural world leans towards this truth with intense focus and urgency.

Psalm 107
An Ancient Ballad

Give thanks to the Lord, for he is good;
his love endures forever.

Let the redeemed of the Lord tell their story —
those he redeemed from the hand of the foe,
those he gathered from the lands,
from east and west, from north and south.

Some wandered in desert wastelands,
finding no way to a city where they could settle.
They were hungry and thirsty,
and their lives ebbed away.
Then they cried out to the Lord in their trouble,
and he delivered them from their distress.
He led them by a straight way
to a city where they could settle.
Let them give thanks to the Lord for his unfailing love
and his wonderful deeds for mankind,
for he satisfies the thirsty
and fills the hungry with good things.

Some sat in darkness, in utter darkness,
prisoners suffering in iron chains,
because they rebelled against God's commands
and despised the plans of the Most High.
So he subjected them to bitter labor;
they stumbled, and there was no one to help.

Then they cried to the Lord in their trouble,
and he saved them from their distress.
He brought them out of darkness, the utter darkness,
and broke away their chains.
Let them give thanks to the Lord for his unfailing love
and his wonderful deeds for mankind,
for he breaks down gates of bronze
and cuts through bars of iron.

Some became fools through their rebellious ways
and suffered affliction because of their iniquities.
They loathed all food
and drew near the gates of death.
Then they cried to the Lord in their trouble,
and he saved them from their distress.
He sent out his word and healed them;
he rescued them from the grave.
Let them give thanks to the Lord for his unfailing love
and his wonderful deeds for mankind.
Let them sacrifice thank offerings
and tell of his works with songs of joy.

Some went out on the sea in ships;
they were merchants on the mighty waters.
They saw the works of the Lord,
his wonderful deeds in the deep.
For he spoke and stirred up a tempest
that lifted high the waves.
They mounted up to the heavens and went down to the depths;
in their peril their courage melted away.
They reeled and staggered like drunkards;
they were at their wits' end.
Then they cried out to the Lord in their trouble,
and he brought them out of their distress.
He stilled the storm to a whisper;

the waves of the sea were hushed.
They were glad when it grew calm,
and he guided them to their desired haven.
Let them give thanks to the Lord for his unfailing love
and his wonderful deeds for mankind.
Let them exalt him in the assembly of the people
and praise him in the council of the elders.

He turned rivers into a desert,
flowing springs into thirsty ground,
and fruitful land into a salt waste,
because of the wickedness of those who lived there.
He turned the desert into pools of water
and the parched ground into flowing springs;
there he brought the hungry to live,
and they founded a city where they could settle.
They sowed fields and planted vineyards
that yielded a fruitful harvest;
he blessed them, and their numbers greatly increased,
and he did not let their herds diminish.

Then their numbers decreased, and they were humbled
by oppression, calamity and sorrow;
he who pours contempt on nobles
made them wander in a trackless waste.
But he lifted the needy out of their affliction
and increased their families like flocks.
The upright see and rejoice,
but all the wicked shut their mouths.

Let the one who is wise heed these things
and ponder the loving deeds of the Lord.

RESURRECTION EGGS

VERSES

1 Sam. 2:6	Mark 12:18-27	1 Cor. 6:14
Job 19:23-27 NIV	John 3:13-17	1 Cor. 15:3-8
Ps. 16:5-6, 8-11	John 5:19-29	1 Cor. 15:20-26
Ps. 18:46	John 6:37-40, 44-58	1 Cor. 15:42-44, 54
Ps. 49:13-15 NIV	John 10:10	Eph. 2:4-7
Prov. 12:28	John 11:17-26	Phil. 3:7-11, 20-21
Isa. 9:2	Acts 2:22-24, 32	Col. 2:9-13
Isa. 25:6-8	Acts 4:33	1 Thes. 4:13-17
Isa. 26:19	Acts 17:24-31	1 Tim. 6:12-14
Ezek. 37:1-14	Acts 24:15-16	2 Tim. 1:8-10
Dan. 12:2-3	Acts 26:8	Heb. 13:20-21
Hos. 13:14a-c NIV*	Rom. 4:16-17	1 Pet. 1:3-5, 17-21
Matt. 22:23-32	Rom. 6:3-5	Rev. 1:18
Matt. 27:51-53	Rom. 8:11, 31-39	

*"I will deliver this people from the power of the grave; I will redeem them from death. Where, O death, are your plagues? Where, O grave, is your destruction?

OPTIONAL VERSES

These are usually read at church during Easter services or the Easter Season.

John 20:1-18	Luke 24:1-12	Matt. 28:16-20
John 20:19-23	Luke 24:13-35	Mark 16:1-8
John 20:24-31	Luke 24:35-53	Mark 16:9-11
John 21:1-14	Matt. 28:1-10	Mark 16:12-13
John 21:15-25	Matt. 28:11-15	Mark 16:14-20

SONGS

I Know That My Redeemer Lives (Hymn)

Christ the Lord is Risen Today (Hymn)

He is Risen (Hymn)

I Believe in Jesus (Praise Song)

In Christ Alone (Praise Song)

Thine Is the Glory (Hymn)

Crown Him with Many Crowns (Hymn)

Glory to the Lamb (Praise Song)

Low in the Grave He Lay (Hymn)

New Song, by Mary

You are My All in All (Praise Song)

Revelation Song (Praise Song)

Baptized in Water (Praise Song)

What the Lord Has Done In Me (Praise Song)

The Lord Almighty Reigns (Praise Song)

Lord I Lift Your Name on High (Praise Song)

My Redeemer (Hymn)

BLOGS

"Missing Miracles"

From *Sara has Something to Say: Culture, Faith, and the Writing Life*,
by Sara Kelm, April 2, 2013
Used with permission

On Good Friday, it occurred to me that I didn't believe in a God who did miracles.

It was not a convenient time to face this fact. My culture was preparing for the celebration of the most amazing miracle of all: either a giant rabbit that delivers candy or the resurrection of a dead man…depending on which religion you follow.

This year, I wasn't prepared for the Easter weekend. I spent the Holy Week roaming around strange East Coast cities. In all of the noise and the crowds, there was little time for considering Jesus….save in the beauty of the towering buildings, the historic sights, the humanity of the teeming subways.

I finally arrived in my Oregon apartment, dirty and exhausted, on Good Friday evening, and I found my Facebook feed peppered with Mary. I didn't know Mary, but she was a student at my alma mater, who by all accounts loved the poor and disliked shoes. And she was missing.

She had gone up to the mountain to go hiking, and no one had heard from her since Sunday evening. Her car was found in the Mount Hood parking lot. All they really knew was that she was missing and had been for days.

Over Facebook, I saw people fear and grieve. I saw a community rise together and affirm the value of an individual. I hurt for those who loved Mary, and I feared what her loss would do to her family and her campus community. I also saw hope and prayer and petitions to God's loving heart, that he would restore her to those who loved her.

That's when I realized I didn't believe Mary was alive. I didn't believe that she could be saved. And I didn't believe that God would save her.

It would take a miracle, and I didn't think God did miracles much anymore.

My faith is complex. I believe in the old miracles, the biblical ones, because I always have. Because regardless of their literal truth, they are embedded with a truth that goes deeper, that tells us something about the heart of God.

At some point, though, I just stopped believing that most of the things attributed to miracles were actually unexplained phenomena. Because so many things can be explained now. Everything attributed to miracle status seemed so easily explained by other means.

But this situation seemed inexplicable and inescapable. I didn't believe God would save Mary. I believed that the snow and the wind and the elements had her life in their hands, and she would not be the victor.

The realization that I didn't believe God did miracles made me feel old and sad, like when that moment when you're holding your Easter basket waiting for the go signal, and you suddenly realize your mother spent hours hiding eggs in the yard last night, just so that you could wade through mud for candy. It's a loss of innocence. A loss of faith.

On the night that Christ breathed his last breath, I grieved for a stranger and for my loss of faith.

On Saturday morning, I woke, a heart heavy with sleep and Mary. I drank tea, unpacked my suitcase, took a shower. I looked outside at the sunshine and left my coat indoors. I went to a coffee shop. And in the middle of my coffee meeting, sunlight streamed in the shop windows, and it was there.

She was alive. They had found her. The internet community rejoiced.

Easter had come early.

In my mind and heart, this stranger, who meant so much to those around me, had been dead. She was gone. Easter would forever be a reminder of loss even while there would be a celebration of life. A town would mourn, a campus would grieve, and hearts would be broken.

But I assumed the end of the story from what I know about life, and I forgot that there are surprise twists that change the direction of the story. A lot of times those twists are bad: an accident, a diagnosis, a pink slip. And just sometimes those twists are good.

Not everything changed. I do not see miracles everywhere I look, and I will always doubt. But it occurred to me that my definition of miracle was too small.

Deep down, I believe that today's miracles are found in doctors and vaccines, split seconds and possibilities. Science, and the goodness of humanity, and coincidence, and how we interpret events can explain a lot. And I think God is pleased with that.

I attribute the rescue to Mary's mind that kept her alive, to her strength and her will. And to the rescuers who knew where to search, after experience and training had taught them how.

But this isn't denying God's hand in this situation. Now I can see the miracles. That Mary's mind is a miracle, and God is in that. The training and the experiences of the rescuers are a miracle, and God is in that.

A miracle doesn't have to mean that God worked alone. It usually doesn't. Instead, God uses the miracles he's already put in place to continue his work. You. Me. Mary.

She's sharing her story now, to news outlets. Her face is bright, almost incandescent in every photo I see. And a community celebrates a life reborn.

A miracle.

"HOLY DOUBT"

From *Mama Unabridged: The whole story on parenting (not just the pretty bits),*
by Abigail, April 2, 2013, Tagged: Mary Owen
https://mamaunabridged.wordpress.com/?s=holy+doubt
Used with permission

This past week, holy week, a student from the university where I teach went missing. Her name is Mary Owen. I'm not here to tell her story (it's a good one, but not mine to tell; you can read more about it here). I want to tell a smaller, quieter story that sits half-hidden in the shadow of the other one—a story about living with doubt during holy week.

I heard that Mary was missing on Friday afternoon from the great oracle of Facebook. She went hiking on Mount Hood the previous Sunday with minimal supplies and was thought to be lost somewhere on the freezing mountain, maybe injured, maybe dead.

I don't actually know her personally, but our circles are intertwined, and when I heard she was missing I felt instantly invested in the story. I couldn't stop thinking about it, so I shared a post on Facebook, asking for prayer—which meant, I quickly realized, that I probably had to pray for her, too.

Here's a little secret. **I'm not very good at praying, at least not the typical ask-for-specific-things-from-God kind of praying**. I'm afraid to believe in that kind of prayer, because as soon as I admit that God works that way, that God chooses to regularly and directly intervene in human affairs and can be swayed by our petitions, well, then I have to face the idea of God choosing NOT to intervene and prevent some really horrific shit, like tsunamis that sweep away cities, and children being sold into sex slavery, and so on. It's easier, and more comfortable, for me to avoid that whole mess by sticking to wordless or contemplative-style prayer—when I pray at all.

But this time I felt compelled to pray for something specific. And I did, all night long. **I held a breastfeeding vigil**. My baby, currently many reincarnations away from the Nirvana of "sleeping through the night," wakes up around 4-5 times to eat between 9 p.m. and 7 a.m.. So that night, Friday night, whenever he woke me up, my thoughts immediately turned to Mary, and I prayed while I nursed.

We're talking really simple prayers, here, almost awkwardly so. None of that flowery, preachy stuff I ceased being able to pull off years ago (*We know, dear Lord, that you are a merciful God and you hold all things in your hands…*).

Just: *Please find her. Let them find her.*

In between nursing sessions, while I slept, I even dreamed about Mary. I dreamed about hiking up the mountain with a bunch of people to rescue her, each of us armed with ski poles and snowshoes, white flakes falling softly all around, a bright beacon of moon guiding us.

In my dreams, I was confident she'd be rescued.

In waking life, I was almost certain that she would be found dead.

Sure, I was praying—but I severely doubted that what I was praying for would happen. I'd checked the weather and the temperatures on Mount Hood; I'd combed over the news stories, trying to imagine a realistic scenario to explain how Mary could still be alive after almost a week in frozen wilderness, with little or no food, underdressed, without shelter, most likely injured. I couldn't think of a convincing one.

On Saturday morning, still assured in my doubt, I was once again feeding my baby and checking Facebook on my phone—and I saw the news that Mary had been found. Alive. After six days of freezing and starving in a hole she'd carved out in the snow, she'd been rescued. Upon reading this, I literally exclaimed: "Holy shit!" (still working on that not-swearing-in-front-of-the-baby thing). I was honestly surprised, almost shocked, to be proven wrong. I'd been so sure that my analysis of the situation was accurate.

There's no way, I'd thought.

This is a constant refrain for me, especially when it comes to matters of faith.

There's no way…

We live in a time and place where jaded, skeptical thinking is presented as far more sophisticated, far more intellectual, than hoping. But the events of this (holy) week have reminded me that my chronic inclinations towards doubt and cynicism are not necessarily the truest mirrors of reality.

Don't misunderstand – this isn't a post about me feeling a complete renewal of faith because GOD ANSWERED MY PRAYER!!! JUST IN TIME FOR EASTER!!! There's more subtlety to it. I *am* feeling a sense of renewal, yes—not because I happened to pray for the thing that came true, but more because ***what I believed would actually happen did NOT come true.***

And there is my doubt, unmasked, revealed to be resting on the arrogant assumption that I can climb high enough to have a God's eye view, when I'm really down here, with the rest of the humans, fumbling around in the dark.

Mary Owen was not the only Mary on my mind this week. There's another one, Mary Magdalene, on her way to the tomb of a dead friend. It's tempting to skip to the happy ending. But I'm compelled by the moment before the end of the story, the moment when Mary gets to the tomb and sees that it's empty, the moment when her heart sinks and she feels sick to her stomach and she wonders *What have they done with his body?*

This is where I am stuck, most of the time, when it comes to faith. **I tend to get trapped in the silent moment before the resurrection, my voice echoing back to me in the stillness of a tomb that has been emptied of God.**

Where is he? What have they done with his body?

Maybe there is more to doubt than cynicism and pessimism—maybe there's hopeful doubt, holy doubt, like that of Mary as she searches in the shadows, wondering what has happened.

I'm no more certain about God or the way God works now than I was last week. I've long since abandoned any quest for certainty. There will always be impenetrable mystery, unanswerable unknowns. But now I'm beginning to realize something: Disbelief is not the only way to respond to the darkness. **Uncertainty also offers the possibility of hope.**

So, I'm going to keep showing up at the tomb, even if most of the time it is just to sit in God's absence. Because sometimes God shows up. And if I'm there, waiting and watching, I might catch a glimpse.

"Mary Magdalene Repentant," by Gustave Dore

PHOTOGRAPHS OF LEG AND LEG GASH

WARNING NOTE: The photographs in Appendix C
may be upsetting or cause trauma to some people.
They should be viewed at the reader's discretion.

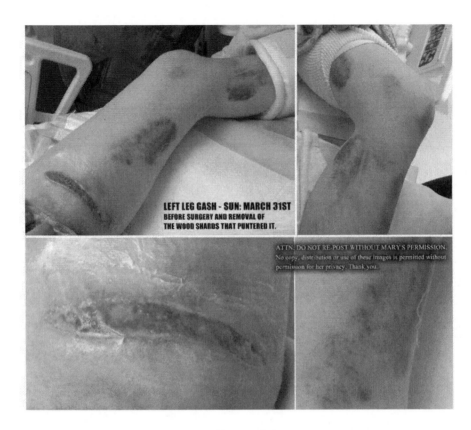

Leg gash and bruises, before surgery

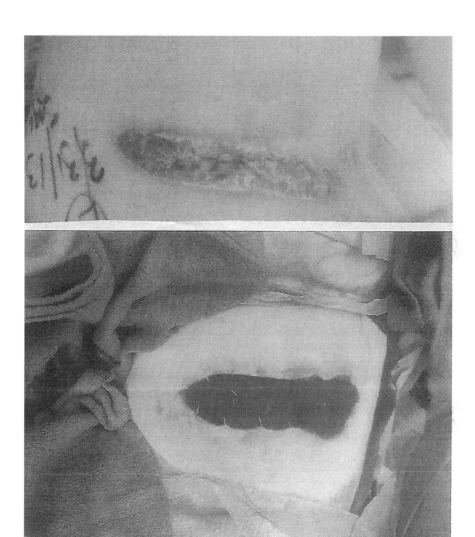

Leg gash pre- and post- surgery

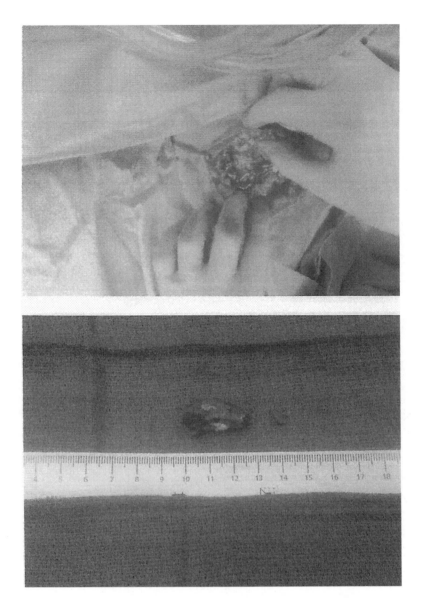

Leg gash during surgery and bits of wood that were removed from it

ACKNOWLEDGEMENTS

A book is the sum of many contributions, and this book has been especially dependent on many people and circumstances outside myself for its existence. I want to first thank my husband, Bruce, for the voluntary, loving support underlying every aspect of this book's creation from beginning to end.

Also, I want to express a big, "Thank you," to the professors at George Fox University who helped me improve my writing skills, both directly, through classes on the subject, and indirectly, through assignments that required writing and/or presentation, including the supposition that any excellence in writing *always* involves editors—other people's eyes on your work. Among my professors I especially want to thank Melanie Mock, PhD, who taught my "Creative Nonfiction Writing" class; Abigail Favale, PhD, who showed me how to "close-read," write my interpretations, and to consider many things more deeply; and Polly Peterson, then Assistant Professor of English, who helped me largely begin to understand the characteristics and vagaries of English grammar and composition. All of this preparation was fundamental to the writing of this book.

A big thank you also to my friends and family members, who were my first readers and editors including Bruce, Mary, Denise, Karie, Jan, Karen, Mary R., and especially you, Laurie! Your help and encouragement gave me a solid start towards publishing.

I am grateful to my developmental editor, Linda Ruggeri, *The Insightful Editor*, who helped so much with an outside perspective, organization, and content (though I had to make the final choices, so don't blame any "lameness" in the book on her); also, to Melinda, the magical formatter of this book. Both Linda and Melinda helped me in person and through the resources they provided, with the timely, invaluable, and necessary guidance I needed for my first experience with the publishing process. A big thank you to also to Jen Anne, Marjory, Jimmie, and to Bruce for your help with copy editing and proofreading as well. Also, I thoroughly enjoyed working with my talented daughter, Rachel, who developed the cover for this book.

Thank you also to our friends, family members, and communities who supported this project with your encouragement, permissions, finances, and prayers, which ultimately allowed it to come to fruition. Each one of you is a blessing in my life, in our family member's lives, and really in all the world. You're our treasures on earth that contribute greatly to our joy here and now.

Before being done, I want to thank the Lord for letting me be a part of what He's doing on earth. He has provided all things for this book. He gave inspiration and helped me work through many of the deficiencies in my writing.

Lord, thank You most of all, because working for and walking with You is the greatest adventure of all. It is never boring, and it is work that's everlasting for those who are touched by it and receive it through You; it is joyful and beautiful forever! May this particular work draw others to You, back to You, and closer to You.

NOTES

Chapter 4

1. "Peak Lists," *Peakbagger.com*, 1987-2021, https://www.peakbagger.com/ListIndx.aspx; and Bivouac.com, accessed January 2021, https://bivouac.com/PeakLists.asp.

2. Lynne Palombo, "Mount Hood Deaths Since 1883," *The Oregonian/OregonLive. com*, February 07, 2012; updated January 10, 2019; http://www.oregonlive.com/pacific-northwest-news/index.ssf/2012/02/mount_hood_climber_deaths.html; and KATU staff, "At least 46 people [24 climbers] have died on Mt. Hood since 2002," KATU.com, February 13, 2018; updated April 7, 2020, https://katu.com/news/local/data-shows-at-least-16-people-have-died-on-mt-hood-in-the-last-16-years.

3. Toutonghi, Pauls. "Mount Hood's Deadliest Disaster," *Outside Magazine*, November 1, 2018, https://www.outsideonline.com/2357451/mount-hood-disaster-1986.

4. Dan Simon and Chris Lawrence, contributors, "Dead Climber recovered from Mount Hood," *CNN.com*, December 18, 2006, https://www.cnn.com/2006/US/12/18/missing.climbers/index.html. See also: Joseph B. Frazier, "Widow reconstructs tragedy: Karen James writes book about deaths on Mount Hood," *The Spokesman-Review*, Spokane, Washington, Friday, November 14, 2008; https://www.spokesman.com/stories/2008/nov/14/widow-reconstructs-tragedy/; Matt Buxton, "Karen James, widow of Mount Hood climber Kelly James, give talk in Portland," *The Oregonian/OregonLive.com*, October 10, 2010; updated January 10, 2019, https://www.oregonlive.com/portland/2010/10/widow_karen_james_returns_to_o.html; and James, Karen. *Holding Fast: The Untold Story of the Mount Hood Tragedy.* Thomas Nelson, 2008. p. 256. ISBN 978-1-59555-175-7.

5. Aaron Mesh, "Where People Fall and Die on Mount Hood," *Willamette Week*, June 21, 2016; updated October 3, 2016; http://www.wweek.com/news/2016/06/22/where-people-fall-and-die-on-mount-hood/. See also Lynne Palombo, "Mount Hood Deaths Since 1883," *The Oregonian/OregonLive.com*, February 07, 2012; updated January 10, 2019; http://www.oregonlive.com/pacific-northwest-news/index.ssf/2012/02/mount_hood_climber_deaths.html.

6. Tom Kloster, "Sandy Glacier Caves: Realm of the Snow Dragon," *WyEast Blog: Mount Hood National Park Campaign*, September 29, 2013, https://wyeastblog.org/2013/09/29/sandy-glacier-caves-realm-of-the-snow-dragon/.

7. "Cornice," *Avalanche.org*, American Avalanche Association and Forest Service, Department of Agriculture, National Avalanche Center, 2017-2020, https://avalanche.org/avalanche-encyclopedia/cornice/.

8. Some examples: Allan Brettman, "Climber killed on Mount Hood was not using ice ax, rescuers say," *The Oregonian/OregonLive.com*, May 10, 2017; updated January 09, 2019; http://www.oregonlive.com/pacific-northwest-news/index.ssf/2017/05/deceased_mount_hood_climber_wa.html. See also "ACCIDENT REPORT FOR THE AMERICAN ALPINE CLUB: Mount Hood fatal fall from the summit," *Traditional Mountaineering.org* and *Alpine Mountaineering.org*, June 2000-June 2009, http://www.traditionalmountaineering.org/Report_Hood_FatalFall.htm; and "ACCIDENT REPORT FOR THE AMERICAN ALPINE CLUB: Mt. Hood Cooper Spur climb ends in tragedy," *TraditionalMountaineering.org* and *AlpineMountaineering.org*, May 23, 1999, http://www.traditionalmountaineering.org/Report_Hood_Cardin.htm.

9. "May 2002: Disaster on Mt. Hood," *Clackamas County Sheriff's Office*, May 30, 2002, https://www.clackamas.us/sheriff/2002SARIncidentRecap.html. See also: Stuart Tomlinson and Eric Mortenson, "'They all disappeared': 3 climbers die on Hood," *The Oregonian/OregonLive.com*, May 31, 2002; updated January 11, 2019, http://www.oregonlive.com/outdoors/index.ssf/2002/05/they_all_disappeared_3_climber.html; and "Fall into Crevasse, Unable to Self-Arrest, Inadequate Protection, Poor Position, Oregon, Mount Hood, Standard Rout," *American Alpine Club website*, 2003, http://publications.americanalpineclub.org/articles/13200308000/Fall-into-Crevasse-Unable-to-Self-Arrest-Inadequate-Protection-Poor-Position-Oregon-Mount-Hood-Standard-Rout.

10. Stuart Tomlinson, "Mount Hood rescuers develop new protocols to save fallen climbers from toxic volcanic vents," *The Oregonian/OregonLive.com*, April 24, 2015; updated January 09, 2019; http://www.oregonlive.com/pacific-northwest-news/index.ssf/2015/04/fumaroles_mount_hood_rescuers.html; see also, "Hot Rocks Fumarole Climber Rescue," *Portland Mountain Rescue*, May 24, 2014, http://www.pmru.org/headlinenews/hot-rocks-fumarole-clibmer-rescue/.

11. Renate Hartog, "Another typical Mount Hood earthquake swarm?" Pacific Northwest Seismic Network, January 18, 2021, https://pnsn.org/blog/2021/01/18/another-typical-mount-hood-earthquake-swarm.

12. "Mount Hood—History and Hazards of Oregon's Most Recently Active Volcano," United States Geological Survey, Fact Sheet 060-00: Online Version 1.0., last modified: May 27, 2010; https://pubs.usgs.gov/fs/2000/fs060-00/; and "Mount Hood: Cascade Volcano Observatory: Hazards," United States Geological Survey: Volcano Hazards Program, U.S. Department of the Interior, page modified: November 20, 2013, https://volcanoes.usgs.gov/volcanoes/mount_hood/mount_hood_hazard_68.html.

13. "Mount Hood: Cascade Volcano Observatory: Mount Hood: Summary," United States Geological Survey: Volcano Hazards Program, U.S. Department of the Interior, page modified: February 2, 2015, https://volcanoes.usgs.gov/volcanoes/mount_hood/mount_hood_geo_hist_96.html.

14. See article by Tom Kloster (endnote 6) above.

15. Rick Bella, "Mount Hood Recovery Mission Brings Back Remains of Climbers Who Went Missing in December 2009," *The Oregonian/OregonLive.com*, August 26, 2010; https://www.oregonlive.com/clackamascounty/2010/08/mt_hood_recovery_mission_finds.html.

Chapter 10

16. *Northwest Cable News (NWCN)* was a 24 hour news service that was headquartered in Seattle, Washington (they're no longer in service). Their news was collected from their "affiliated channels: Seattle, Washington's: *KING-TV, KONG*; Spokane, Washington's: *KREM, KSKN*; Boise, Idaho's: *KTVB*, and Portland, Oregon's: *KGW*. Their news report about Mary being missing was probably taken from *KGW*'s interview of Bruce on Friday, 29 March 2013. *KGW*: "Newberg woman missing, possibly alone on Mt. Hood: A 23-year-old woman is missing and is believed to have gone hiking alone on Mt. Hood several days ago, officials said..." the links to the *NWCN News* station and this news report on Mary's incident are no longer active.

17. S— Eddy's son Joshua Steven Eddy was only 19 years and 2 months old when he died. Following is the address to his past blog, "The Bright and Hopeful Unknown," http://joshyeddy.blogspot.com/. Josh's last article, "To Surrender a Precious Dream," can be found at: https://joshyeddy.blogspot.com/2012/04/to-surrender-precious-dream.html. Following is a link to another blog written by a person who did not know Josh personally, but who was deeply touched by his life: "Joshua Steven Eddy, Go with God," *Keep Calm and Walk by Faith*, Tuesday, May 29, 2012, http://walkbyfaithkkw2011.blogspot.com/2012/05/joshua-steven-eddy-go-with-god.html.

Chapter 11

18. "Mt. Hood Meadows Avalanche Dogs Organization," *Facebook*, accessed February 2021, https://www.facebook.com/Mt-Hood-Meadows-Avalanche-Dogs-155079924547382/. See also Mary Loos, "Mt. Hood resorts training dogs ahead of snow season," *KATU.com*, Sunday, November 20, 2016, https://katu.com/news/local/mt-hood-resorts-training-avalanche-dogs-ahead-of-snow-season.

19. Robert Lindsey, "Two Climbers May Have Survived Because of Positions in Snow Cave," *The New York Times*, May 17, 1986, accessed 8 December 2019, https://www.nytimes.com/1986/05/17/us/two-climbers-may-have-survived-because-of-positions-in-snow-cave.html.

20. "Mt. McLoughlin Trail," *Rogue-Siskiyou Forest Service*, accessed 17 July 2018, https://www.fs.usda.gov/recarea/rogue-siskiyou/recarea/?recid=69818.

21. Heather Steeves, "Search for missing Mount Hood hiker to resume Saturday," *The Oregonian / Oregonlive.com*, posted and updated March 29, 2012, https://www.oregonlive.com/clacka-mascounty/2013/03/police_searching_for_missing_m_1.html .

Chapter 16

22. To hear a recording of Mary's song, sung by Mary, visit the Mountain Rescue: https://www.mountainrescue.online/bonus-features.

Chapter 18

23. Truth is, none of us is perfect in love or justness, except Jesus. We all do thoughtless and wrong things. How does a God of perfect love or justness ever put up with any of us!?! Yet He does, through Jesus; but He requires that we forgive others if we want to be forgiven by Him (Matt. 5:6, 14-15; 18:21-35; 26:28; Mark 11:25; Luke 1:77; 6:37; 7:36-48; 11:4; 17:3-4; 23:32-34; 24:45-49; Acts 2:38; 10:43; 13:38). To see these verses, copy or type these verse references into: Biblegateway. Zondervan/Harper Colin's Publishers. https://www.biblegateway.com/.

Chapter 19

24. "Mount Hood Climbing Accidents," *Wikipedia.org*, Wikipedia: Free Online Encyclopedia, accessed May 2018, https://en.wikipedia.org/wiki/Mount_Hood_climbing_accidents. Article included the following references:

   • Emily Fuggetta, "6 days stranded on Mount Hood leave hiker Mary Owen with frostbite, new outlook on life," *The Oregonian / OregonLive.com*, March 31, 2013.

- Huffington Post staff, "Hiker Mary Owen Survives 6 Days In A Snow Cave On Oregon's Mount Hood," *Huffington Post*, April 1, 2013.
- Neal Karlinsky, "Hiker Survived 6 Days in Mount Hood Snow Cave," *ABC News*, April 1, 2013.
- David Boroff, "Oregon college student Mary Owen rescued after spending six days on snowy Mount Hood," *New York Daily News*, April 1, 2013.

Chapter 20

25. See the following articles: Jamie Farnsworth Finn, "Young adult brain development: What you need to know," *TODAY*, January 31, 2020, https://www.today.com/parenting-guides/young-adult-brain-development-t177740; Vaishnavi Patil, "What's the Difference Between Teenage Brains and Adult Brains?" *ScienceABC*, February 1, 2021, https://www.scienceabc.com/humans/teenage-brain-development-behavior-explained-frontal-lobe-function.html; "At What Age Is the Brain Fully Developed?" Mental Health Daily, accessed March 11, 2021, https://mentalhealthdaily.com/2015/02/18/at-what-age-is-the-brain-fully-developed/.

Chapter 21

26. Summary of Snowtrapped, "About (Snowtrapped)," *Channel 5*, Channel 5 Broadcasting Ltd 2020, accessed 15 July 2020, https://www.channel5.comMed/show/snowtrapped/.
27. Neal Karlinsky, "Hiker Survived 6 Days in Mount Hood Snow Cave," *ABC News*, April 1, 2013, https://abcnews.go.com/blogs/headlines/2013/04/hiker-survived-6-days-in-mt-hood-snow-cave/.
28. *Huffington Post* staff, "Hiker Mary Owen Survives 6 Days In A Snow Cave On Oregon's Mount Hood," Huffington Post, April 1, 2013, https://www.huffpost.com/entry/hiker-mary-owen-rescued_n_2992917.

BIBLIOGRAPHY

Abigail. "HOLY DOUBT," *Mama Unabridged: The whole story on parenting (not just the pretty bits)*. Wordpress (blog), April 2, 2013. Used with permission. https://mamaunabridged. wordpress.com/?s=holy+doubt.

"ACCIDENT REPORT FOR THE AMERICAN ALPINE CLUB: Mount Hood fatal fall from the summit." *Traditional Mountaineering.org and Alpine Mountaineering.org*, June 2000-June 2009. http://www.traditionalmountaineering.org/Report_Hood_FatalFall.htm.

"ACCIDENT REPORT FOR THE AMERICAN ALPINE CLUB: Mt. Hood Cooper Spur climb ends in tragedy." *Traditional Mountaineering.org and Alpine Mountaineering.org*, May 23, 1999. http://www.traditionalmountaineering.org/Report_Hood_Cardin.htm.

Back Packing Light staff. "How to Survive Frostbitten Feet." *Backpackinglight.com.* Beartooth Media Group, Inc., April 1, 2013 [link to article and comments no longer available].

Bella, Rick. "Mount Hood Recovery Mission Brings Back Remains of Climbers Who Went Missing in December 2009." *The Oregonian/OregonLive.com*, August 26, 2010. https://www. oregonlive.com/clackamascounty/2010/08/mt_hood_recovery_mission_finds.html.

Brettman, Allan. "Climber killed on Mount Hood was not using ice ax, rescuers say." *The Oregonian/ OregonLive.com*, May 10, 2017; updated January 09, 2019. http://www.oregonlive.com/ pacific-northwest-news/index.ssf/2017/05/deceased_mount_hood_climber_wa.html.

Buxton, Matt. "Karen James, widow of Mount Hood climber Kelly James, give talk in Portland." *The Oregonian/OregonLive.com*, October 10, 2010; updated January 10, 2019. https://www. oregonlive.com/portland/2010/10/widow_karen_james_returns_to_o.html.

Clackamas County Sheriff's Office (CCSO). "A Q&A with Mary Owen." *YouTube*, April 17, 2013. https://www.youtube.com/watch?v=918-W6pmlyg.

Cook, David C. "Everyday Supernatural," p.209. Quoted in a guide for this book by the same name, by Mike Pilavachi and Andrew John Croft, through Soul Survivor (Publishing), Watford, Herts, UK, 2017. https://static1.squarespace.com/

static/576843ee6a4963a2b8c7a785/t/5992ff11cd0f686525d683d7/1502805779177/ Everyday+Supernatural+Spirit+Led+Small+Group+Guide.pdf.

"Cornice." *Avalanche.org*. American Avalanche Association and Forest Service, Department of Agriculture, National Avalanche Center, 2017-2020. https://avalanche.org/ avalanche-encyclopedia/cornice/.

Davenport, Chris. "Tree Well Demo." *YouTube*, March 2, 2017. https://www.youtube.com/ watch?v=qnbju_AGwe4.

Eddy, Joshua Steven. "The Bright and Hopeful Unknown." *Blogspot*, 2012. http://joshyeddy.blogspot. com/.

Eddy, Joshua Steven. "To Surrender a Precious Dream." *The Bright and Hopeful Unknown, Blogspot*, April 2012. https://joshyeddy.blogspot.com/2012/04/to-surrender-precious-dream.html.

"Fall into Crevasse, Unable to Self-Arrest, Inadequate Protection, Poor Position, Oregon, Mount Hood, Standard Rout." *American Alpine Club website*, 2003. http://publications. americanalpineclub.org/articles/13200308000/Fall-into-Crevasse-Unable-to-Self-Arrest- Inadequate-Protection-Poor-Position-Oregon-Mount-Hood-Standard-Rout.

FOX 12 Oregon / KPTV staff. "Missing Mt. Hood Hiker Has Not Been Heard from Since Last Sunday." *FOX 12 Oregon / KPTV.com*, March 29, 2013.

Francke, Tyler J. "George Fox University student Mary Owen says she learned a lot of difficult lessons while stranded for more than six days on Mount Hood." *Newberg Graphic*, Wednesday, April 10, 2013.

Francke, Tyler J. "Message from hiker Mary Owen's mom." *News Blog, Wordpress*, April 6, 2013. https://tylerjfrancke.wordpress.com/2013/04/06/message-from-hiker-mary-owens-mom/.

Frazier, Joseph B. "Widow reconstructs tragedy: Karen James writes book about deaths on Mount Hood." *The Spokesman-Review*, Spokane, Washington, Friday, November 14, 2008. https:// www.spokesman.com/stories/2008/nov/14/widow-reconstructs-tragedy/.

Fuggetta, Emily. "6 days stranded on Mount Hood leave hiker Mary Owen with frostbite, new outlook on life." *The Oregonian / OregonLive.com*, March 31, 2013. https://www.oregonlive. com/portland/2013/03/6_days_stranded_on_mount_hood.html.

Getty, Keith and Stuart Townend. "In Christ Alone." *Thankyou Music (PRS)*, copyright © 2002 (adm. worldwide at CapitolCMGPublishing.com excluding Europe with is adm. by Integrity Music, part of the David C Cook family. Songs@integritymusic.com). All rights reserved. Used by permission.

GFU staff writer. "George Fox sends students on annual service trips." *George Fox University*, accessed 26 January 2021. https://www.georgefox.edu/featured_stories/Summer%20 Serve%202013.html.

GFU staff writer. "Information and prayers sought for missing student Mary Owen." *George Fox University News Blog*, March 28–30, 2013. http://blogs.georgefox.edu/newsreleases/?p=6142.

Goss, Winston. "Tree Well Near-Death Experience." *YouTube*, February 12, 2016. https://www. youtube.com/watch?v=NY6STzbolTU.

Gritters, Jenni. "The Best Gaiters for Snow, Hiking & Mountaineering." *REI Co-op Journal*, October 17, 2018. https://www.rei.com/blog/hike/best-gaiters-for-hiking-snowshoeing-mountaineering .

Hartog, Renate. "Another typical Mount Hood earthquake swarm?" *Pacific Northwest Seismic Network*, January 18, 2021. https://pnsn.org/blog/2021/01/18/ another-typical-mount-hood-earthquake-swarm.

Heather De Rosa. "Ministry Opportunities at George Fox." *Bruin Blog*, posted February 13, 2013. https://blogs.georgefox.edu/bruinblog.

"Hot Rocks Fumarole Climber Rescue." *Portland Mountain Rescue*, May 24, 2014. http://www.pmru. org/headlinenews/hot-rocks-fumarole-clibmer-rescue/.

Huffington Post staff. "Hiker Mary Owen Survives 6 Days In A Snow Cave On Oregon's Mount Hood." *Huffington Post*, April 1, 2013. https://www.huffpost.com/entry/ hiker-mary-owen-rescued_n_2992917.

James, Karen. *Holding Fast: The Untold Story of the Mount Hood Tragedy*. Thomas Nelson, 2008. p. 256. ISBN 978-1-59555-175-7.

Karlinsky, Neal. "Hiker Survived 6 Days in Mount Hood Snow Cave." *ABCNews. go.com*, April 1, 2013. https://abcnews.go.com/blogs/headlines/2013/04/ hiker-survived-6-days-in-mt-hood-snow-cave/.

KATU Staff. "At least 46 people have died on Mt. Hood since 2002." *KATU.com*, February 13, 2018; updated April 7, 2020. https://katu.com/news/local/ data-shows-at-least-16-people-have-died-on-mt-hood-in-the-last-16-years.

KATU Staff. "Hiker, 23, Reported Missing on Mount Hood for Days." *KATU.com/news/*, March 29, 2013.

KATU Staff. "Hiker found alive: 'We are just praising God and are so happy.'" *KATU.com/news/*, March 30, 2013.

KATU Staff. "Miracle on the Mountain." *KATU.com/news/*, March 30, 2013.

Kelm, Sarah. "Missing Miracles." *Sara has Something to Say: Culture, Faith, and the Writing Life.* Wordpress Blog, April 2, 2013.

Kloster, Tom. "Sandy Glacier Caves: Realm of the Snow Dragon." *WyEast Blog: Mount Hood National Park Campaign*, September 29, 2013. https://wyeastblog.org/2013/09/29/ sandy-glacier-caves-realm-of-the-snow-dragon/.

KOIN staff. "Hiker Likely Missing on Mount Hood." *KOIN Local 6, koinlocal6.com*, March 29, 2013.

KOIN staff. "Search continues for missing hiker at Mount Hood." *KOIN Local 6, koinlocal6. com*, reported March 29; posted March 30, 2013. https://www.youtube.com/ watch?v=Ab9YfD_dqsA.

Lewis, C. S. "Miracles." *Goodreads*. Goodreads Inc., accessed June 4, 2020. https://www.goodreads. com/quotes/381786-death-and-resurrection-are-what-the-story-is-about-and.

Lindsey, Robert. "Two Climbers May Have Survived Because of Positions in Snow Cave." *The New York Times*, May 17, 1986. https://www.nytimes.com/1986/05/17/us/two-climbers-may-have-survived-because-of-positions-in-snow-cave.html.

Loos, Mary. "Mt. Hood resorts training dogs ahead of snow season." *KATU News*, Sunday, November 20, 2016. https://katu.com/news/local/mt-hood-resorts-training-avalanche-dogs-ahead-of-snow-season.

"May 2002: Disaster on Mt. Hood." *Clackamas County Sheriff's Office*, May 30, 2002. https://www.clackamas.us/sheriff/2002SARIncidentRecap.html.

Merriam-Webster. Merriam-Webster Inc., 2021. https://www.merriam-webster.com/dictionary.

Mesh, Aaron. "Where People Fall and Die on Mount Hood." *Willamette Week*, June 21, 2016; updated October 3, 2016. http://www.wweek.com/news/2016/06/22/where-people-fall-and-die-on-mount-hood/.

"Mount Hood: Cascade Volcano Observatory: Hazards." *United States Geological Survey: Volcano Hazards Program*. U.S. Department of the Interior, page modified November 20, 2013. https://volcanoes.usgs.gov/volcanoes/mount_hood/mount_hood_hazard_68.html.

"Mount Hood: Cascade Volcano Observatory: Mount Hood: Summary." *United States Geological Survey: Volcano Hazards Program*. U.S. Department of the Interior, page modified February 2, 2015. https://volcanoes.usgs.gov/volcanoes/mount_hood/mount_hood_geo_hist_96.html.

"Mount Hood Climbing Accidents." *Wikipedia.org*. Wikipedia: Free Online Encyclopedia, accessed May 2018. https://en.wikipedia.org/wiki/Mount_Hood_climbing_accidents. Article included the following references:

[70] Fuggetta, Emily. "6 days stranded on Mount Hood leave hiker Mary Owen with frostbite, new outlook on life." *The Oregonian / OregonLive.com*, March 31, 2013.

[71] *Huffington Post* staff. "Hiker Mary Owen Survives 6 Days In A Snow Cave On Oregon's Mount Hood." *Huffington Post*, April 1, 2013. https://www.huffpost.com/entry/hiker-mary-owen-rescued_n_2992917.

[72] Karlinsky, Neal. "Hiker Survived 6 Days in Mount Hood Snow Cave." *ABC News*, April 1, 2013. https://abcnews.go.com/blogs/headlines/2013/04/hiker-survived-6-days-in-mt-hood-snow-cave/.

[73] Boroff, David. "Oregon college student Mary Owen rescued after spending six days on snowy Mount Hood." *New York Daily News*, April 1, 2013.

"Mount Hood—History and Hazards of Oregon's Most Recently Active Volcano." *United States Geological Survey*, Fact Sheet 060-00: Online Version 1.0., last modified May 27, 2010. https://pubs.usgs.gov/fs/2000/fs060-00/.

"Mount Hood, Satellite View." *Google Maps*. Imagery Maxar Technologies, 2020, State of Oregon, Map data, United States, 2020. https://www.google.com/maps/place/Mt+Hood/@45.3736141,-121.7047059,3144m/data=!3m2!1e3!4b1!4m5!3m4!1s0x54be1c5501719a05:0x831d7.

"Mt. Hood Meadows Avalanche Dogs Organization." *Facebook*, accessed February 2021. https://www.facebook.com/Mt-Hood-Meadows-Avalanche-Dogs-155079924547382/.

"Mt. McLoughlin Trail." *Rogue-Siskiyou Forest Service*, accessed 17 July 2018. https://www.fs.usda.gov/recarea/rogue-siskiyou/recarea/?recid=69818.

"Missing Person, Case Report." Newberg-Dundee Police Department, Report Date/Time: 3/28/2013, 5:24:00 PM; Mary removed from LEDS/NCIC as a missing person, March 30, 2013.

NBC News staff. "Missing Mount Hood hiker found alive on Sandy Glacier." *NBC News/nbcnews.com,* March 30, 2013.

Nicholson, William. "William Nicholson's, C. S. Lewis in 'Shadowlands.'" *Goodreads*. Goodreads Inc., accessed July 2018. https://www.goodreads.com/quotes/343027-to-put-it-another-way-pain-is-god-s-megaphone-to.

NWCN/KGW News staff. "Woman Missing, Possibly Alone on Mt. Hood." *NWCN.com / KGW.com*, March 29, 2013.

Oregonian / Oregonlive.com staff. "Police Searching for Missing Mt. Hood Hiker." *The Oregonian / Oregonlive.com*, March 29, 2013.

"Oregon National Guard: 130509-Z-OT568-038," Flikr, SmugMug+Flickr, 23 June 2012[3], May 2018, https://www.flickr.com/photos/oregonmildep/8724052359.

"Oregon National Guard: 130509-Z-OT568-073," Flikr, SmugMug+Flickr, 23 June 2012[3], May 2018, https://www.flickr.com/photos/oregonmildep/8724052129/in/photostream/.

"Oregon National Guard: 130509-Z-OT568-101," Flikr, SmugMug+Flickr, 23 June 2012[3], May 2018, https://www.flickr.com/photos/oregonmildep/8725172496/in/photostream/.

Palombo, Lynne. "Mount Hood Deaths Since 1883." *The Oregonian/OregonLive.com*, February 07, 2012; updated January 10, 2019. http://www.oregonlive.com/pacific-northwest-news/index.ssf/2012/02/mount_hood_climber_deaths.html.

"Papua New Guinea." Word Made Flesh International, 2014-2021. https://wordmadeflesh.org/about/staff/papua-new-guinea-staff/.

"Peak Lists." *Bivouac.com.*, accessed January 2021. https://bivouac.com/PeakLists.asp.

"Peak Lists." *Peakbagger.com*, 1987-2021. https://www.peakbagger.com/ListIndx.aspx.

Portland Mountain Rescue staff. "Lost Mt. Hood Climber." *PMRU.org*. Portland Mountain Rescue: Saving lives through rescue and mountain safety education, March 29, 2013. https://pmru.org/?s=20130329.

Rodgers, Richard and Oscar Hammerstein II. "Maria." *Genius.* Genius Media Group, 2021. https://genius.com/Peggy-wood-marni-nixon-portia-nelson-anna-lee-and-evadne-baker-maria-lyrics. See also, https://genius.com/Julie-andrews-prelude-the-sound-of-music-lyrics.

Simon, Dan and Chris Lawrence, contributors. "Dead Climber recovered from Mount Hood." *CNN.com*, December 18, 2006. https://www.cnn.com/2006/US/12/18/missing.climbers/index.html.

Snowtrapped summary. "About (Snowtrapped)." *Channel 5*. Channel 5 Broadcasting Ltd., accessed July 15, 2020. https://www.channel5.comMed/show/snowtrapped/.

Spafford, Horatio, music composed by Philip Bliss, article by Mel Johnson. "The Story Behind the Hymn 'It Is Well With My Soul.'" *GodUpdates, Share Inspiration*, March 7, 2016. https://www.godupdates.com/story-behind-it-is-well-with-my-soul/#story-behind-it-is-well.

Steeves, Heather. "Search for Missing Mount Hood Hiker to Resume Saturday." *The Oregonian / Oregonlive.com*, March 29, 2013. https://www.oregonlive.com/clackamascounty/2013/03/police_searching_for_missing_m_1.html.

Switchfoot. "Gone." *AZLyrics*, accessed November 2021. AZLyrics: https://www.azlyrics.com/lyrics/switchfoot/gone.html.

Terry, Lynne. "Family of missing hiker, 23, overjoyed she's found after week alone on Mount Hood." *The Oregonian / Oregonlive.com*, March 30, 2013. http://www.oregonlive.com/pacific-northwest-news/index.ssf/2013/03/family_of_missing_hiker_23_ove.html.

Terry, Lynne. "Search teams fan out on Mount Hood." *The Oregonian / Oregonlive.com*, March 30, 2013.

Terry, Lynne. "Searchers find missing hiker, 23, on Mount Hood." *The Oregonian / Oregonlive.com*, March 30, 2013. https://www.oregonlive.com/pacific-northwest-news/2013/03/searchers_find_missing_hiker_2.html.

Tomlinson, Stuart and Eric Mortenson. "'They all disappeared': 3 climbers die on Hood." *The Oregonian/OregonLive.com*, May 31, 2002; updated January 11, 2019. http://www.oregonlive.com/outdoors/index.ssf/2002/05/they_all_disappeared_3_climber.html.

Tomlinson, Stuart. "Mount Hood rescuers develop new protocols to save fallen climbers from toxic volcanic vents." *The Oregonian/OregonLive.com*, April 24, 2015; updated January 09, 2019. http://www.oregonlive.com/pacific-northwest-news/index.ssf/2015/04/fumaroles_mount_hood_rescuers.html.

Toutonghi, Pauls. "Mount Hood's Deadliest Disaster." *Outside Magazine,* November 1, 2018. https://www.outsideonline.com/2357451/mount-hood-disaster-1986 .

"Tree Well Safety Education." *Canada West Ski Areas Association*, January 16, 2019. https://cwsaa.org/2019/01/16/tree-well-safety-education/.

"Tucker Sno-Cat® Snow Machines." *Tucker Sno-Cat® Corporation*, 2019. http://sno-cat.com/.

Unknown. "Joshua Steven Eddy, Go with God." *Blogspot, Keep Calm and Walk by Faith*, Tuesday, May 29, 2012. http://walkbyfaithkkw2011.blogspot.com/2012/05/joshua-steven-eddy-go-with-god.html.